CH00722092

THE VICTORIAN TAXPAYER
AND THE LAW

The central element of the taxpayer's relationship with the law was the protection it afforded to ensure only the correct amount of tax was paid, that it was legally levied and justly administered. These legal safeguards consisted of the fundamental constitutional provision that all taxes had to be consented to in Parliament, local tax administration, and a power to appeal to specialist tribunals and the courts. The book explains how these legal safeguards were established and how they were affected by changing social, economic and political conditions. They were found to be restrictive and inadequate, and were undermined by the increasing dominance of the executive. Though they were significantly recast, they were not destroyed. They proved flexible and robust, and the challenge they faced in Victorian England revealed that the underlying, pervasive constitutional principle of consent from which they drew their legitimacy provided an enduring protection for the taxpayer.

CHANTAL STEBBINGS is Professor of Law and Legal History at the University of Exeter and a Fellow of the Royal Historical Society. She is also a General Commissioner of Income Tax. In the past she has served as Dean of the Faculty of Law at the University of Exeter, Visiting Professor at the University of Rennes, France and a Fellow of the Institute of Taxation.

CAMBRIDGE TAX LAW SERIES

Tax law is a growing area of interest, as it is included as a subdivision in many areas of study and is a key consideration in business needs throughout the world. Books in the Cambridge Tax Law series expose and shed light on the theories underpinning taxation systems, so that the questions to be asked when addressing an issue become clear. Written by leading scholars and illustrated by case law and legislation, they form an important resource for information on tax law while avoiding the minutiae of day-to-day detail addressed by practitioner books.

The books will be of interest for those studying law, business, economics, accounting and finance courses in the UK, but also in mainland Europe, USA and ex-Commonwealth countries with a similar taxation system to the UK.

Series Editor
Professor John Tiley
Queens' College, Director of the Centre for Tax Law.

Well known internationally in both academic and practitioner circles, Professor Tiley brings to the series his wealth of experience in tax law study, practice and writing. He was made a CBE in 2003 for services to tax law.

THE VICTORIAN TAXPAYER
AND THE LAW

A Study in Constitutional Conflict

CHANTAL STEBBINGS

CAMBRIDGE
UNIVERSITY PRESS

CAMBRIDGE UNIVERSITY PRESS
Cambridge, New York, Melbourne, Madrid, Cape Town, Singapore, São Paulo, Delhi

Cambridge University Press
The Edinburgh Building, Cambridge CB2 8RU, UK

Published in the United States of America by Cambridge University Press, New York

www.cambridge.org
Information on this title: www.cambridge.org/9780521899246

© Chantal Stebbings 2009

This publication is in copyright. Subject to statutory exception
and to the provisions of relevant collective licensing agreements,
no reproduction of any part may take place without
the written permission of Cambridge University Press.

First published 2009

Printed in the United Kingdom at the University Press, Cambridge

A catalogue record for this publication is available from the British Library

Library of Congress Cataloguing in Publication data
Stebbings, Chantal.
The Victorian taxpayer and the law : a study in constitutional conflict / Chantal Stebbings.
p.   cm. – (Cambridge tax law series)
ISBN 978-0-521-89924-6 (hardback)   1. Taxing power–Great Britain–History.
2. Tax protests and appeals–Great Britain–History.   3. Tax administration and procedure–
Great Britain–History. I. Title. II. Series.
KD5375.S74 2009
343.4204′2–dc22   2009007869

ISBN 978-0-521-89924-6 hardback

Cambridge University Press has no responsibility for the persistence or
accuracy of URLs for external or third-party internet websites referred to
in this publication, and does not guarantee that any content on such
websites is, or will remain, accurate or appropriate.

For my son, Mark

CONTENTS

ACKNOWLEDGEMENTS

This project was funded by the award of a Major Research Fellowship by the Leverhulme Trust. I most gratefully acknowledge this generous support, without which the sustained period of research and writing would not have been possible. I would like to thank Professor John Tiley CBE FBA, Professor of the Law of Taxation and Fellow of Queens' College, University of Cambridge, for his expert encouragement of this work, and for making me so welcome on my frequent visits to the Centre for Tax Law in Cambridge. My thanks to Mr David Wills, Librarian of the Squire Law Library, University of Cambridge, for his generous assistance with my many queries; to Mr Roger Brien of the Devon and Exeter Institution Library for his constant thoughtfulness in facilitating the writing of this book; and to friends and colleagues at universities all over the world who have willingly discussed aspects of this work with me and whose knowledge and expertise have been invaluable. Any remaining errors are, of course, my own. Finally, my special thanks again to my ever-supportive family who have borne with the problems of Victorian taxpayers for the past four years: to Mark and Jennie whose help and insight, in the midst of their own studies, I have greatly valued, and to my husband Howard who has again read every draft of every chapter with his usual enthusiasm, perception and unfailing love.

TABLE OF STATUTES

TABLE OF CASES

ABBREVIATIONS

Cases: The named reporters of cases have been cited according to the standard abbreviations in Donald Raistrick, *Index to Legal Citations and Abbreviations*, 2nd edition (London: Bowker-Saur, 1993).

BTR	*British Tax Review*
CIR	*Commissioners of Inland Revenue*
DRO	*Devon Record Office*
HCPP	*House of Commons Parliamentary Papers*
Parl. Deb.	*Parliamentary Debates*
TNA: PRO	*The National Archives: Public Record Office*

The establishment of the taxpayer's safeguards in English law

Prologue

One of America's greatest judges famously observed that 'taxes are what we pay for civilised society',[1] and from the earliest times English men and women were called on to pay for the costs of managing the state in an orderly way, providing an infrastructure of good government and defence.[2] As the effective government of a state depended to a great extent on the condition of its finances, the state's power to tax its subjects was central to its relationship with them, and the law of tax its principal and voluminous formal expression. The imposition of a tax, whether novel or merely an increase in the rate or incidence, was always perceived and accepted as an act of considerable constitutional importance. It affirmed the power and legitimacy of the state. To tax was to govern, and, implicitly, to do so by right, and as such was an expression of sovereignty. In taxation, above all, the interests of the individual most closely and repeatedly came into direct conflict with those of central government. Tensions between the state and the subject in this respect were inevitable, and not merely because the payment of taxes, however worthy or necessary the object, was disliked by most and constituted a very real hardship to many. Tensions were deep seated for three reasons. First, the exaction of taxes by the state by its nature violated the fundamental right of the subject to private property, one of the three absolute rights vested in the English people[3] that constituted an aspect of their personal liberty.[4] The right

---

[1] *Compañía General de Tabacos* v. *Collector* 275 US 87 (1927) at 100 *per* Holmes J.
[2] J. S. Mill, *Principles of Political Economy*, 6th edition, People's Edition (London: Longmans, Green & Co., 1896), Book V, p. 483.
[3] Sir William Blackstone, *Commentaries on the Laws of England*, 1783 edition printed for W. Strahan and T. Cadell, London and D. Prince, Oxford, 4 vols. (New York: Garland Publishing Inc., 1978), vol. i, p. 138, and see generally pp. 127–40.
[4] See generally Jane Frecknall Hughes, 'The Concept of Taxation and the Age of Enlightenment', in John Tiley (ed.), *Studies in the History of Tax Law II* (Oxford and Portland, Oreg.: Hart Publishing, 2007), pp. 256–65.

was highly valued by the English and it occupied a prominent place in political thought.[5] As it was prima facie inviolable and guarded by the law,[6] it was a common foundation of objections to any new taxation.[7] Nevertheless, taxation was demanded as 'a sacrifice of part of the public property … for the preservation of the whole'.[8] Sacrifice indeed, and a necessary evil. Secondly, the balance of power between the state and the subject was by its very nature an unequal one, and in no area was this more keenly felt by the individual than in taxation. Taxpayers were for the most part ordinary people of moderate means, but even the wealthy were too weak and poor as individuals to withstand the mighty organs of the state.[9] When the state argued necessity, the individual taxpayer could have little effective response. The political and administrative history of Britain shows the state increasing its power, authority and resources as its financial needs grew, with the position of the subject remaining, inevitably, subordinate and growing correspondingly in vulnerability. Thirdly, the highly personal nature, especially of direct taxation, and the mechanics of assessment and collection, demanded and engendered a close and continuous relationship between the state and the taxpayer. This made taxation a highly visible and tangible expression of potent state power. These three factors combined to make tax a highly sensitive issue in the relationship between government and governed. Indeed, the history of tax law is the history of the reconciliation of the power of the state and the right of the subject. Taxpayers acknowledged that they paid tax to the state in return for defence and stable government,[10] but the inherent tensions in their relationship with the state, and its necessary intimacy, led them to question whether that arrangement included any provision to ensure the state did not abuse its unequal position and that the demands of the public revenue were not favoured at their expense.[11]

---

[5] W. R. Cornish and G. de N. Clark, *Law and Society in England 1750–1950* (London: Sweet & Maxwell, 1989), p. 3.

[6] 9 Hen. III c. 29 (1225).

[7] For example the triple assessment was condemned as 'a profligate contempt of property': *Parliamentary History* vol. 33, cols. 1111–12, 14 December 1797 *per* Charles James Fox.

[8] *Ibid.*, col. 1075, 4 December 1797 *per* William Pitt. See Frecknall Hughes, 'Concept of Taxation', pp. 262–3.

[9] See *The Times*, 29 June 1864, p. 9 col. f; *ibid.*, 7 July 1864, p. 14 col. a.

[10] For Locke's theory of social contract, see Frecknall Hughes, 'Concept of Taxation', pp. 261–2.

[11] John Booth, *The Inland Revenue … Saint or Sinner?* (Lymington: Coracle Publishing, 2002), where the author argues that the balance is firmly in favour of the Board of Inland Revenue.

The law of tax was clearly primarily, and in its essential nature, one of constraint, expressing a power which has been described as 'the most pervasive and privileged exercise of the police power of the state'.[12] It compelled the payment of taxes with penal sanctions, and provided for the compulsory disclosure of personal information regarding an individual's property and income. It was the very power of that constraint which raised a correspondingly strong demand by the taxpayer[13] for a protective element in his relationship with the law. As Bracton had stated in the thirteenth century, even the king stood under not only God but the law,[14] and the place of law was integral to the English model of government. Governments were the servants of the law, not its masters, and law was, as William Blackstone observed, 'the supreme arbiter of every man's life, liberty, and property'.[15] It was thus to the law that the taxpayer looked for protection. Only the law could ensure the government did not abuse its immensely powerful position. It was in the state's interests to promote this protective character of the law. While the state equally had to be protected against too lenient an assessment, compliance to tax was of self-evident importance, and it could best be achieved by providing the taxpayer with systems to ensure that he was taxed accurately and according to the letter of the legislation, for legal safeguards went a long way towards ensuring public co-operation. Furthermore, the absence of legal protection could allow abuse by the state of its taxation powers leading to the inevitable surfacing of the fundamental tensions and the consequent release of popular resentment. There was plenty of evidence for this. Used oppressively, taxation gave rise to popular anger and revolt, and disputes between the state and its subjects over the nature or extent of taxation lay at the heart of the political revolutions of the Western world.[16] The English civil war, the American war of independence and the French revolution were all the result, to varying degrees, of the unrestrained exercise of the powerful instrument of taxation by central government. The power and needs of the state, both fiscally and politically, made the establishment of legal safeguards for the taxpayer

---

[12] John Tiley, *Revenue Law*, 4th edition (Oxford: Hart Publishing, 2000), p. 9.

[13] As to the existence of 'The Taxpayer' see James Coffield, *The Tax Gatherers* (London: Hutchinson, 1960), p. 10.

[14] George E. Woodbine (ed.), *Bracton on the Laws and Customs of England*, Samuel S. Thorne (trans.), 4 vols. (Cambridge, Mass.: Harvard University Press, 1968), vol. ii, p. 33.

[15] Blackstone, *Commentaries*, vol. i, p. 141.

[16] See H. C. G. Matthew, 'Disraeli, Gladstone, and the Politics of Mid-Victorian Budgets', *Historical Journal*, 22 (1979), 615 at 615–16.

a matter of necessity and defined the nature of the relationship between the taxpayer and law.

Taxpayers required more than the economic and moral considerations which yielded notions of fairness, equality and good administration[17] which were certainly of considerable importance in the formulation of tax policy and the development of an ideology of taxation.[18] They wanted safeguards of law and they acquired a role in the imposition of tax through the fundamental constitutional safeguard of parliamentary democracy, and an undisputed right to pay only what Parliament had consented to, as expressed in the legislation of that body, neither more nor less. This ensured that the state taxed only within those limits, that it acted legally, not arbitrarily, in the imposition of tax. They enjoyed protection against excessive or unjust assessment through two supporting tax-specific legal safeguards, namely local administration and the overarching enforcing power of the judiciary. The three legal safeguards, namely the constitutional safeguards of Parliament, the administrative safeguard of localism, and the judicial safeguard of the regular courts of law, constituted the bulwarks of the law safeguarding the taxpayer from the abuse of the state and its taxing organs.

A new commercial and industrial age

Most aspects of the three fundamental legal safeguards of Parliament, local administration and the judiciary, were conceived and established in a world very different from that of the Victorian taxpayer in nineteenth-century England. The context of their establishment was an agricultural economy, with domestic commerce and industry generally being small-scale, local and often family-based and requiring little capital. Workers operated either singly or in small groups, largely in their own homes, with unsophisticated tools and machines and forms of power which were all limited in extent, reliability or time. Only foreign commerce was

---

[17] Notably Adam Smith's four canons of taxation: Adam Smith, *An Inquiry into the Nature and Causes of the Wealth of Nations* (R. H. Campbell, A. S. Skinner, W. B. Todd (eds.), 2 vols. (Oxford: Clarendon Press, 1976), vol. ii, Book V, Chapter 2, pp. 825–8. See H. Lloyd Reid, *The British Tax-Payers' Rights* (London: T Fisher Unwin, 1898), p. 210. Notions of fairness pervaded contemporary debate on taxation: Arthur Herald, *The Income Tax in Utopia* (Letchworth: Garden City Press Ltd. 1917), p. 5; *Young* v. *IRC* (1875) 1 TC 57 at 61.

[18] See G. S. A. Wheatcroft, 'The Attitude of the Legislature and the Courts to Tax Avoidance', *Modern Law Review* 18 (1955), 209 at 212 for popular views on tax avoidance; Henk Vording, 'The Normative Background for a Broad Concept of Tax' in Bruno Peeters (ed.), *The Concept of Tax*, IBFD series no. 3 (Amsterdam: IBFD, 2008), pp. 30–48.

important in scale and in its use of capital. Society reflected this agrarian economy. Land was the foundation of political power, social status and material wealth; the main focus of society was the village or the small town and the population was small, and communications poor.[19] The fiscal system reflected this. Immediately prior to the Victorian period public revenue was raised primarily through the indirect excise and customs duties, while direct taxation was limited to times of national emergency, generally war. The principal direct tax was the land tax, originally a tax on real and personal property and incomes[20] but it became a tax purely on land in the nature of a perpetual charge by the end of the eighteenth century.[21] Though it was levied every year, and constituted a real burden on landowners,[22] the tax reduced in importance and effectiveness, and in 1798 provision was made for its redemption.[23] The demands of war forced William Pitt to seek other methods of raising revenue, and he increased the already large number of assessed taxes on luxury goods, including the famous window and inhabited house taxes, and extended them to servants, horses, carriages, coaches and carts.[24] These taxes were rendered complex and relatively unproductive by the many exemptions they allowed, and in 1798 he turned to a new and conceptually important tax, the triple assessment based on multiples of a taxpayer's assessed tax charge of the previous year.[25] The eighteenth century closed, however, with the introduction by William Pitt of a general charge on all leading branches of income,[26] namely the new income tax. The tax

[19] See generally, M. J. Daunton, *Progress and Poverty* (Oxford University Press, 1995).
[20] 38 Geo. III c. 5 s. 2 (1797).
[21] See CIR Thirteenth Report, *HCPP* (1870) (82, 82–1) xx 193, 377; Charles Wilson, *England's Apprenticeship 1603–1763* (London: Longman, 1965), pp. 130–1; Pretor W. Chandler, *The Land Tax: its Creation and Management* (London: Reeves & Turner, 1899); W. R. Ward, *The English Land Tax in the Eighteenth Century* (London: Oxford University Press, 1953); Paul Langford, *Public Life and the Propertied Englishman 1689–1798* (Oxford: Clarendon Press, 1991), pp. 339–66; J. V. Beckett, 'Land Tax or Excise: The Levying of Taxation in Seventeenth- and Eighteenth-Century England', *English Historical Review* 100 (1985), 285; William Phillips, 'No Flowers, By Request', *BTR* (1963), 285.
[22] See R. A. C. Parker, 'Direct Taxation on the Coke Estates in the Eighteenth Century', *English Historical Review* 71 (1956), 247.
[23] 38 Geo. III c. 60 (1798). See *Parliamentary History*, vol. 33, cols. 1434–54, 9 May 1798; Anon., *Considerations on the Act for the Redemption of the Land Tax* (London: J. Payne, 1798).
[24] For a history of these taxes see Stephen Dowell, *A History of Taxation and Taxes in England*, 4 vols. (London: Longmans, Green & Co, 1884), vol. iv.
[25] 38 Geo. III c. 16 (1798).
[26] 39 Geo. III c. 13 (1799). For the history of income tax, see B. E. V. Sabine, *A History of Income Tax* (London: George Allen & Unwin Ltd, 1966); Peter Harris, *Income Tax in*

failed, and needed substantial procedural reform by Henry Addington in 1803 to make it succeed.[27] The revenue from the customs, excise and stamp duties together, however, far exceeded that from the direct taxes.[28] Governments favoured indirect taxation not only because it was easy to collect but because it was thought to constitute an accurate taxation of wealth. The greatest proportion of the public revenue was contributed by the ancient customs,[29] imposed on spirits, beer, wine and tobacco, paid by the merchant on certain imported articles and the cost passed on to the consumer. The excise, introduced as part of the financial measures of the civil war in 1643, was of particular importance in the eighteenth century[30] and applied to a wide range of articles of domestic consumption and raw materials, including beer, malt, spirits, soap, salt, glass, tea, coffee, tobacco, and paper. Of all the taxes of the period, the excise was the most unpopular primarily because it tended to be imposed on items of necessity rather than luxury as part of the purchase price and so could not easily be avoided, and its administration was obtrusive. '[I]ts very name,' observed Blackstone, 'has been odious to the people of England',[31] and violent excise riots had been experienced after the tax's introduction.[32] Like the customs, the excise was increased throughout the eighteenth century[33] and reached its peak in the early nineteenth century, before declining, as the customs did, in the face of the free trade movement. Stamp duties, introduced in 1694 to finance the war against France,[34] were imposed on

Common Law Jurisdictions, Cambridge Tax Law Series (Cambridge University Press, 2006); B. E. V. Sabine, 'Great Budgets: Pitt's Budget of 1799', *BTR* (1970), 201; CIR Thirteenth Report, *HCPP* (1870) (82, 82–1) xx 193, 377 at pp. 326–7.

[27] 43 Geo. III c. 122 (1803). See generally A. Farnsworth, *Addington: the Author of the Modern Income Tax* (London: Stevens and Sons, 1951).

[28] Patrick K. O'Brien, 'The Political Economy of British Taxation, 1660–1815', *Economic History Review*, 41 (1988), 1.

[29] For a history of the customs duties see First Report, Commissioners of Customs, *HCPP* (1857) (2186) iii 301 at pp. 358–76. See generally Ronald Max Hartwell, 'Taxation in England during the Industrial Revolution', *Cato Journal*, 1 (1981), 129 at 145; Sir John Craig, *A History of Red Tape* (London: Macdonald & Evans Ltd, 1955), pp. 91–6; William Phillips, 'Anything to Declare', *BTR* (1965), 226.

[30] Hartwell, 'Taxation in England', 145; Craig, *Red Tape*, pp. 99–101.

[31] Blackstone, *Commentaries*, vol. i, p. 321. See Wilson, *England's Apprenticeship*, pp. 129–30.

[32] Michael J. Braddick, 'Popular Politics and Public Policy: the Excise Riot at Smithfield in February 1647 and its Aftermath', *Historical Journal*, 34 (1991), 597; Stephen Matthews, 'A Tax Riot in Tewkesbury in 1805', *BTR* (2002), 437.

[33] See generally Edward Carson, 'The Development of Taxation up to the Eighteenth Century', *BTR* (1984), 237; Graham Smith, *Something to Declare* (London: Harrap, 1980).

[34] 5 & 6 Will. & M. c. 21 (1694). See generally R. S. Nock, '1694 And All That', *BTR* (1994), 432.

the vellum, paper or parchment on which legal transactions were written, on various licences, postage stamps, pamphlets and newspapers.[35] The duty was either a fixed amount depending on the nature of the item in question, or was an ad valorem duty depending on the value involved. Probate duty had been introduced in 1694 as a stamp duty on the grant of probate or letters of administration, while legacy duty, originally a stamp duty, dated from 1780[36] and became a tax on moveable property. Both applied mainly to personalty passing by death.

When Victoria came to the throne in 1837, profound economic and social changes in the fabric of national life were transforming Britain from an agricultural economy to the leading industrial nation in the world and the essentials of this process were already in place. Developments in technology had established the potential for replacing natural power with steam power for the production of quality iron and the mechanisation of industry. Developments in communications took the form of better roads and the development of canals. Overseas trade had grown with the opening of new markets in America, India and the Far East. The coal, iron and cotton manufacturing industries all grew rapidly, and the development of the railways was astonishing, all stimulated by an expansion in markets and available labour resulting from a trebling of the population. Mass production and heavy industry came to dominate, and towns and cities grew up around centres of industry, while London became the centre of new financial and commercial institutions. All these changes and developments interlinked, and industrial and economic development were self-perpetuating. Britain's commercial and industrial prosperity, as well as her confidence and global influence, were evident at the time of the Great Exhibition of 1851, and reflected in the contemporary statistics of production.[37] The country's economy continued to grow throughout the century,[38] and by 1870 it had far outstripped its European neighbours and the United States. A new fund of commercial wealth was created. There was a decline in the political, economic and social value of land, and an increased tendency to express wealth in terms of money, and new investments in the form of the shares and debentures of joint stock banks, public

---

[35] See generally Pauline Sadler and Lynne Oats, '"This Great Crisis in the Republick of Letters" – The Introduction in 1712 of Stamp Duties on Newspapers and Pamphlets', *BTR* (2002), 353.

[36] 20 Geo. III c. 28 (1780). See too 36 Geo. III c. 52 (1796). For a history of these duties see CIR First Report, *HCPP* (1857) (2199 sess. 1) iv 65 at Appendix 10.

[37] Cornish and Clark, *Law and Society*, p. 5.

[38] CIR Fifteenth Report, *HCPP* 1872 (646) xviii 259 at p. 318.

utilities and Britain's expanding empire.[39] These new commercial opportunities considerably increased the complexities of wealth and business. Better communications and postal services increased the pace of work to an unprecedented degree, and business methods were of rapidly growing sophistication. The industrial revolution changed the commercial and industrial life of the country, and shaped its society, its politics, its outlook and its priorities.

These new social and economic conditions challenged almost every aspect of the English legal system,[40] a system which was essentially medieval in substance, structure, procedures and institutions. The legal process and legal institutions were forced to change as a result of wider political, social and economic pressures. The enormous and rapid growth in the population and the migration from the countryside to towns which became overcrowded and diseased[41] were problems of social regulation of the greatest magnitude, and tested the very structures of government. New and appalling working conditions in factories[42] and mines and the exploitation of children gave rise to new public health and safety issues, and the crushing pervasive influence of poverty challenged the old poor laws.[43] New relationships in the workplace were not addressed by the old law of master and servant, while crowded cities and the erosion of the family by new work practices were believed to lead to increased crime, with which the old criminal law was not equipped to deal efficiently. Traditional legal institutions for the preservation of wealth and the support of the family were tested as commercial pressures came into conflict with moral imperatives.[44] A new commercial economy challenged a law of property based entirely on landownership, found bankruptcy laws

---

[39] See P. L. Cottrell, *British Overseas Investment in the Nineteenth Century* (London: Macmillan, 1975).

[40] See generally W. Blake Odgers, 'Changes in Domestic Legislation', in Council of Legal Education (eds.), *A Century of Law Reform* (London: Macmillan & Co. Ltd, 1901), pp. 131–41; Derek Fraser, *The Evolution of the British Welfare State* (London: Macmillan, 1973), pp. 28–50; David Roberts, *Victorian Origins of the British Welfare State*, reprint of Yale University Press edition 1960 (Hamden, Connecticut: Archon Books, 1969), pp. 38–9.

[41] Poor Law Commissioners, *Report on an Inquiry into the Sanitary Condition of the Labouring Population of Great Britain* (London: HMSO, 1842).

[42] First Report of the Central Board of Commissioners for inquiring into the Employment of Children in Factories, *HCPP* (1833) (450) xx 1 at p. 36.

[43] See generally S. G. and E. O. A. Checkland (eds.), *The Poor Law Report of 1834* (Pelican Books, 1974), Introduction.

[44] See generally C. Stebbings, *The Private Trustee in Victorian England* (Cambridge University Press, 2002).

inadequate, a law of commercial association rudimentary and a property law inhibiting the full exploitation of land and minerals. Finally the legal process was one of infinite slowness, technicality and expense, unfit to serve a new dynamic economy and society. These demands on the existing law and legal process were all novel and required a significant degree of adaptation and, in some cases, fundamental changes in principle.

Taxation and the law of tax in 1837 were not immune to these momentous social and economic pressures. Tax had to operate in this new commercial climate in which not only would individuals' tax affairs inevitably grow in complexity, but the taxpayer population was itself growing rapidly. In an age when the objective of nearly all taxation was still simply to raise government finance, the fiscal challenge of the new Victorian age was the traditional one of insufficient yield. The wars against France in the mid and late eighteenth century had created a fiscal crisis for early Victorian governments and when Sir Robert Peel began his second Tory administration in 1841, the Treasury was empty. The debt resulting from the wars was still taking over half of the total gross central government expenditure, and navy and army costs were high. A series of bad harvests and depressed wages had increased the demand for relief from the established indirect taxes, and the earlier remission of a number of taxes to promote Whig free trade had absorbed what surplus there was. The problem facing the government was not only to secure new sources of public revenue, but equally to ensure its steady and consistent flow to sustain the rapid and widespread social reforms and to meet the increased expenditure of a developing bureaucratic state. The need was therefore to increase the public revenue from taxation to satisfy pressing military and domestic demands. It was the industrial revolution which provided both the solution and the challenge. The solution lay in the new commercial wealth of the transformed British economy; the challenge lay in how to tap it. The challenge was compounded, however, by two difficulties.

First, the existing taxes did not yield sufficient revenue to meet the government's long-term demands. This was despite the increased commercial activity and wealth which naturally gave rise to higher yields, and despite the increase in the range and rate of most taxes in the eighteenth and early nineteenth centuries, and a measure of consolidation and innovation. In particular, though the land tax continued to yield a steady revenue, it was undermined by its methods of administration and was limited in the extent to which it was suited or could be made to suit the increasing demand for public revenue. It had long become unrealistic through being based on out-of-date valuations and had become of little fiscal significance.[45]

Secondly, the public's attitudes were not conducive to new or increased taxes. The popular perception in pre-Victorian England was one of heavy personal taxation.[46] The triple assessment, along with the permanence of the land tax and then the income tax, constituted a heavy burden on the wealthier classes at the dawn of the nineteenth century.[47] The income tax had been in suspension since 1816 and its reintroduction was not necessarily straightforward. Pitt had faced acute problems in introducing it in 1799, and any reintroduction after such a long period would almost amount to the institution of a new tax, with all the political and practical problems associated with it. In 1837 the compulsory taxation of income was still a novelty, for only a small proportion of the working population could remember its introduction less than forty years before, and most had no experience of it at all. Ideological objections to direct income taxation as inquisitorial, though weaker, were still widely held, and the tax was one which, as a commentator was to observe some forty years later, 'touches to the very quick the sensitiveness of the taxpayer'.[48] Furthermore, a direct influence of the industrial revolution was the impact of centralisation. The addressing of the new social problems through the intervention of central government led to a growth in state bureaucracy. While state intervention to address major public social issues began only in the 1830s, tax had been the first sphere of government activity to see a significant growth in bureaucracy. Blackstone had observed in the 1760s that the management of the revenue by the crown had given rise to a 'multitude' of officers who had 'extended the influence of government to every corner of the nation', an influence he called 'most amazingly extensive'.[49] Not only were taxpayers aware that a growth in state bureaucracy had to be paid for and would result in increased taxation, they disliked state interference in its own right. It was contrary to their orthodox belief in laissez-faire, and their traditional faith in local government and local institutions. Since substantive national taxation was the ultimate expression of centralisation,

---

[45] See CIR Twenty-ninth Report, *HCPP* (1886) (4816) xx 279 at pp. 307–8.
[46] See the famous words of Sidney Smith quoted by Monroe: H. H. Monroe, *Intolerable Inquisition? Reflections on the Law of Tax* (London: Stevens & Sons, 1981), pp. 18–19.
[47] John Habakkuk, *Marriage, Debt, and the Estates System, English Landownership 1650–1950* (Oxford: Clarendon Press, 1994), pp. 522–3.
[48] Leone Levi, 'On the Reconstruction of the Income and Property Tax', *Journal of the Statistical Society of London*, 37 (1874), 155 at 157.
[49] Blackstone, *Commentaries*, vol. i, p. 336.

of state interference with private property, taxation was unpopular from that perspective. It was in this context that tax law had to adapt in order to meet the immediate challenge to provide a substantive and procedural tax framework to respond to an acute financial need. And thereafter, it had to ensure that the existing tax law regime, and any new developments in this respect, suited the demands of its increasingly technical, demanding and dynamic commercial field of operation.

The fiscal response

The inevitable response to the immediate fiscal challenge of the Victorian age was to increase the rate of some existing taxes and to introduce new ones. Though the assessed taxes continued to be levied and the redemption of the land tax continued apace,[50] Peel was convinced the solution to the 'great public evil' of the growing deficit lay in the reintroduction of income tax. In 1842,[51] despite popular protests, he revived Pitt's income tax of 1799[52] as extensively modified in both principle and process by Addington in 1803.[53] The 1842 Act was in effect a reprint of the 1806 Act,[54] which itself was virtually unchanged from that of 1803, and the tax itself was to be administered according to the provisions of the Taxes Management Act 1803. Income tax was also 'the key that would unlock the Free Trade cupboard',[55] and indeed it allowed him the political space to reform the customs and excise and remove a number of those imposts.[56] Within income tax itself he addressed the problem of the failure fully to tax commercial income by introducing a new method of assessment.[57] Just over a decade later a new succession duty was introduced, the first new tax of the reign, primarily to remove a glaring anomaly in the regime of taxation at death. The Succession Duty Act 1853 taxed all successions to property which took place as a consequence of death, and thereby for the first time brought all real and personal property, whether settled or not,

---

[50] See CIR First Report, *HCPP* (1857) (2199 sess. 1) iv 65 at Appendix 14.

[51] 5 & 6 Vict. c. 35.

[52] 39 Geo. III c. 13. See generally B. E. V. Sabine, 'Great Budgets III: Sir Robert Peel's Budget of 1842', *BTR* (1971), 50.

[53] 43 Geo. III c. 122 (1803).   [54] 46 Geo. III c. 65.

[55] G. M. Trevelyan, *British History in the Nineteenth Century and After (1782–1919)*, 2nd edition (London: Longmans, Green & Co., 1937), p. 267.

[56] See generally J. H. Clapham, *An Economic History of Modern Britain: Free Trade and Steel 1850–1886* (Cambridge University Press, 1932), pp. 398–9.

[57] The Special Commissioners: see below, pp. 105–9.

into charge.[58] It was primarily an extension of the legacy duty to real property, which had been chronically under-taxed.[59] These duties increased progressively, and the end of the century saw the introduction, amid acrimonious debate and sustained opposition, of the new estate duty on the aggregate net value of all property passing on a person's death.[60] Though it provided small revenue in relation to the other taxes, it soon proved its fiscal worth.[61]

The introduction of new taxes, the reintroduction of old ones and the increase in some existing ones was not novel and was not a response to a challenge arising directly from the new industrial and commercial conditions. Governments had always been doing this in times of financial need. The formal response to the financial crisis in 1842, however, defined the essential character of the fiscal policy of the new age. The reintroduction of the income tax marked the beginning of the formative period of modern taxation, a period of some sixty years in which the legal foundations of British tax were constructed and refined, creating an enduring basis on which legislators of the following century and beyond had to operate to craft a new fiscal system in radically different global conditions. The basis of taxation achieved by the Victorians and begun by Peel was one of pervasive and permanent direct taxation, with an increasing prominence and scope of a compulsory general income tax and a relative decline both in the fiscal importance of indirect taxation[62] and the ideological adherence to voluntaryism. The income tax was at the centre of this new regime, a tax which despite a modest yield was, only fifteen years after its reintroduction, described by the Commissioners of Inland Revenue as 'the most important of all the duties under our management'.[63] Despite a consistent political adherence to its theoretically temporary nature,[64] it would become in practical terms permanent, taking its place as the dominant tax of the modern world, with soaring rates after the First World War and the consequent development of the modern and unstoppable phenomenon of

---

[58] John Stuart Mill had regarded inheritances and legacies as 'highly proper subjects for taxation': J. S. Mill, *Principles of Political Economy*, Book V, chapter II, section 3.

[59] *Parl. Deb.*, vol. 127, ser. 3, cols. 259–71, 12 May 1853 (HC).

[60] For the history of the death duties up to 1884, see CIR Twenty-eighth Report, *HCPP* (1884–5) (4474) xxii 43 at pp. 102–12. See generally William Phillips, 'Three Score Years and Ten', *BTR* (1964), 152.

[61] CIR Thirty-ninth Report, *HCPP* (1896) (8226) xxv 329 at p. 386.

[62] H. C. G. Matthew, *Gladstone* (Oxford: Clarendon Press, 1997), pp. 121–5.

[63] CIR First Report, *HCPP* (1857) (2199 sess. 1) iv 65 at p. 94.

[64] See generally Clapham, *Economic History*, pp. 399–405.

tax avoidance or 'taxmanship'.[65] An effective administrative system, successive governments with the determination to implement such a tax regime, and an overall, if not universal, popular acceptance all played their part. The Victorian taxation regime was one of considerable scope and depth which marked a change of fiscal culture, with respect both to the substance of taxation and its machinery.[66]

In the process of this inevitable and necessary reappraisal and reform of the tax laws, procedures and practices, and the creation of a new fiscal culture, the legal safeguards could be vulnerable. This was the real concern. When considered with a new self-motivating commercial dynamism, an inexorable growth in the bureaucratic authority of the state and a legal system faced with a sustained demand for change, the need for taxpayers to ensure they were taxed strictly within the law became an issue of considerable importance. The three legal safeguards which the law provided for taxpayers at the dawn of the Victorian age were safeguards of principle which had been established in English law, to varying degrees, for over five hundred years and which had endured largely unchanged. It remained to be seen how these legal safeguards, conceived in a narrow and rigid socio-economic context of a different age, and just as entrenched as other legal institutions, would be affected in the inevitable adaptation of tax law and practice.

The parliamentary safeguards

The substantive constitutional safeguard

The fundamental protection of the taxpayer was that the tax demanded of him or her was lawful, and the cardinal principle of English taxation was that it could only legally be levied with the consent of the people's representatives in Parliament. This intimacy between the legality of taxation and the taxpayer's consent through Parliament was central to the protective relationship between the taxpayer and the law. To demand that a tax be levied only with the consent of Parliament, that is by legislation properly enacted imposing a tax, was an essential right, liberty and privilege of the English people. It was 'the undoubted birthright of

---

[65] Carl S. Shoup, 'Some Distinguishing Characteristics of the British, French, and United States Public Finance Systems', *American Economic Review*, 47 (1957), 187 at 194. See generally David Stopforth, 'Settlements and the Avoidance of Tax on Income – the Period to 1920', *BTR* (1990), 225.

[66] See Matthew, 'Politics of Mid-Victorian Budgets'.

free Subjects',[67] and only thus could their right to private property be interfered with.

The need for the consent of taxpayers to direct taxation[68] was well established in the thirteenth century, reflected in law, custom and political practice and rarely departed from by the monarch.[69] The need for that consent to be expressed through the House of Commons was settled by the fourteenth, for by then the status of the members of that house as the representatives of the people was accepted in political and constitutional theory, and, moreover, finding expression in parliamentary practice.[70] It has been shown that the notion that every subject contributed to the decision to tax through his representatives in Parliament was not a fanciful one, and that by the standards of the age, English taxpayers enjoyed a measure of actual representation.[71] By the fifteenth century, Parliament consisted not only of the leading churchmen and lay peers, but smaller landowners and the principal members of the counties and main urban centres. As such it represented the entire community, and the representatives' function was to express their communities' concerns and grievances, and, of course, to consent on their behalf.[72] In legal theory taxpayers, like all subjects, were deemed to be present in person.[73] In this sense, therefore, taxpayers consented in a real way to the undermining of their right to personal property by the imposition of taxes upon them.

This fundamental constitutional protection of parliamentary consent was established beyond question by the civil war and lay at the heart of that conflict. At no time in history was the protection of the taxpayer of such central national importance as in the politically turbulent seventeenth century when it was intimately bound up with the struggle between the Stuarts and their Parliaments on the question of the supremacy of the prerogative. It was in the context of a courageous and resolute determination to be taxed only with parliamentary consent that the fundamental freedoms of the English were secured. Tax accordingly played a central

[67] *Darnel's Case* (1627) 3 ST 1 at 85 *per* Sir Dudley Diggs.
[68] For early distinctions in indirect taxation, see A. L. Brown, *The Governance of Late Medieval England 1272-1461* (London: Edward Arnold, 1989), pp. 226–7.
[69] *Ibid.*, pp. 224–5; Jeffrey Goldsworthy, *The Sovereignty of Parliament* (Oxford: Clarendon Press, 1999), pp. 46–7, 69–70; Martin Daunton, *Trusting Leviathan: the Politics of Taxation in Britain, 1799–1914* (Cambridge University Press, 2001), pp. 1–8.
[70] Brown, *Governance of Late Medieval England*, pp. 228–9.
[71] Goldsworthy, *Sovereignty of Parliament*, pp. 69–70.
[72] Brown, *Governance of Late Medieval England*, pp. 232–5.
[73] See Goldsworthy, *Sovereignty of Parliament*, pp. 96–7.

role in the destruction of absolute kingship and the establishment of the legal supremacy of Parliament and a constitutional monarchy.[74] Fiscal issues took on a constitutional dimension. In the face of an unwilling or non-existent Parliament, and where the borders of prerogative powers were fluid and uncertain, monarchs exploited their royal prerogative powers to raise money.[75]

The extensive debate as to the legality of indirect taxation in the Commons in 1610[76] made it clear that the king was not permitted at law to impose customs duties on his subjects within the realm without the consent of Parliament outside the exercise of the prerogative to regulate foreign trade.[77] Above all, however, it was the period of Charles I's personal rule which raised popular passions against arbitrary taxation. He raised money through a variety of means, all arguably illegal as undertaken without the consent of Parliament.[78] Whereas the king had some theoretical room for manoeuvre in relation to the indirect taxes, since tonnage and poundage had been approved by the decision in *Bates' Case*,[79] there was none in relation to the direct taxes. In 1637 the great case of ship-money,[80] following the levy in 1629 of money for naval defence on coastal towns, tested the fundamental principle of parliamentary consent. The demand of a compulsory money payment into general navy funds rather than ships themselves[81] was, in the view of many, nothing less than a tax, and a tax made by the king without the consent of the people in Parliament. As such it was contrary to the provisions of the Petition of Right consented to by the king himself only a few years earlier.[82] John Hampden, a landowner and parliamentarian from Buckinghamshire, who had refused to pay the

---

[74] Cornish and Clark, *Law and Society*, pp. 6–12.

[75] See generally Derek Hall, 'Impositions and the Courts 1554–1606', *Law Quarterly Review* 69 (1953), 200; Wilson, *England's Apprenticeship*, pp. 92–6.

[76] See *Parliamentary Debates in 1610, edited from the notes of a Member of the House of Commons by Samuel Rawson Gardiner*, Camden Society, First Series 81 (London: Camden Society, 1862).

[77] See David W. Williams, 'Three Hundred Years On: Are our Tax Bills Right Yet?', *BTR* (1989), 370 at 375 on the prerogative powers of taxation.

[78] T. F. T. Plucknett, *Taswell-Langmead's English Constitutional History*, 11th edition (London: Sweet & Maxwell Ltd., 1960), pp. 365–72; Richard Cust, *The Forced Loan and English Politics, 1626–1628* (Oxford: Clarendon Press, 1987).

[79] *Bates' Case* (1606) 2 ST 371.

[80] See generally Edward Hyde, *History of the Rebellion and Civil Wars in England*, W. Dunn Macray (ed.), 2 vols. (Oxford: Clarendon Press, 1888) vol. i, p. 92; W. J. Jones, *Politics and the Bench: the Judges and the Origins of the English Civil War* (London: George Allen and Unwin Ltd., 1971).

[81] See the writ to London, in *R. v. Hampden* (1637) 3 ST 825 at 830–3.

[82] 3 Car. I c. 1 (1628). See *Darnel's Case* (1627) 3 ST 1 at 221–4.

forced loan of 1627, refused to meet the crown's demand for 20 shillings' ship-money. This led to one of the most important and celebrated trials in English fiscal and constitutional history. The issue which the court had to decide was whether in exercising his powers and duty to protect the realm, the king was subject to the rights of his subjects in their property. It was a case in which the royal prerogative was unequivocally pitted against the liberty of the subject in the property in his goods. Sir John Finch reflected the opinion of his brother judges when he observed it was 'the greatest case that ever came in any of our memories, or the memory of any man'.[83]

Hampden refused to pay on principle. Ship-money, he argued, had been levied, and subjects' property interfered with, without the consent of Parliament, contrary to a long line of statutes from Magna Carta to the Petition of Right. The danger was clear, for if the king could demand 20 shillings without the consent of Parliament, he could demand £20. Though ultimately the court found for the king, by the narrowest possible margin, the judges relied on the absolute authority of the monarch because they were unable to refute the statutory authority for parliamentary consent to taxation.[84] While it was clear that the king could not impose taxes on his subjects at all times and in all circumstances, for they 'are subjects, not slaves, freemen, not villains, to be taxed *de alto et basso*',[85] to say that the king could never tax his subjects other than with the consent of Parliament was to go too far. The law was the 'trust servant' of the king, to be used to govern his people, and so it 'knows no such king-yoking policy'.[86] When the kingdom was in immediate danger taxes could be levied without the consent of Parliament,[87] in other words only as an incident to his prerogative right to defend the realm. It was, however, the fearless and learned judgment of Sir George Croke which was to prove the most enduring.[88] He found unequivocally for Hampden that the king's demand was contrary to the common law and to the statutes of the country since it was not sanctioned by Parliament. Neither prerogative nor necessity could make it legal. It was the consent of every man's representative in Parliament which drew a distinction between the goods of a bondsman and those of a

---

[83] *R. v. Hampden* (1637) 3 ST 825 at 1217 *per* Sir John Finch.

[84] Though there were weaknesses in these authorities: see Ian Ferrier, 'Ship-Money Reconsidered', *BTR* (1984), 227 at 229.

[85] *R. v. Hampden* (1637) 3 ST 825 at 1090 *per* Sir Robert Berkley.   [86] *Ibid.*, at 1098.

[87] Sir John Finch at *ibid.*, 1224–43 gave the strongest and most unequivocal judgment for the king.

[88] *R. v. Hampden* (1637) 3 ST 825 at 1127–81.

free man, and it was a principle of taxation which permeated the common law and a series of statutes since Magna Carta.

Though the decision was for the king, Sir George Croke's judgment was a moral and political victory for Hampden and a powerful affirmation of the principle of parliamentary consent. Despite a legitimate argument that the case did not challenge the principle of parliamentary consent since it did not concern a tax at all,[89] the importance of the case went beyond the actual decision and in the longer term raised the fundamental basis on which the king could tax his people. It forced the king to recall Parliament in 1640 where it established its total control, both in substance and procedure, over taxation.[90] This was ultimately confirmed in the Bill of Rights 1689, which did not deny the existence of the royal prerogative, but laid down that if it imposed a new charge upon the subject, then parliamentary consent was required. '[L]evying money for or to the use of the Crown by pretence of prerogative', it declared, 'without grant of Parliament … is illegal.'[91] This, like all the rights laid down in the Bill of Rights, were 'true, ancient and indubitable rights and liberties' of the English people.[92] Parliamentary authority, meaning the consent of Commons, Lords and crown, came to be the exclusive legal basis of the right to tax and the liability to pay.[93] It was, as Locke stated in his theory of government, a fundamental law of nature limiting the power of the state,[94] and legitimising the interference with an individual's private property.[95] It provided the ultimate safeguard of the taxpayer against arbitrary taxation by the state.

The procedural safeguards of Parliament

While the legality of tax was ensured in substance by the requirement for parliamentary consent, for that safeguard to be effective in practical terms it was equally important that rigorous procedures were adopted.

---

[89] See D. L. Keir, 'The Case of Ship-Money', *Law Quarterly Review* 52 (1936), 546; Conrad Russell, 'The Ship Money Judgments of Bramston and Davenport', *English Historical Review* 77 (1962), 312 at 313; Hyde, *History of the Rebellion*, vol. i, p. 85.

[90] 16 Car. I c. 14 (1640); 16 Car. I c. 8 (1640) See too F. W. Maitland, *The Constitutional History of England* (Cambridge University Press, 1926), p. 96.

[91] 1 Will. & M. sess. 2 c. 2 s. 4 (1689).   [92] *Ibid.*

[93] See Goldsworthy, *Sovereignty of Parliament*, pp. 106, 200–1 and the authorities there cited.

[94] John Locke, *Two Treatises of Government*, 2nd edition, P. Haslett (ed.) (Cambridge University Press, 1970), Book II, section 142.

[95] *Ibid.*, Book II, sections 138–40.

Accordingly the absolute rights of which the right to taxation only by consent was an aspect were protected by the constitution, powers and procedures of Parliament itself.[96] So sophisticated did these procedures become, notably in the passage of tax measures and the role of the House of Commons, that they came to constitute a legal safeguard in their own right. From the seventeenth century there were established a regulated process of motion, free debate in a committee of the whole house, formal debate in the Commons, and a report stage to inform the members and allow further and more reflective consideration.[97] Debate in committee, where the rate could be reduced, and a third reading of the bill in the Commons preceded the procedure through the Lords and the royal assent. Only then would the tax be legally imposed on the subject. This meticulous and detailed procedure ensured that taxation measures were fully publicised to the people through their elected representatives, that they were fully debated, analysed and examined, and that the government had to defend and explain their measures to the representatives of the people. They were designed to afford protection against any hasty or inconsidered imposition of a tax on the people by ensuring that no taxation was imposed on the subject without full and proper consideration and reflection by the House of Commons.[98] Inherent in the whole process was a series of checks, reviews and examinations whereby the substantive constitutional protection of the taxpayer was effected.

The involvement of both houses of Parliament in the imposition of taxes in this way created considerable tensions, since from the fourteenth century the Commons insisted that the Lords should play no part in the imposition of taxes.[99] It was a right the Commons guarded jealously.[100] Although the Lords had amended bills of supply from the mid sixteenth century,[101] the Commons had always claimed the right not only that all

---

[96] Blackstone, *Commentaries*, vol. i, p. 141.
[97] John Hatsell, *Precedents of Proceedings in the House of Commons*, 2nd edition, 4 vols. (London: T. Payne, T. Cadell, W. Davies, 1796), vol. iii, p. 158.
[98] *Ibid.*, p. 157. See generally, Dennis Morris, '"A Tax by Any Other Name"; Some Thoughts on Money, Bills and Other Taxing Measures', *Statute Law Review* 22 (2001), 211 and 23 (2002), 147.
[99] For the history of money bills see Henry Hallam, *The Constitutional History of England*, 1846 edition published by J. Murray, London, 2 vols. (New York: Garland Publishing Inc., 1978), vol. ii, pp. 192–8.
[100] Brown, *Governance of Late Medieval England*, pp. 229–30.
[101] Hatsell, *Precedents of Proceedings*, vol. iii, pp. 100–32.

bills imposing a charge on the people had to originate with them,[102] a right acknowledged by the Lords in 1640, but also that the Lords could not make any amendments to bills imposing a tax upon the people. The Lords, said the Commons, could reject, but not amend. And indeed, numerous bills for the imposition of new or increased duties, or for the repeal of duties, on various commodities had been rejected by the Lords with no objection by the Commons. They exercised this right for the benefit and the protection of the people, a right acknowledged by Blackstone[103] and accepted by the Commons. But the Commons denied that the Lords had any right to amend a money bill, and whenever the Lords did so, the Commons rejected it outright, ignored it and allowed it to lie neglected, or issued a fresh bill themselves.[104] In 1671 the issue arose over a bill laying a tax on sugar. The Lords amended it by reducing the rate, and in a subsequent conference the Commons unanimously resolved that the Lords had no right to interfere and change the rate, and produced detailed authorities and precedents to that effect.[105] In 1678 the Commons claimed that the Lords should be entirely excluded from amending all bills of supply. In his *Precedents of Proceedings in the House of Commons*, first published in 1785, John Hatsell stated the rules which guided the practice of Parliament in taxing bills.[106] These rules limited the role of the Lords in money bills and were 'clear, and indubitable rights', based 'on ancient practice and admitted precedents', and confirmed in the Commons by the 'constant and uniform practice of Parliament'.[107] At the end of the eighteenth century the Commons maintained these limitations as privileges of their own, establishing their supremacy in tax matters. The House of Lords tacitly, if not expressly, accepted the privilege the House of Commons claimed to have the sole authority to amend money bills.[108] Thus although, as Maitland observed, this privilege, so staunchly maintained by the Commons, had an obscure and uncertain provenance, it nevertheless was observed in parliamentary usage and in practice made the House of Commons the predominant chamber.[109]

---

[102] Blackstone called the Commons' right to originate money bills its 'antient indisputable privilege': Blackstone, *Commentaries*, vol. i, p. 169.
[103] *Ibid.*   [104] See Hatsell, *Precedents of Proceedings*, vol. iii, pp. 105–6.
[105] For the precedent of 1671 see the Report of the Select Committee to search the Journals of Houses of Parliament to ascertain the Practice of each House with regard to Bills imposing or repealing Taxes, HCPP (1860) (414) xxii 1 at p. 7; Hatsell, *Precedents of Proceedings*, vol. iii, pp. 110, 368–93.
[106] Hatsell, *Precedents of Proceedings*, vol. iii, pp. 138–9.
[107] *Ibid.*, p. 139.   [108] *Ibid.*, p. 132.
[109] Maitland, *Constitutional History*, pp. 310–11.

The administrative safeguard of localism

The charge to tax and its rate and scope having been laid down by Parliament, the practical implementation of the tax was the next and final stage. The administration of tax comprised two principal elements of assessment and collection, and it was the assessment stage at which potential abuses had to be guarded against. This stage included the disclosure of the property in question, its valuation where appropriate, the incorporation of any allowances or exemptions and the application of the rate to the property. It included an adjudicatory element in the form of an appeal against an assessment. Though theoretically a mechanical exercise, the administration of an impost was the essential stage of the raising of taxes, and its outcome was the measure of a tax's success or failure. Sound administration through efficient and expeditious machinery was thus essential for the government to raise a consistent and steady flow of revenue. For taxpayers it was the stage at which there was a direct interface with the taxing authority, where as individuals they actively felt the impact of a tax. As such it was an operation of considerable delicacy which was often as important to them as the actual substance of the tax. The safeguard provided by the law in the direct taxes was that of localism: the administration of tax by the taxpayer's peers rather than by central government, including the granting of powers of appeal from the assessing bodies by an aggrieved taxpayer to some other, usually higher and theoretically independent, adjudicating body. This method of administration ensured that taxation was not an uncontrolled arbitrary instrument in the hands of the state and as such constituted the second, and the principal, of the law's safeguards for the taxpayer.

The nature of the system

From the earliest period of English taxation legislative provision for the administration of direct national taxes was firmly based on local lay control, with some, though minimal, central professional supervision.[110] Prior to the Victorian period, bodies of lay commissioners were well established institutions in English fiscal life,[111] having been used continuously in relation to the direct taxes since the thirteenth century, and intermittently

---

[110] See E. V. Adams, 'The Early History of Surveyors of Taxes', *Quarterly Record* (1956), 290 at 292–3.

[111] See W. R. Ward, *The Administration of the Window and Assessed Taxes 1696–1798* (Canterbury: Phillimores, 1963), pp. 1–2.

in relation to indirect taxes.[112] By the close of the eighteenth century the principle of localism was the accepted basis of tax administration and entrenched in relation to the direct taxes. With few exceptions they were to be administered by local laymen known as commissioners. These ad hoc public bodies, each explicitly designed to implement a specific tax, and created by the statute which imposed the tax, were the oldest and first of those quasi-judicial bodies which came to be known as administrative tribunals and were to form an essential part of the civil justice system from the mid nineteenth century.

The local lay commissioners appointed to administer the land tax constituted the model for, and basis of, all subsequent lay tax commissioners. Their function was to execute the legislation, to supervise and co-ordinate the assessment to and collection of the tax. To do so their parent Act laid down the necessary administrative powers and structures, notably to appoint subordinate officials[113] to undertake the practical work of valuation, assessment and collection. The commissioners controlled the process, whereby a certain quota was set for each district and the assessors appointed by them had to make their assessments so as to raise that sum. True to the tradition of localism, it was these commissioners who were given the additional burden of executing the various assessed taxes imposed on a large number of luxury items,[114] following the established pattern of appointing and supervising the subordinate assessors. The same structures were imposed when in 1798 they were entrusted with the execution of the Triple Assessment Act.[115] The same system of local administration was employed by Pitt for his new income tax of 1799.[116] Though his local lay commissioners, the General Commissioners, so called because they were to carry out 'the general purposes of [the] Act', were a new body, they were unambiguously based on the Land Tax Commissioners, being appointed by and from those commissioners. Furthermore, Commercial Commissioners were appointed to assess commercial income, a matter of considerable sensitivity.[117] When Addington introduced the schedular system into income taxation in 1803, whereby income was taxed

---

[112] See Brown, *Governance of Late Medieval England*, pp. 69–72.

[113] 38 Geo. III c. 5 s. 8 (1797); 4 Will. & M. c. 1 s. 8 (1692).

[114] The foundation of their jurisdiction lay in the legislation of the houses and windows taxes of 1747: 20 Geo. II c. 3 s. 6. See Ward, *Window and Assessed Taxes*, pp. 8–9.

[115] 38 Geo. III c. 16.

[116] 39 Geo. III c. 13. Anon., *Observations upon the Act for Taxing Income* (London: Bunney and Gold, 1799), pp. 33–5; B. E. V. Sabine, 'The General Commissioners', *BTR* (1968), 18.

[117] See generally, Anon., *Observations*, pp. 56–61.

according to its source,[118] he refined Pitt's system and amended the number, powers and functions of the commissioners. He retained the General Commissioners and extended their powers, abolished the Commercial Commissioners, and introduced Additional Commissioners to make assessments of commercial income. These reforms were designed purely to make the administrative machinery simpler, and left the principle of localism untouched.

It was inevitable that during the essentially administrative process of assessing taxpayers disputes would arise. These would be as to a decision to bring property into charge, a denial of an allowance or a deduction, or an inaccurate assessment. Provision had to be made for their resolution not only to ensure the legislation was implemented and the tax raised, but also to ensure its popular acceptance. Taxes were generally unpopular, and even the implementation of familiar machinery, though it helped ensure compliance, did not suffice. A provision for dispute-resolution where grievances could be raised and properly addressed went far towards pacifying hostile public opinion and achieving the acquiescence of the tax-paying public. It was in itself a powerful political tool. Where a tax was controversial, as with the compulsory and inquisitorial income tax, those disputes would have to be carefully and sensitively provided for in order to make the tax acceptable to the public and indeed to Parliament. Provision for appeals would reassure the public that any grievances they might have would be clearly and unambiguously addressed in an acceptable way. The responsibility for hearing and determining such disputes was naturally given to the lay commissioners. This appellate stage of the administrative process was perceived by both taxpayers and the government as the principal, though not the only, protective element in the localist system.

The Land Tax Act gave the commissioners a general power to resolve disputes that arose in the course of the administration of the tax.[119] Similarly in their administration of the assessed taxes, they were empowered to hear and determine the appeals of persons who felt themselves aggrieved by

---

[118] 43 Geo. III c. 122 ss. 31, 66, 84, 175 (land, annuities and dividends, profits from any property, profession, trade or vocation, and public offices, employments, pensions and annuities). For the early evolution of taxation at the source, see Piroska E. Soos, 'Taxation at the Source and Withholding in England, 1512 to 1640', *BTR* (1995), 49. See too William Phillips, 'A New Light on Addington's Income Tax', *BTR* (1967), 271.

[119] 38 Geo. III c. 5 ss. 8, 23, and see too ss. 17, 18, 28 (1797). This adjudicatory and appellate jurisdiction was no innovation, powers similar in nature and scope being found in the seventeenth century land tax legislation: see 4 Will. & M. c. 1 s. 20 (1692); *Re Glatton Land Tax* (1840) 6 M & W 689.

being over-rated by the assessors or subject to a miscalculation of the triple assessment.[120] The hearing and determination of appeals was given to a discrete body of commissioners by Pitt when he introduced his legislation for the redemption of the land tax in 1798,[121] though it left the principle of localism untouched. As far as appeals in income tax were concerned, Pitt favoured the same two-tier system, placing the appellate jurisdiction in a separate and higher body, the Commissioners of Appeal.[122] The jurisdiction extended to complaints by taxpayers aggrieved by assessments made upon them by the General Commissioners and complaints by the government official, the surveyor. Addington abolished them in 1803 and transferred their powers to the General Commissioners, making them both the supreme assessing body, as before, and also the supreme appellate body.[123]

The adoption of localism

There existed compelling reasons for this consistent insistence on the local administration of all direct taxes, taxes which were, unlike indirect taxes, largely unavoidable, attached to the essential fabric of taxpayers' lives, and starkly felt by them. The first was that it satisfied a strong popular desire for local control of public affairs, and the possession of institutions which reflected it. Traditionally there existed a powerful ideological allegiance to local interests and local autonomy.[124] The English had always valued local self-government, and its institutions were perceived as enshrining their very liberties. Reflecting this was a profound historic culture of amateur participation in both local government and the administration of justice. Self-government was part of the fabric of English life and was engrained in society, having developed through usage over hundreds of years, and finding political acceptance and statutory expression. Justices of the Peace were the embodiment of localism and the system depended entirely on them. They were unelected and unpaid local landowners with no formal legal knowledge, who undertook public duties, both administrative and judicial, for no remuneration, motivated by feelings of public and social obligation and with a strong sense of independence. They became

---

[120]   20 Geo. II c. 3 ss. 12, 21 (1747); 38 Geo. III c. 16 s. 54 (1798).
[121]   38 Geo. III c. 60 s. 121. When the sum in question exceeded £500 of stock, an aggrieved party had to appeal to the Court of Chancery or Exchequer.
[122]   39 Geo. III c. 13 s. 16 (1799).   [123]   43 Geo. III c. 122 s. 144.
[124]   See Fraser, *British Welfare State*, p. 109.

the principal law enforcement agency in the provinces,[125] constituting the face of the administration of justice in the eyes of the great proportion of the population.

Secondly there were practical reasons for favouring local tax administration. If new machinery had to be developed to administer any tax, the process was time-consuming and costly, with no guarantee of efficiency or success, and with the danger of further alienating the tax-paying public. Indeed, it was not a realistic possibility where, as in the eighteenth century, the bureaucratic machinery of central government was virtually non-existent. England had the advantage of a long-established system of tax administration which was thoroughly tested, familiar to the tax-paying public, developed to a considerable level of sophistication and found to be relatively efficient. The reduction to a minimum of the expense of tax collection was the aspiration of any government and was firmly accepted as a desirable feature of any tax.[126] If new expense could be avoided, it went some way to securing support for a new impost. So when Pitt introduced the triple assessment he was able to reassure the house that '[t]o enforce it, no new power will be delegated, no new office created, no new expenses incurred'.[127]

Finally, such strong ideological and cultural foundations, along with a degree of formal legitimacy, made the adoption of local tax administration by successive governments a political necessity.[128] All taxes were unpopular, but taxpayers objected to them on a variety of grounds: perceived unfairness, an excessively high rate, an inquisitorial nature, an absence of real necessity, or an absolute unavoidability of liability. These were not legal rights as there was no unambiguous right to a fair, low, non-inquisitorial, necessary or avoidable tax, but their infringement made taxpayers less willing to pay. Where a tax displayed one or more of these features particularly strongly, public resentments had to be appeased to ensure any degree of compliance. If there were significant opposition then avoidance, evasion and simple non-compliance would rise and the yield would suffer. Every government knew that taxes could not be levied without the practical agreement of the tax-paying public. Success often depended not on the substance of a tax, but on its machinery of implementation, for it

---

[125] Elie Halevy, *A History of the English people in 1815* (London: Ark Paperbacks edition, 1987), pp. 33–4; J. P. Dawson, *A History of Lay Judges* (Cambridge, Mass.: Harvard University Press, 1960).

[126] See Pitt's comment with respect to the stamp duty in the budget debate of 1797: *Parliamentary History*, vol. 33, col. 432, 26 April 1797.

[127] *Ibid.*, vol. 33, col. 1049, 24 November 1797.

[128] Daunton, *Trusting Leviathan*, pp. 180–204.

was often that which determined the popular response to a tax and made it acceptable or unacceptable. The taxpayer of the eighteenth and nineteenth centuries was possibly concerned more with the process than the principle of taxation. The importance of acceptable and efficient machinery was not to be underestimated in the fiscal policy of any jurisdiction. As James Bayard observed in the United States Congress in 1798, 'it was not so much the letter of a tax law which was offensive to the people, as the hand of the tax gatherer which compelled them to pay',[129] a point of which Pitt was only too aware when introducing his income tax.[130] Where a tax depended on the willingness of taxpayers to make honest returns of their property or income, a fair, impartial and efficient machinery of taxation was essential, for it gave the public confidence that everyone was paying their due taxes and promoted public co-operation.

To use a traditional means of tax administration which was familiar and understood by all taxpayers and sympathetic to their concerns, which satisfied their desire for local control and which was overtly protective in conception, was a powerful pacifier in view of widespread concern and distrust and one which few legislators in the nineteenth century felt able to undermine. When Pitt introduced the triple assessment in 1797, he observed that its administration would 'entirely depend upon laws now existing, laws long in force, laws familiar to those who will be the objects of its provisions'.[131] Similarly in relation to his new and highly controversial income tax[132] the following year, he was acutely aware that the closest adherence to the traditional principle of tax administration was the price he had to pay to secure the tax's successful passage through Parliament. He accordingly consciously used existing and familiar forms and processes to make his involuntary and inquisitorial tax, with all its accompanying sensitivities to the disclosure of private financial matters, politically acceptable.

The protective nature of localism

Traditionally, the system of local tax administration was perceived both officially and popularly as an effective legal institution for the protection

---

[129] *Annals of Congress*, 5 Cong., 2 sess., 1231, 5 March 1798 *per* James Bayard. See too *ibid.*, 13 Cong., 1 sess., 367, 29 June 1813 *per* Charles Ingersoll.

[130] *Parliamentary History*, vol. 34, cols. 6–24, 3 December 1798. See too *Parl. Deb.*, vol. 61, ser. 3, col. 1025, 21 March 1842 (HC) *per* Charles Buller.

[131] *Parliamentary History*, vol. 33, col. 1049, 24 November 1797.

[132] See William Phillips, 'The Real Objection to the Income Tax of 1799', *BTR* (1967), 177; William Phillips, 'The Origin of Income Tax', *BTR* (1967) 113 at 114–15.

of the taxpayer. Its protective elements were twofold, namely the independence of the local lay commissioners from central government, and their local knowledge.

Its essential character was non-governmental, for the commissioners were independent of the government. Where one of the parties in an administrative or judicial process was the government, as in taxation, this independence was of some moment. It had two facets: it consisted of functional independence, namely the extent to which the commissioners were subject to the authority of central government, and personal independence, namely the extent to which they were financially and politically independent of central government. It was above all this independence which protected the taxpayer in law. If the taxes were administered by commissioners who represented the taxpayers and had no allegiances to central government, those commissioners would have no reason to act in the interests of the crown in an improper way. The functional independence of the commissioners was primarily ensured by their statutes of creation. The parent statutes placed the formal and final responsibility of administration of the tax in question in the hands of the commissioners, with the practical administrative duties of valuing, assessing and collecting undertaken by officials appointed by, and subordinate to, the commissioners themselves.[133] The giving of an appellate jurisdiction to the commissioners themselves only emphasised the extent of their control of tax administration, particularly since the statutes invariably provided their determination was final,[134] and in many instances made no provision for appeal to the regular courts of law at all.

This functional independence was not undermined by the statutory powers given to the executive, for while the fiscal tribunals reflected an early division of power between central control and local administration, the formal role given to the executive by the tax legislation was expressly subordinate to that of the local commissioners. The Land Tax Commissioners constituted the purest example of localism in tax administration since virtually no interference from any official of the central government was permitted under the legislation. Central government was more actively involved in the administration of the assessed taxes, for statute directed that the Treasury was to appoint salaried officers, called surveyors, to supervise the execution of the legislation by the

[133] 38 Geo. III c. 5 s. 8 (1797) (land tax); 20 Geo. II c. 3 ss. 6–10 (1747) (assessed taxes).

[134] 38 Geo. III c. 5 s. 8 (1797) (land tax); 20 Geo. II c. 3 s. 13 (1747) (assessed taxes), though see the provisions of the amending Act 21 Geo. II c. 10 s. 10 (1748); 38 Geo. III c. 16 s. 54 (1798) (triple assessment).

local commissioners and acting under the direct control and instruction of the tax office in London.[135] Along with the power to inspect properties, amend assessments and impose surcharges, this was a development that would prove of considerable significance for the future of localism. In relation to the income tax, Pitt was aware that the system would collapse without some central control and assistance. He knew it needed mutual co-operation between local and central agencies, and realised that professional surveyors were essential to the system's efficient working. Accordingly the surveyor was given the responsibility for bringing any doubts as to the correctness of the assessments to the attention of the commissioners[136] and the power to inspect returns to establish it. He was, however, to remain subordinate to the commissioners.[137] Functional independence would be rendered largely nugatory if the commissioners were not also personally independent, in the sense of not having any private or pecuniary interest in their appointment. This was achieved through ensuring they were not appointed by the government and were unpaid for their work. Like Justices of the Peace, they saw their functions as a civil and social duty and an honour to perform. It was possible because only commissioners who were personally financially independent were eligible for appointment. They all had to satisfy high property qualifications[138] and as such were sufficiently rich and disinterested to devote their leisure to the public service.

The second protective element inherent in the localist system of tax administration was local knowledge, enabling the commissioners to make accurate assessments and also ensuring that all property which should be assessed to tax was indeed fully and accurately subjected to the impost. Traditionally no expert knowledge of any kind was required of a magistrate, it being considered that he would judge well enough by the light of common sense and a familiarity with, and connection to, the locality in which he functioned. In tax it went somewhat further. Orthodox fiscal thought held it was of essential importance in arriving at correct assessments to possess knowledge of local people and local economic conditions, of the level of wages in particular trades, of individuals' profits, of their methods of business, of local land values, and

---

[135] See Adams, 'Surveyors', 294–5, 300–1.
[136] *Parliamentary History*, vol. 34, col. 7, 3 December 1798.   [137] *Ibid.*, col. 102.
[138] 38 Geo. III c. 5 ss. 92–3 (1797) (Land Tax Commissioners); 20 Geo. II c. 3 s. 6 (1747); 17 Geo. III c. 39 s. 7 (1777); 18 Geo. III c. 26 s. 10 (1778); 25 Geo. III c. 47 s. 11 (1785) (Assessed Taxes Commissioners); 39 Geo. III c. 13 ss. 23–26 (1799) and 43 Geo. III c. 122 s. 12 (1803) (General Commissioners of Income Tax).

of everyday matters and problems in local commercial life. In the land tax, the assessed taxes and the income tax, local knowledge formed the acknowledged basis of the administrative machinery.[139] It was of particular importance in relation to the highly sensitive taxation of commercial income. It required the appointment of local property-owning merchants, but that inevitably meant that such commissioners would become familiar with the financial affairs of men who might well be their rivals in trade. This proved to be an intractable problem for successive legislators from the late eighteenth century. Pitt addressed the issue by the creation of a separate tribunal, the Commercial Commissioners, who had to satisfy a high property qualification and were selected by and from the commercial community to deal entirely, exclusively, and secretly with its income.[140] Commercial knowledge was not expressly required, but was implicit in the machinery of appointment by the commercial community, achieving commercial expertise without undermining the localist principle. Local knowledge was also ensured by the property qualifications themselves, since these addressed both quantum and location.[141] Residence gave commissioners an extensive knowledge of their locality, its property and its people.

The legislature was not as clear in its policy as to legal expertise despite it being clear that no body of commissioners, particularly in their appellate role, could function effectively without it. Although the appeals before the commissioners were typically small and simple questions of fact, they still demanded the skills of sifting evidence and judging its value from an independent and neutral perspective, skills which only trained lawyers possessed. Such skills were made available to the fiscal commissioners through the medium of their clerk. Though the clerk's statutory functions were invariably laid down as purely ministerial, comprising the receipt, filing, copying and storage of the key documentation, the position developed into a more substantive contribution to the legal process of the tribunal. The tax commissioners came to look to their clerk for legal advice, both substantive and procedural, and the clerk often became a key figure in the assessment process.[142]

[139] *Parliamentary History*, vol. 33, col. 1073, 4 December 1797.
[140] 39 Geo. III c. 13 ss. 95–118 (1799).
[141] 38 Geo. III c. 48 s. 2 (1798) (Land Tax Commissioners); 39 Geo. III c. 13 s. 25 (1799) and 43 Geo. III c. 122 s. 17 (1803) (General Commissioners of Income Tax).
[142] See Minutes of Evidence before the Departmental Committee on Income Tax, *HCPP* (1905) (2576) xliv 245, qq. 1978, 2014 *per* Arthur Chamberlain JP, putting forward the views of the Birmingham Chamber of Commerce on income tax.

The inherent protection arising from the commissioners' independence and local knowledge would have been undermined had the commissioners been, as individuals, lacking in integrity, moral rectitude and ability. Legislators thought it prudent to require all commissioners to take an oath to execute their powers 'faithfully, impartially, and honestly, according to the best of [their] skill and judgment',[143] thereby underlining the probity, honesty and impartiality with which the commissioners would carry out their duties. But a high calibre of commissioner and subordinate staff was fundamental to the authority and efficacy of the tax tribunals, and in its own right reinforced the safeguard to the taxpayer. It was of real importance in the absence of the rigorous training and well-established practices for appointment found within the legal profession, especially since the tax tribunals did not possess the same formal processes to provide procedural protection to taxpayers as the courts of law enjoyed. The substantial property requirement ensured, according to the accepted values of the time, that the men filling these responsible and powerful posts with wide and confidential powers were able, trustworthy and honourable. Personal wealth was perceived as an indication of moral worth. It did at least in general ensure a measure of education and a sense of public responsibility. More certainly perhaps it ensured that individuals were not tempted into corruption by the sums of money they handled. When Pitt introduced his revolutionary and unpopular income tax in 1799 he took overt care in the appointment and qualification of the commissioners, assuring the house that they would be 'persons of a respectable situation in life; as far as possible removed from any suspicion of partiality, or any kind of undue influence; men of integrity and independence'.[144] It was highly unlikely, he observed, that such men would 'wantonly abuse their trust' or 'indulge in idle or injurious curiosity'.[145] As a result of these requirements, most General Commissioners were wealthy men of some social standing in their county, often members of the gentry or professional men. In the commercial centres, and indeed in most towns, the leading merchants were appointed.[146] The permitted qualification through the ownership of personal estate, particularly in the cities, opened the ranks of lay justice to the new commercial fortunes. Most General Commissioners were also Justices of the Peace and Land Tax Commissioners, and were almost invariably considerably involved in civic life. The tax tribunals constituted

---

[143] See for example 38 Geo. III c. 16 s. 60 (1798); 43 Geo. III c. 122 Schedule F (1803).
[144] *Parliamentary History*, vol. 34, col. 6, 3 December 1798.
[145] *The Times*, 4 December 1798.
[146] See Adams, 'Surveyors', 299–300.

a self-perpetuating civic elite as a result of their appointment and renewal from their own ranks.

The judicial safeguards

The third major safeguard established in English law was judicial in nature. Eighteenth-century legal theory was dominated by the doctrine of the rule of law,[147] and on this was based the constitutional theory of the separation of powers.[148] After the revolution of 1689, the theory was refined and developed through Montesquieu's analysis of the English constitution in his *L'Esprit des Lois* published in 1748[149] and the influence of John Locke.[150] It subjugated the crown and made Parliament supreme. Legislation was the province of Parliament, administration that of the executive, and adjudication, being the state's power to resolve disputes between its subjects or itself and its subjects, that of the judges of the regular courts of law. Only the judges were permitted by the constitution to do justice in the sense of exercising the judicial power of the state. Their constitutional role, therefore, was to enforce the law made by Parliament. Of course, if that law were ambiguous, in applying it the judges would necessarily have to interpret it, and so another judicial function was to interpret the law. The legal supremacy of Parliament established by the constitutional upheavals of the seventeenth century left the judges in the position merely of finding the meaning of the statute law, for they could not, constitutionally, make law themselves. In these two ways the judges protected the rights of the individual by ensuring the true meaning of the legislation was adhered to, and by having disputes determined by expert and trained individuals of high calibre. Furthermore, the judges had the power to supervise the proceedings of inferior courts. The judicial safeguard was thus threefold in nature, comprising an interpretative, an

[147] For an analysis of the meaning of the term, see Sir William Wade and Christopher Forsyth, *Administrative Law*, 9th edition (Oxford University Press, 2004), pp. 20–42; H. W. Arthurs, 'Rethinking Administrative Law: A Slightly Dicey Business', *Osgoode Hall Law Journal* 17 (1979), 1 at 3; W. Burnett Harvey, 'The Rule of law in Historical Perspective', *Michigan Law Review* 59 (1961), 487.

[148] See Sir Ivor Jennings, *The Law and the Constitution*, 5th edition (London: University of London Press Ltd, 1959), pp. 18–28.

[149] Charles Louis de Secondat, Baron de Montesquieu, *De L'Esprit des Lois*, 1748 (Paris: Librairie Garnier Frères, 1949), Livre xi, Chapitre vi, 'De la Constitution d'Angleterre'. See Jennings, *Law and the Constitution*, pp. 18–28; C. K. Allen, *Law and Orders* (London: Stevens and Sons Ltd, 1947), pp. 6–18.

[150] See generally M. J. C. Vile, *Constitutionalism and the Separation of Powers* (Oxford: Clarendon Press, 1967), pp. 76–118.

adjudicatory and a supervisory element. Though the case of ship-money had severely damaged the public perception of the judges, for 'those persons who should have been as dogs to defend the sheep, have been as wolves to worry them',[151] the existence and implementation of the separation of powers gradually ensured that their standing improved, and they were generally regarded as independent of the executive.[152] The judges thereby constituted one of Blackstone's 'outworks or barriers'[153] which protected the subject's absolute rights, including the right to private property which gave rise to the principle of consent to taxation.

Statutory interpretation

As the Bill of Rights 1689 made clear, a taxpayer could only be taxed by the express authority of Parliament. Tax was, therefore, entirely a creature of statute, which it was the constitutional function of the judges to interpret. The earliest approach to this process, the mischief rule, was a broad and purposive one which looked beyond the mere words of the statute, and sought the reason why a particular statute had been passed.[154] It permitted the judges to construe a statute so as to 'suppress the mischief, and advance the remedy … according to the true intent of the makers of the Act, *pro bono publico*',[155] and was regarded by Blackstone[156] as 'the most universal and effectual way of discovering the meaning of a law', at least when the words were 'dubious'. The 'reason and spirit' of the law should be looked to. Another approach, the golden rule, was the broadest and least restrictive. It could be adopted where the words gave rise to an absurdity which in the opinion of the judge Parliament could not have intended, to find a different meaning by allowing the addition or removal of words.[157]

In relation to tax Acts, however, both these rules were rejected. The normal approach adopted by English judges prior to the nineteenth century to the interpretation of such legislation, and indeed to most statutes, was one which permitted recourse only to the words of the enactment to reveal the intention of Parliament, an approach known as the application

---

[151] *R. v. Hampden* (1637) 3 ST 825 at 1260.
[152] See generally A. H. Manchester, *A Modern Legal History of England and Wales 1750–1950*, (London: Butterworths, 1980), pp. 79–83.
[153] Blackstone, *Commentaries*, vol. i, p. 141.
[154] See D. J. Llewelyn Davies, 'The Interpretation of Statutes in the Light of their Policy by the English Courts', *Columbia Law Review* 35 (1935), 519 at 520–2.
[155] *Heydon's Case* (1584) 3 Co 7a at 7b.   [156] Blackstone, *Commentaries*, vol. i, p. 61.
[157] See Parke B in *Becke* v. *Smith* (1836) 2 M & W 191 at 195.

of the literal rule. After all, as Bacon observed, '[t]he statute law is the will of the legislature in writing'.[158] It was the safest, and certainly the easiest, approach to adopt in an unfamiliar area. They interpreted taxing Acts 'with no guide except a grammar book and a dictionary'.[159] It was true that such Acts did not readily lend themselves to interpretation by the mischief rule because they addressed no clear mischief. They were not clear remedial statutes, and traditionally their sole purpose was to raise money for the crown. However, the principal reason for eschewing the purposive rules, other than the judges' considerations for safety in construction, was that they both potentially undermined the fundamental constitutional principle that a subject could be taxed only by Parliament, and, implicitly, by its clear words.

A purposive construction would allow a case which was not within the letter of a statute to come within it if the legislator was found reasonably to have intended it,[160] the reason being that 'the law-maker could not set down every case in express terms'.[161] But that is exactly what a law-maker had to do in a taxing Act, for the law demanded an explicit expression of the charge. The words of the statute could be neither enlarged nor restricted to include or exclude any particular case. Only the strict and literal approach to statutory interpretation was consistent with this fundamental principle. Furthermore, only if the judges interpreted this authority to tax strictly on the basis of the words in the Act could the taxpayer be assured as far as possible of that predictability of taxation inherent in the notion of parliamentary taxation. It was this strict interpretation which constituted the safeguard for the taxpayer by keeping within the letter of the law, recognising the importance of tax and its inherent undermining of individual rights. A tax, therefore, had to be imposed expressly and clearly by the words of the statute, and this fundamental right of the taxpayer was reiterated constantly before the Victorian period. The instances where a subject was to be charged should, observed Lord Ellenborough CJ in 1807, be 'fairly marked out'.[162]

Where the words were clear and unambiguous, and the meaning plain, the judges adopted it and a taxpayer came within them however great the hardship upon him or her. The consequences of the statute's construction could not be considered, for that would consist of an assumption of

---

[158] Matthew Bacon, *A New Abridgment of the Law*, Henry Gwillim (ed.), 5th edition, 7 vols. (London: A. Strahan, 1798), vol. vi, tit. Statute, p. 364.
[159] Vinelott J, 'Interpretation of Fiscal Statutes', *Statute Law Review* 3 (1982), 78 at 80.
[160] Bacon, *Abridgment*, p. 380.   [161] *Ibid.*, p. 386.
[162] *Warrington* v. *Furbor* (1807) 8 East 242 at 245.

legislative authority.[163] Indeed there was no room for liberality even in an exemption.[164] Even where the application of the literal meaning gave rise not merely to hardship but to an absurdity or anomaly, the strictest approach was traditionally maintained if the words were clear. In 1800, for example, Lord Kenyon CJ refused to accept a stamp of ninepence on a promissory note where the stamp should have been for eightpence, for '[t]he words of the Stamp Acts are express, and can admit of no other interpretation'.[165] In such cases the application of the literal rule was neutral in action and effect since the approach, if not the words, favoured neither the revenue authorities nor the taxpayer, though as the adoption of the literal rule was narrow in its effect, it generally acted in favour of the taxpayer. An approach which looked to a tax Act's spirit, on the other hand, would favour the taxing authorities, since it permitted the judges to look at the reasons why a particular statute was passed and thereby reveal the intention of the executive, which conceived and framed the Act. Similarly, had the judges adopted the mischief rule, with the mischief being that the state had collected insufficient tax, it would inevitably have meant that their construction would favour the public revenue.

The words of a taxing Act were, however, frequently obscure or ambiguous, and gave room for the judges to adopt an approach which favoured one party at the expense of the other. There was a constant tension between the interests of the taxpayer and those of the state, but support for the interests of the state was relatively slight in cases of conflict. Occasionally contemporary views showed concern for the public revenue, and in 1809 the editor of Blackstone's *Commentaries* observed that in ambiguous cases the judges construed tax Acts in favour of the public revenue, and that this was 'agreeable to good policy and the public interests'.[166] This, however, was the exception. The constitutional importance of imposing a tax on the subject and its significance in relation to the subject's liberty of property were such that where the meaning of a provision was ambiguous, the taxpayer was given the benefit of the doubt. This canon of interpretation of taxing Acts followed from the basic principle that a subject could only be taxed by parliamentary authority, and it was settled law by the early years of the nineteenth century.[167]

---

[163] Bacon, *Abridgment*, p. 391.
[164] *AG v. Coote* (1817) 4 Price 183.   [165] *Farr v. Price* (1800) 1 East 55 at 57.
[166] Blackstone, *Commentaries*, Edward Christian (ed.), 15th edition, 4 vols. (London: T. Cadell and W. Davies, 1809), vol. i, p. 324 n. It seems that this observation was not included in the following edition.
[167] *Gildart v. Gladstone* (1809) 11 East 675.

Adjudication

In their adjudicative capacity, the judges heard and determined disputes between subjects and between the subject and the crown. In the case of tax disputes, however, unlike other branches of English law, the specialist local tribunals determining disputes in relation to the direct taxes constituted the primary formal adjudicative safeguard for the taxpayer. The extent of the safeguard which the judges could provide in their adjudicative capacity depended, therefore, on whether the tax legislation permitted a further appeal to the regular courts. ·

Prior to the Victorian period, appeals to the courts from the decisions of the local tax tribunals were only exceptionally permitted. This was unsurprising, for there was no tradition at common law of proceedings in the nature of appeals to a superior court submitting that the inferior body's decision was wrong in fact or law. So, despite the right of appeal being described in 1723 as 'the glory and happiness of our excellent constitution',[168] the presumption was quite the other way. The orthodox view was that appeals were neither necessary nor desirable. Juries were involved in most civil and criminal trials, and they were widely accepted as being the best and the final arbiters of fact.[169] Indeed, juries were another illustration of lay involvement in the administration of justice in England and the value placed on regional knowledge in this respect. There was also the practical consideration that the finding of facts involved assessing the credibility of witnesses, and that could not be determined from written notes, while rehearing or ensuring a complete record of the evidence would be a prohibitively expensive, impracticable and lengthy process.[170] But while there should be no appeals on questions of fact, the determination by the judges of questions of law was their legitimate and appropriate function. The size of the judiciary was small, its status high, and legal issues were left to them with confidence.[171] If appeals were to be permitted in any sphere, however, they had to be expressly provided for by statute. Against this background, the general view was that there should not be

---

[168] *R. v. Cambridge University* (1723) 1 Stra 557 at 564 *per* Pratt CJ.
[169] See H. J. Stephen, *New Commentaries on the Laws of England*, 1844 edition printed for Henry Butterworth, London, 4 vols. (New York: Garland Publishing Inc., 1979), vol. iii, pp. 622–3. See too First Report of the Judicature Commissioners', *HCPP* (1868–9) (4130) xxv 12; Cornish and Clark, *Law and Society*, pp. 19–21.
[170] Minutes of Evidence. Second Report of the Judicature Commissioners, *HCPP* (1872) (631) xx 245, Answers to Questions 23–28. See too Report of the Royal Commission on the Income Tax, *HCPP* (1920) (615) xviii 97 at para. 590.
[171] See Stephen, *New Commentaries*, vol. iii, pp. 622–3.

any appeal from the determinations of disputes by the tax tribunals to the courts of law, and the parent Acts of most of those tribunals reflected this view. The determinations of all the various bodies of tax commissioners were provided to be final. The finality of the Land Tax Commissioners' appellate determinations ran through the whole land tax,[172] with no right of appeal, even one limited to a point of law. This model was adopted in relation to the income tax when it was introduced in 1799, and the policy continued by the legislation of 1803.[173]

The approach in the eighteenth century to the establishment of the judicial safeguard of appeal in relation to tax, however, was not consistent. While all statutes provided for the initial finality of the lay tribunals' determinations, that finality was sometimes qualified and appeals allowed. From the mid eighteenth century, if either the surveyor or the taxpayer were dissatisfied with the commissioners' determination in relation to the assessed taxes or the triple assessment he could appeal to the central courts of law. The appeal was by way of case stated, a method based on the well-established common law procedure of leaving questions of fact to be decided finally by the jury, while allowing in certain instances a review on a question of law to a 'court of high standing'.[174] The issue to be determined by the judges was whether the determination was contrary to the 'true Intent and Meaning of [the] Act',[175] and in light of the judges' finding, the commissioners' determination was amended or confirmed. This power was widely used, and the resulting case law was extensive.

Supervisory jurisdiction

The taxpayer certainly expected the system of tax appeals to include procedural safeguards to ensure his rights in natural justice to be given a fair hearing in his challenge of any decision. Such procedures were largely guaranteed in the regular courts of law, with their inherent requirements of formal evidence, demanding standards of proof, detailed provisions for the conduct of proceedings and legal representation to test evidence. The

---

[172] 38 Geo. III c. 5 ss. 8, 17, 23, 28 (1797).   [173] 43 Geo. III c. 99 s. 29.

[174] A procedure known as the special case. See generally The Law Society, *A Compendium of the Practice of the Common Law* (London: R. Hastings, 1847), pp. 383–4; M. J. Pritchard, 'Nonsuit: A Premature Obituary', *Cambridge Law Journal* (1960), 88 at 92–6; C. Stebbings, 'The Appeal by way of Case Stated from the Determinations of General Commissioners of Income Tax: An Historical Perspective', *BTR* (1996), 611.

[175] 21 Geo. II c. 10 s. 10 (1748). This provision was to be read into, or was reproduced exactly in, a number of later Acts, such as 17 Geo. III c. 39 s. 22 (1777); 18 Geo. III c. 26 s. 42 (1788).

lay fiscal tribunals, both local and executive, enjoyed no such safeguards, the outcome of the desire of the executive to have tax appeals settled swiftly at the earliest opportunity. With the simple and informal procedures which both taxpayer and executive desired came the danger that acceptable standards of fairness would be undermined. The judges were given powers of judicial review to ensure that the proceedings of inferior courts were correct and jurisdictionally sound. These powers embraced the extent and exercise of the tribunal's powers and procedures and constituted another potentially powerful safeguard for the taxpayer against any procedural shortcomings in the appellate process before the various bodies of tax commissioners.

The requirements that a court should act only within its jurisdiction, and that its proceedings should adhere to the requirements of natural justice, were ancient and established precepts of judicial process in English law. The rule that a man could not be a judge in his own cause, that he should be independent and impartial, was firmly established[176] and it came to apply to all inferior jurisdictions through the supervisory jurisdiction of the Court of King's Bench. It was reflected in the context of the tax tribunals in their parent Acts, which made provision for oaths of impartiality, the avoidance of conflicts of interest[177] and generally to ensure obvious abuses of procedure did not occur and that the process was demonstrably fair. But in the common law itself, procedures existed whereby the decisions of the inferior regular courts could be reviewed. The writ of error[178] was an order of the King's Bench requiring the record of proceedings in an inferior common law court of record to be sent to it for review for errors of law.[179] The writ, and the analogous writ of false judgment for courts which were not of record,[180] were widely used.[181] Though the writ of error was firmly established in the eighteenth and early nineteenth centuries and

[176] See Coke CJ in *Dr Bonham's Case* (1610) 8 Co Rep 113b at 118a and Holt CJ in *City of London* v. *Wood* (1702) 12 Mod 669 at 687.

[177] See for example 38 Geo. III c. 5 s. 23 (1797); 38 Geo. III c. 16 s. 61 (1798).

[178] See generally *Jaques* v. *Caesar* (1670) 2 Wms Saund 100 n.

[179] See generally Sir Edward Coke, *The First Part of the Institutes of the Laws of England*, 1628 edition, 2 vols. (New York: Garland Publishing Inc., 1979), vol. ii, p. 288b; Bacon, *Abridgement*, vol. iii, tit. Error A3; *Groenvelt* v. *Burwell* (1698) 1 Salk 144; *Scott* v. *Bye* (1824) 2 Bing 344; *Bruce* v. *Wait* (1840) 1 Man & G 1 at 2 n (a).

[180] See Sir F. Pollock and F. W. Maitland, *The History of English Law*, 2nd edition 1898 reissued (Cambridge University Press, 1968), vol. ii, pp. 666–8; *Dyson* v. *Wood* (1824) 3 B & C 449.

[181] See generally Joseph Dixon (ed.), *Lush's Practice of the Superior Courts of Law*, 3rd edition, 2 vols. (London: Butterworths, 1865), vol. ii, pp. 657–86.

constituted an important though technical and cumbersome safeguard for the individual litigant, it was not one to which the taxpayer could have recourse in relation to the proceedings of the local tax tribunals. This was because none of the tax tribunals was a court of common law. None enjoyed that status through being a court of record, and none was of such a nature that it could claim the status on general principles. The various bodies of tax commissioners constituted new jurisdictions established by Act of Parliament to administer specialist rules in the limited sphere of tax, and to do so by methods quite different from those of the common law courts. The common law courts employed writs, pleadings and jury trial; their proceedings were in Latin, their judgments were formal and their judges learned in the law. Tax tribunals, on the other hand, enjoyed a large degree of informality, proceeded in English, avoided written pleadings and jury trial, and were staffed by laymen ignorant of the rules of law. These distinctions in procedure were fatal to their use of both error and false judgment.

The common law, however, provided alternative safeguards in the prerogative writs of mandamus, prohibition and certiorari. Mandamus, which possessed a non-judicial character derived from its original purpose in controlling borough and city authorities, ordered a court to perform some public duty or to show why it had failed to do so. It could issue to ensure that a statutory discretion was exercised, or properly exercised. Prohibition addressed the boundaries of jurisdictions and the interpretation of the charters or statutes on which those jurisdictions were founded, and prohibited the inferior court in question from going beyond its proper jurisdiction.[182] It also lay for error on the face of the record or breach of the rules of natural justice. Certiorari proved particularly important in the search for an alternative to error.[183] In 1700 Holt CJ said that certiorari could lie to bodies which did not proceed according to the common law, and he called it 'as good as a writ of error'.[184] It would enable the superior court to do justice where the inferior court had not.[185] Certiorari ordered that the records of causes in the inferior courts be brought into the King's Bench which, armed with this information, reviewed their proceedings

---

[182] See *Re Crosby Tithes* (1849) 13 QB 761; *Worthington* v. *Jeffries* (1875) 10 LR CP 379; *Mayor and Aldermen of City of London* v. *Cox* (1867) LR 2 HL 239; *Hall* v. *Norwood* (1663) 1 Sid 165. See too *Chabot* v. *Lord Morpeth* (1844) 15 QB 446.

[183] For early history of certiorari, see Frank J. Goodnow, 'The Writ of Certiorari', *Political Science Quarterly*, 6 (1891) 493 at 493–501.

[184] *Groenvelt* v. *Burwell* (1700) 12 Mod 386 at 389.

[185] See counsel's argument in *R.* v. *Coles* (1845) 8 QB 75 at 79.

and decisions.[186] Along with prohibition and mandamus it ensured that inferior courts kept within their jurisdiction, that any error that appeared on the face of the record of the proceedings was addressed, and that they observed the rules of natural justice.[187] The King's Bench did this 'by the common law'[188] by reason of its 'great superiority',[189] in other words by its inherent power. The reason for this jurisdiction was public policy; the courts could not allow these inferior bodies to remain uncontrolled by the superior courts.[190] This supervisory jurisdiction was widely exercised in the seventeenth and eighteenth centuries, and early authorities established that there were three fundamental requirements to the application of certiorari: that the tribunal should be a court proceeding according to the common law; that it should be a court of record; and that it should, indeed, be a court. All three presented a considerable legal barrier to the use of the writ by the tax tribunals since prima facie they satisfied none of them.

By the beginning of the Victorian period two of the three legal obstacles had been overcome. First, though their informal statutory procedures had denied them the use of the writ of false judgment, it had been established that the court in question did not need to be a court of the common law for certiorari to lie. The second requirement of a court of record had been more problematic to overcome. Lack of this had denied them the use of the writ of error, and eighteenth-century legal opinion maintained it was equally necessary for certiorari.[191] Coke had defined a court of record as a court of justice having the power to hold pleas according to the course of the common law and whose proceedings were recorded on parchment,[192] while Blackstone concentrated mainly on the recording

---

[186] *R. v. Inhabitants in Glamorganshire* (1701) 1 Ld Raym 580; see too S.C. *The Case of Cardiffe Bridge* (1700) 1 Salk 146.

[187] R. M. Jackson, *The Machinery of Justice in England*, 7th edition (Cambridge University Press, 1977), pp. 167–8. See generally Louis L. Jaffe and Edith G. Henderson, 'Judicial Review and the Rule of Law: Historical Origins', *Law Quarterly Review* 72 (1956), 345; S. A. de Smith, 'The Prerogative Writs', *Cambridge Law Journal* 11 (1951), 40; Edith G. Henderson, *Foundations of English Administrative Law* (Cambridge, Mass: Harvard University Press 1963).

[188] *Groenvelt* v. *Burwell* (1697) 1 Ld Raym 454 at 469.   [189] 12 Mod 386 at 390.

[190] See generally J. H. Baker, *An Introduction to English Legal History*, 4th edition (London: Butterworths LexisNexis, 2002), pp. 135–54.

[191] *Per* Holt CJ in *Groenvelt* v. *Burwell* (1699) Carth 491 at 494; *R. v. Lediard* (1751) Sayer 6; Sir John Comyns, *A Digest of the Laws of England*, 4th edition (Dublin, 1793), vol. ii, tit. Certiorari A.1.

[192] Coke, *Institutes*, vol. ii, p. 260 a.

of the proceedings on parchment[193] and the indisputable nature of these records. The requirement for a court of record was left unresolved as to its necessity for the application of certiorari, with some legal writers maintaining it and others not even alluding to it. Since no tax commissioners were established as courts of record, insistence on that status in the sense in which Coke and Blackstone regarded it would have been fatal to the application of certiorari to them. In practice, the absence of formal status as a court of record became essentially a matter of procedure. The requirement was conveniently converted into a requirement for the existence of a record, and tribunals overcame the absence of a record by using the writs of false judgment. These writs compelled inferior tribunals not of record to make up a record, and while they did not transform them into courts of record in the traditional sense of the term, they did provide a record sufficient for the purposes of certiorari.[194] And though only a court of common law could use the writ of false judgment to acquire a record,[195] new jurisdictions did employ it on the basis that while tribunals did not follow common law procedures, they did follow the substantive common law and could accordingly competently be reviewed by the superior common law courts. Certainly the tax commissioners did, in the sense that they administered the law of England, albeit statute law, and were bound by the fundamental rules of the common law as to evidence, natural justice and judicial precedent.

The third legal requirement, that of status as a court, was not satisfied by the tax tribunals prior to the nineteenth century, and it remained to be seen whether the Victorian judiciary would address it. It was, furthermore, well established that certiorari would not lie in relation to administrative acts, for throughout the eighteenth century there were instances where the judges had refused it on these grounds.[196] As in pre-Victorian England the administration of tax was regarded in its entirety as a purely ministerial process and the appellate function of the commissioners not distinguished, certiorari was not a safeguard available to the taxpayer.

Access to the legal safeguards

The extent to which taxpayers could fully exploit the protective relationship they enjoyed with the law depended largely on their awareness of the

---

[193] Blackstone, *Commentaries*, vol. iii, p. 24.
[194] *Edwards* v. *Bowen* (1826) 5 B & C 206; *Ex parte Phillips* (1835) 2 Ad & E 586.
[195] *Scott* v. *Bye* (1824) 2 Bing 344.
[196] *R.* v. *Lediard* (1751) Sayer 6; *Miller* v. *Seare* (1777) 2 Black W 1141.

safeguards it provided, how far they understood them, and the ease of their access to the relevant processes.

Access to tax law

Access to the safeguards was not entirely a matter within the taxpayer's personal control. While the fundamental safeguard of parliamentary consent was generally known, England had no single document which laid down the framework of rules of government or its fundamental values in relation to taxation. The constitution, which had evolved over hundreds of years, was instead contained in a small number of overtly constitutional documents, in a great many detailed rules in statutes and in case law, as well as governmental and parliamentary practices and usage.[197] Being neither classified nor codified, English taxpayers had no obvious practical way in which they could find out the basic constitutional principles governing taxation and so they could not achieve a general view of it.

As to the charge to any tax and the machinery for its assessment and collection, these were laid down by statute, in accordance with the safeguard of parliamentary consent. Tax legislation prior to the Victorian period, while not as voluminous as it was to become, was nevertheless inaccessible to the ordinary taxpayer. Taxation was one of the principal subjects of legislation, and in the overall and relatively small body of statute law it held a prominent place in terms of volume. Statutes were physically accessible to the educated propertied and professional classes, since some were published[198] and others privately copied and distributed. A series of the statutes, though not necessarily a complete one, could generally be found in the relatively common private libraries and reading rooms in most towns and cities. Educated taxpayers would also have access to the parliamentary reports in *The Times*, which followed the passage of all new and important legislation including tax measures.[199] This was supplemented by articles, correspondence and the occasional report of a tax case in those same publications and, indeed, in local newspapers.

Intellectual access, on the other hand, proved an almost insurmountable barrier as far as ordinary taxpayers were concerned. First, a taxpayer

[197] See generally Émile Boutmy, *Studies in Constitutional Law*, translated from 2nd French edition by E. M. Dicey (London: Macmillan & Co, 1891); R. C. van Caenegem, *An Historical Introduction to Western Constitutional Law* (Cambridge University Press, 1995).
[198] See Manchester, *Modern Legal History*, p. 32.
[199] See for example the report of Pitt's introduction of income tax: *The Times*, 4, 15, 20 December 1798, 1, 9 January 1799; 15 March 1799.

could not assume the latest tax Act contained the whole law. Most Acts referred to the provisions of earlier Acts on the same subject and were often subject to the provisions of separate management Acts. The land tax Acts were relatively few in number, but those for the assessed taxes were both numerous and fragmented. Though the income tax of 1799 was novel and its legislative enactment relatively self-contained, even there the 1799 Act was not the only one relating to the tax. There were two amending Acts passed later in 1799,[200] and furthermore all taxes under the control of the Board of Stamps and Taxes were subject to the Taxes Management Acts of 1803, 1808 and 1810. These were incorporated by reference into the principal substantive Acts. Though the Board of Stamps and Taxes itself produced a pamphlet entitled 'A Plain, Short and Easy Description of the Different Clauses in the Income Tax so as to Render It Familiar to the Meanest Capacity',[201] most taxpayers found the legislation intellectually inaccessible. In 1816 Henry Brougham remarked that 'a mere abstract of the revenue laws furnished matter for a large volume, [and] that even a mere index filled a volume of no small bulk'.[202] Customs Acts were notoriously numerous, with new ones every session introducing modifications to the tariff of all kinds and causing 'intricacy and confusion' which was the despair of taxpayers and officials alike.[203] In 1797, 1,200 articles were subject to duty, and the laws filled six large folio volumes.[204] Between 1797 and 1815 a further 600 Customs Acts were passed. There were attempts to consolidate the law in the seventeenth and early eighteenth centuries, but they were unsatisfactory and the whole system became 'a bewildering and appalling chaos'.[205] A digest of the customs laws published in 1815 was the most successful, and was used as the official handbook for customs officials until Victoria's reign.[206] Nevertheless, it was well known that customs law was so intricate, and imperfectly understood even by the officials administering it, that generally merchants were uncertain as to how much duty they were to pay.[207] The excise and stamp duty legislation was similarly extensive and complex.

Not only would it be difficult for the taxpayers to locate all the Acts applicable to their own particular situation, the intellectual task of reading

---

[200] 39 Geo. III c. 22; 39 Geo. III c. 42.

[201] See B. E. V. Sabine, 'The New Taxpayer's Charter or Taxation without Tears', *BTR* (1991), 411.

[202] *Parl. Deb.*, vol. 33, ser. 1, col. 856, 2 April 1816 (HC).

[203] First Report of the Commissioners of Customs, *HCPP* (1857) (2186) iii 301 at p. 323.

[204] *Ibid.*, at p. 323.   [205] *Ibid.*, at p. 324.   [206] *Ibid.*, at p. 325.

[207] *Ibid.*, at p. 374. See generally Edward Carson, 'The Complication of the Customs Duties in the Eighteenth Century', *BTR* (1982), 315.

and understanding them as a coherent body would be very difficult indeed. The task would be made more difficult by the nature of the enactments. The statutory provisions were lengthy, each section following the traditional convention of being expressed in one continuous sentence with no punctuation, were rarely in a logical order, were sometimes contradictory and were couched in often archaic language. The expression of complex and technical law in an obsolescent form, and the need to integrate the provisions of the different Acts, ensured tax law was the intellectual preserve of the lawyers.[208] As far as the tax-paying public was concerned, the law appeared inaccessible, incoherent, illogical and utterly obscure.

Tax law was statutory in nature and that, combined with the paucity of permitted appeals to the regular courts of law in tax matters, resulted in a small jurisprudence of tax. There were important cases where the judges had had to interpret the tax legislation, and where these were reported by one or more of the private law reporters of the eighteenth and early nineteenth centuries, their content would have been theoretically available to the taxpayer, though generally incomprehensible to any but a trained lawyer. The extensive case law of the assessed taxes was, on the other hand, shortly and clearly expressed, but its practical availability was largely limited to professional lawyers and government servants since law libraries to which the public had access were largely unknown.

Even if the formal primary sources of tax law were inaccessible to taxpayers, the local nature of the tax tribunals, where most determinations of disputed issues as to the practical application of the law took place, could have provided them with both some theoretical knowledge of the tax law in question and some practical knowledge of the localist system of administration. This was indeed so in relation to the land tax and the assessed taxes, whose hearings were open to the public, but not in relation to the income tax. So sensitive were English taxpayers to the disclosure of personal financial information either to the government or to the general public that the only way Pitt could ensure the safe passage of his bill through Parliament was to make extensive provision for the secrecy of the administrative process.[209] Not only did he appoint local commissioners who were men of integrity, he insisted that they, and all persons involved in the administration of the tax, should take an oath of non-disclosure.

---

[208] Minutes of Evidence taken before the Royal Commission on the Income Tax, *HCPP* (1919) (288) xxiii, q. 16,028 *per* A. M. Bremner, barrister, on behalf of the General Council of the Bar of England.

[209] See C. Stebbings, 'The Budget of 1798: Legislative Provision for Secrecy in Income Taxation', *BTR* (1998) 651.

Though the effect on individual commissioners and officers of such oaths in law was limited,[210] the restriction of the evidence to those who were sworn to secrecy and the provision that all witnesses were to be examined 'apart'[211] constituted legal authority for the holding of all hearings in private. It followed that any report of the proceedings would not be available to the public.

The accessibility of the appeal processes

The primary safeguard of the appeal process to the lay commissioners was clearly only of any value to taxpayers if they were aware of the existence of their right to appeal. The Acts made provision for public information and were scrupulous in this respect. The date, time and place of the appeal meetings were traditionally publicised by an announcement in church immediately after divine service and the affixing of notices to the church door, in the market place or on the cross in the locality.[212] As the number and availability of newspapers increased, relevant notices appeared in the local journals. Once taxpayers were made aware of their right to appeal, the ease with which they could initiate an appeal was central to the safeguard. In the eighteenth century it was a direct and simple matter, consisting of a relatively informal written communication to the commissioners or some subordinate official stating the desire to appeal or object.[213]

Expense was a key factor in the accessibility of the localist safeguard of appeal. In the eighteenth and early nineteenth centuries it was well established that it constituted an inexpensive and therefore accessible process. First, the appeal hearings were held locally, and taxpayers avoided the considerable expense experienced by litigants to the regular courts in London in travel, board and lodging, and lost earnings. The local tax tribunals sat in hundreds of small divisions throughout the country and were never at any great distance from the taxpayer. Secondly, as the procedures in

---

[210] They were promissory oaths, namely oaths relating to an intention to do, or not to do, something in the future, and so their breach would not result in a prosecution for perjury. Penalties were laid down for acting without having taken the oath: £100, 39 Geo. III c. 13 s. 22 (1799). For government officers breaching their oath the outcome would be dismissal.

[211] 39 Geo. III c. 13 s. 98 (1799). See too 39 Geo. III c. 22 s. 22 (1799), the implication being that this was limited to those persons for whom the Act provided an oath.

[212] 38 Geo. III c. 5 s. 8 (1797) (land tax); 43 Geo. III c. 122 s. 145 (1803) (income tax).

[213] 38 Geo. III c. 5 s. 8 (1797) (land tax); 38 Geo. III c. 16 s. 63 (1798) (triple assessment); 43 Geo. III c. 122 s. 144 (1803) (income tax).

the local tax appeal hearings were simple and informal, and the issues usually of fact rather than law, legal representation was not necessary to enable a taxpayer to participate. Furthermore, though it was permitted in land and assessed taxes hearings, and in excise cases, it was prohibited by statute in the case of income tax.[214] The reason was one of public policy in the light of thousands of potential litigants and the need to keep the process swift so as to assess and collect the tax efficiently and regularly to finance government expenditure. This avoided the greatest expense of regular litigation.

While the local appeal processes were highly accessible to the taxpayer in the eighteenth century, access to the regular courts of law in those few instances where appeals were permitted was most difficult. Though the special case, from which the case stated was derived, was praised in the eighteenth century as a speedy and inexpensive process,[215] that was only relative, and access to the regular courts of law was in most cases prohibitively expensive. A commentator in 1798 criticised the expense and delay of appeals to the Court of Chancery in relation to the redemption of the land tax, and observed that 'the remedy from these two circumstances alone must be worse than the disease'.[216] So technical, complex, inflexible, slow and expensive was the process of the regular courts of law that it was criticised throughout the eighteenth century and beyond as amounting almost to a denial of justice.[217]

Conclusion

The taxpayer's legal safeguards were fully established in English law over a hundred years before Victoria's accession. They were few in number, were safeguards of principle rather than detail, were established early in the history of taxation, and remained static in their legal expression. The new conditions in Victorian England would inevitably, whether deliberately or unconsciously, lead to the re-evaluation of the safeguards. The question was how and if they could or would be maintained in their full

---

[214] 43 Geo. III c. 99 s. 26 (1803).   [215] Blackstone, *Commentaries*, vol. iii, p. 378.
[216] Anon., *Considerations*, pp. 13–14.
[217] See Henry Brougham's lengthy and masterly speech on the state of the courts of the Common Law in 1828: *Parl. Deb.*, vol. 18, new series, cols. 127–247, 7 February 1828 (HC) and *ibid.*, cols. 833–97, 29 February 1828 (HC); First Report of the Common Law Commissioners, *HCPP* (1829) (46) ix 1; First Report of the Commissioners for Inquiring into the Process, Practice and System of Pleading in the Superior Courts of the Common Law, *HCPP* (1851) (1389) xxii 567.

vigour, and whether taxpayers would be sensitive to or accepting of any reform. The Victorian period would show whether legislators and judges would be proactive in their support of the safeguards, or slow and reactive, or even hostile. It was conceivable that the safeguards might be perceived by more modern governments as too restrictive and constituting an impediment to the development of a fiscal policy to suit a new industrial age. Changing political values and the widening of the franchise would affect parliamentary consent; a local system of tax administration would have to find its place in a society with an increasingly national identity, the weakening of local allegiances and a growth in the power of central government. A conservative judiciary and public policy considerations would affect the nature of judicial control of tax tribunals, and it remained to be seen whether tax law and its institutions would be embraced by the legal system or kept on the periphery as savouring too much of the administrative and insufficiently of the legal. Finally, it was not clear whether any movement for a more accessible legal system would include tax law and its institutions.

This book examines how these safeguards, established in English law for the benefit of the taxpayer, were affected and shaped by the new legal, fiscal, economic, social and political conditions of the nineteenth century so as to evolve to their modern form. It explores the extent to which the traditional legal safeguards were adopted or adapted, and how far the law was passive or proactive in ensuring they were maintained and appropriate to the new conditions. It examines their legal expression, and the rules and doctrines surrounding them to assess whether they attained any legal coherence. It explores the interaction of formal statutory provision, judicial methods, professional practices, and the role of the executive to assess the extent to which the safeguards were undermined or whether they were able to establish themselves as fundamental legal safeguards of principle in English law and the legal process. It reveals the nature of the traditional external barriers between tax and law, administration and law, and legal practice and legal theory, and that of the internal divisions between individual taxes and between direct and indirect imposts, and their effect on the development of the legal safeguards. It assesses the degree of protection they were able to afford to the Victorian taxpayer and how effectively they maintained the balance between the state and the taxpayer. Finally, it examines the legal legacy of the safeguards. The study reveals the place of tax law and its institutions within the legal system as a whole, and addresses the popular and professional perceptions of tax law. The study concludes by examining the extent to which the legal safeguards had a constitutional provenance, and whether there existed any underlying code of taxpayer protection in English law.

The establishment and maintenance of legal safeguards to ensure a taxpayer pays the correct amount of a legally levied tax is an issue which is still of considerable importance in the modern world. Its significance as an area of political and legal concern has grown as the modern world meets challenges of equal importance to those faced by the Victorians. The harmonisation of tax law in the European context, an increased globalisation in commercial matters in general, the increasing complexity of tax law and a general rise in tax rates are all modern challenges to taxpayer and taxing authority alike. Their context renders the legal safeguards more potent, for they must now be considered in the light of new emphases on the protection of individual human rights, access to justice, and the openness and accountability of government. The protection of the taxpayer is today a central issue in modern fiscal thinking and planning. It is an issue, however, which is as old as taxation itself and which faced its first, and perhaps severest, test in the Victorian period as the fiscal order of the modern world took shape.

2

The taxpayer's constitutional safeguards of Parliament

Introduction

At the beginning of the Victorian age the fundamental safeguard for the taxpayer was the precondition necessary to all taxes, namely that a tax could only be imposed by the express words of an Act of Parliament. Parliamentary consent, laid down unequivocally in the Bill of Rights, was the cardinal rule of English constitutional law to prevent arbitrary taxation by the state. It has been seen[1] that this constitutional principle, once established, was effected by means of procedural rules of parliamentary practice ensuring that a tax measure enjoyed strict and numerous successive stages of free debate in both the House of Commons and the House of Lords, a scrutiny which could be neither attenuated nor abrogated. So fundamental a principle was it that after the Bill of Rights it was never again challenged in substance. Wilde CJ said in 1850 that it had been 'so often the subject of legal decision that it may be deemed a legal axiom, and requires no authority to be cited in support of it'.[2] Nevertheless the nineteenth century saw the undermining of this safeguard, both substantially and procedurally, through a number of overt statutory reforms of parliamentary process and a more insidious development within the administration of the law itself.

The undermining of parliamentary consent

The role of the executive

Central government desired efficiency and strong control over the administration of taxes. Above all it desired that taxes be administered in a uniform manner so that taxpayers in all parts of the country were subjected to the tax laws in the same way. It had to ensure that all the duties were

---

[1] See above, pp. 13–19.   [2] *Gosling* v. *Veley* (1850) 12 QB 328 at 407 *per* Wilde CJ.

collected promptly so as to ensure a steady flow of revenue to the exchequer. The administration of taxes inevitably involved the department of
the executive which had overall responsibility for them, and that necessarily imported a role for the central government which was the demanding authority, the recipient and the consumer. The executive itself directly
administered the customs, excise and stamp duties, but even in the case
of the locally administered taxes it could not be quiescent or benign and
leave the task entirely to the lay regional commissioners. Even the most
local of all taxes, the land tax, had to have some central direction in order
to decide on the amount of money the tax sought to raise, to make regulations ensuring it was properly levied and collected within the local system, and to make sure that once collected the money was safely received
and put to its designated use.

The organs of central government charged with the administration of
the different taxes at the beginning of the Victorian period were the various boards.[3] The excise was in the hands of three boards for England and
Wales, Scotland and Ireland until their consolidation into one Board of
Excise in 1823,[4] and the customs boards were similarly amalgamated. In
1833 the boards of stamps and of taxes were merged.[5] The major consolidation, however, which would endure throughout the nineteenth century,
was of the Board of Stamps and Taxes with the Board of Excise to make
the Board of Inland Revenue in 1849.[6] Three classes of duty were in its
charge: first, the excise, consisting in the middle of the nineteenth century of duties on many articles including spirits, malt, paper, carriages
and various trade licences; secondly, the stamps, being duties on deeds,
general financial instruments, probates of wills, and letters of administration, legacy and succession duty, and various licences and certificates;
and lastly the taxes, comprising the assessed taxes on luxury items such as
servants, carriages, horses, dogs, hair powder and armorial bearings, as
well as the land and income taxes. The board had to appoint, train, organise and monitor a large staff over the whole country, efficiently to perform
their duties, ensure that interpretations and policies relating to all new
legislation were formulated and disseminated, and deal with an incessant

---

[3] See generally Sir John Craig, *A History of Red Tape* (London: Macdonald & Evans Ltd,
1955), Chapter 9.

[4] 4 Geo. IV c. 23 (1823).   [5] 4 & 5 Will. IV c. 60 (1834).

[6] 12 & 13 Vict. c. 1; See generally Wyn Griffith, *A Hundred Years, The Board of Inland
Revenue 1849–1949* (London: Inland Revenue, 1949), pp. 2–6. The excise was removed
from the Board of Inland Revenue in 1909 and transferred to a Board of Customs and
Excise.

and various mass of inquiries from the public. It did this in the context of an unrelenting demand by the government for a consistent stream of public revenue, a growing body of increasingly complex and uncodified statute law, and a commercial context which was daily becoming more sophisticated as the industrialisation of Britain developed at an astonishing pace. It was a formidable task, and one which grew steadily throughout the nineteenth century.

The legal duty of the commissioners who comprised the Board of Inland Revenue was laid down in its parent Act, the past Acts of the board's constituent parts, the numerous Acts relating to specific taxes, and in the letters patent of their appointment.[7] The Act of 1849 gave the new commissioners the 'care and management' of all the duties in their charge.[8] Though the term was one of essential importance and was familiar to the tax establishment,[9] the duties and powers which the board assumed under this overarching duty were not legally secure. The term was not defined in the Act, nor in any earlier legislation, and neither had it been the subject of judicial consideration. The Act also gave the commissioners all necessary powers to execute the taxing Acts, including those powers which had been in the hands of the old boards, and confirmed the validity of all rules, orders and regulations the old boards had made and the new board would make.[10] The legislature thus imposed on the Commissioners of Inland Revenue a statutory duty of immense breadth, with undefined and equally extensive powers covering virtually any act in the administration of taxes. This, with a lack of legal definition, and the board's desire for control and uniformity, was potentially worrying for the taxpayer for it inevitably led to the development of internal practices for the daily implementation of the legislation.

The broad and undefined statutory power given to the board both demanded and permitted the development of internal rules and practices covering every aspect of the board's administration of taxes, and, furthermore, masked their insidious nature. The board justified its actions on the basis of practicality and common sense, and sought legal justification in the 'care and management' provision. Through official regulations, instructions and circulars distributed to its staff and

---

[7] See, for example, the patent appointing the Commissioners of Excise in 1833, reprinted in Twentieth Report of the Commissioners of Excise Inquiry, *HCPP* (1836) (22) xxvi 179 at p. 340.
[8] 12 & 13 Vict. c. 1 s. 1 (1849). See too 53 & 54 Vict. c. 21 s. 1 (1890).
[9] See 7 & 8 Geo. IV c. 55 s. 4 (1827); 4 & 5 Will. IV c. 60 s. 8 (1834).
[10] 12 & 13 Vict. c. 1 s. 3 (1849); 53 & 54 Vict. c. 21 s. 1(2) (1890).

reinforced through local channels,[11] to which it demanded obedience, the board formulated and disseminated its policy to implement the tax laws, controlled the activities of its officers, and resolved problems arising in the course of the administration. It interpreted obscure legislation and applied judicial decisions to address the everyday problems of tax administration. The practice whereby the board on its own authority allowed remissions of tax to certain individuals or groups of taxpayers was relatively rare in the nineteenth century[12] but would come to be of particular importance in the next.[13] As the term suggests, the practice consisted almost without exception[14] of according relief from taxation to taxpayers, and as these remissions did not impose a charge on the individual taxpayer directly, and only remotely by theoretically increasing the charge on the general body of taxpayers, the fundamental right to be taxed only with the consent of Parliament was not infringed. The board justified them on the basis that they were favourable to the taxpayer in that they mitigated hardship or injustice, that they were subject to the scrutiny of Parliament through the Public Accounts Committee, and that their subject-matter was generally so minor as not realistically to be eligible for parliamentary time. Nevertheless their underlying principle was in the nineteenth century already recognised as significant, dangerous and illegal.[15]

There was always the danger that the board might not be neutral in its practice, since it was in its interests to maintain taxation in its full vigour. It could materially affect the impact of taxation on the body of taxpayers

[11] For example, the board instructed surveyors as to the proper basis of assessment under Schedules A and B of the Income Tax Act 1842 through an open letter in the local newspapers: *Trewman's Exeter Flying Post*, 5 January 1843.

[12] Examples include the board's mitigation of the harsh effect of the Succession Duty Act 1853 s. 11: CIR Second Report, HCPP (1857–8) (2387) xxv 477 at pp. 502–3; the remission of certain assessed taxes and customs duties for foreign ambassadors: Second Report and Minutes of Evidence before Committee of Public Accounts, HCPP (1897) (196) viii 5, qq. 423–6 *per* Sir E. W. Hamilton; the remission of estate duty following the death of Alexander III, Emperor of Russia in 1894: *ibid.*, pp. 9–12; John Booth, *The Inland Revenue ... Saint or Sinner?* (Lymington: Coracle Publishing, 2002), pp. 167–75.

[13] By then commonly known as extra-statutory concessions. See generally Sir Alexander Johnston, *The Inland Revenue* (London: George Allen & Unwin, 1965), pp. 67–8; David W. Williams, 'Extra Statutory Concessions', BTR (1979), 137; Booth, *Inland Revenue*, pp. 17–19; 145–75; G. S. A. Wheatcroft, 'The Attitude of the Legislature and the Courts to Tax Avoidance', *Modern Law Review* 18 (1955), 209 at 220–1; H. W. R. Wade, *Constitutional Fundamentals* (London: Stevens & Sons, 1980), p. 57.

[14] The exception was the composite rate system for building societies.

[15] Second Report and Minutes of Evidence before Committee of Public Accounts, HCPP (1897) (196) viii 5, at pp. 5–12, and qq. 359–463, 878–1006.

in a way that Parliament may not have even envisaged and which it had not expressed in a formal instrument as the law required.[16] The board could take its own view as to the scope or weight of judicial decisions. A striking instance was in relation to the *Bradley Haverstoe* decision in 1851 where the Court of Queen's Bench held that an assessment to the land tax should be determined by an equal pound rate on all properties throughout the division, rather than following the traditional practice of levying it unequally so as to reflect changing property values. The board refused to regard the decision as 'authoritative' on the basis that the court had no jurisdiction to rule on that particular issue and it was 'imperfectly informed'.[17] The board here took its own view of the law, in the face of an apparently clear judicial decision, informed legal opinion and the misgivings of local tax commissioners. It did so for entirely pragmatic reasons of convenience, for it would have upset an old and universal practice of land tax assessment upon which basis property had been bought and sold.

These internal practices could have the effect of administering a tax mildly or harshly, to raise more or less revenue as the board chose. The circulars interpreting new tax legislation and circulated to its officers ensured that a uniform official view prevailed, a view which could favour the taxpayer or favour the state, for example by allowing or denying exemptions if the wording were sufficiently fluid. These internal rules of administration, the customs and practices of the administration, were by their very nature extra-statutory. If they acquired a quasi-legal character, and were used so as to impose tax and not merely mitigate it, they could undermine the fundamental legal right of the taxpayer to be taxed only by an Act of Parliament. The board could, through the development of such internal practices, be led by the needs of the exchequer for increased revenue into adopting a stricter policy of administration to make the taxes more productive;[18] it could respond to the constant demands to control public expenditure and reduce or refine its establishment accordingly, which could affect its implementation of the tax laws. Furthermore, as was observed somewhat cynically in the house in 1860, 'it increases their duty, adds to their staff, and, perhaps, establishes

---

[16] See H. H. Monroe, 'The Constitution in Danger', *BTR* (1969), 24 at 30.

[17] Letters relative to Judgment of Court of Queen's Bench in Case of *Queen* v. *Commissioners of Land Tax for Bradley Haverstoe*, HCPP (1851) (528) xxxi 329 at p. 337.

[18] For the board's practice of acquiring information from employers to verify the tax returns of their employees see Robert Colley, 'Mid-Victorian Employees and the Taxman: A Study in Information Gathering by the State in 1860', *Oxford Journal of Legal Studies* 21 (2001), 593.

a claim to higher salaries'.[19] It could, in short, be influenced by political or economic pressures to adopt particular policies in the administration of tax. This law-making by the central boards was extra-statutory and as such it undermined the legal right of the taxpayer to be taxed only by parliamentary authority. These practices, however necessary they might be, and indeed however sensible or favourable to the taxpayer, were unauthorised by Parliament. This unified and close central control was a formidable barrier to the individual taxpayer who disagreed with the board's interpretation and application of the tax legislation. With a bureaucracy generally unwilling to admit mistakes and totally conversant with complex and technical law and practice, the balance was heavily against the taxpayer.

The taxpayer's anxiety was not misplaced, for any legal control of the board's activities in ensuring the care and management of the public revenue was minimal. Whereas the type of taxation and the rate of taxes were political issues which were decided by the government, and were matters in which Parliament in the nineteenth century took a keen and largely effective interest through its normal legislative processes, the mechanics of administration were the concern of the Treasury.[20] The control of the Treasury over the work of the board, though reiterated in a number of sources, was both vague and slight. With respect to the Commissioners of Inland Revenue themselves, it was not expressed in their parent Act of 1849, though it had been included in most of the constituent Acts of earlier boards,[21] and was included in their letters patent of appointment.[22] This control was expressed in Treasury minutes, which were then embodied in regulations. The relationship of the revenue boards to Parliament was distinct from other departments of the executive, because the appointment of the commissioners by the crown gave them a degree of independence which civil servants did not generally enjoy,[23] and the taxpayers depended

---

[19] *Parl. Deb.*, vol. 157, ser. 3, col. 384, 12 March 1860 (HC) *per* John Maguire.

[20] See Booth, *The Inland Revenue*, pp. 30–6; Sir Norman Chester, *The English Administrative System 1780–1870* (Oxford: Clarendon Press, 1981), p. 225.

[21] 5 & 6 Will. & M. c. 21 ss. 11, 13 (1694); 4 Geo. IV c. 23 s. 8 (1823); 7 & 8 Geo. IV c. 53 s. 2 (1827); 7 & 8 Geo. IV c. 55 s. 10 (1827); 3 & 4 Will. IV c. 13 s. 6 (1833); 39 & 40 Vict. c. 36 s. 2 (1876); 43 & 44 Vict. c. 19 s. 12 (1880); 53 & 54 Vict. c. 21 s. 1(2) (1890); 56 Geo. III c. 98 (1816).

[22] Twentieth Report of the Commissioners of Excise Inquiry, *HCPP* (1836) (22) xxvi 179 at p. 340; Treasury Minutes relative to Consolidation of Boards of Stamps and Taxes, *HCPP* (1833) (647) xxxii 655 at p. 661.

[23] Johnston, *Inland Revenue*, p. 21.

on the vigilance of their representatives and the scrutiny of the Public Accounts Committee for their protection in Parliament.[24]

This independence of the revenue boards and the light control of the Treasury had been developing well before the nineteenth century.[25] The House of Commons was acutely aware of it and expressed its concern in relation to the Board of Excise in 1836. Though the constitutional status of the board was as a sub-department of the Treasury, the nature of its practice gave it the appearance of an independent department. The manner in which the board executed its functions gave it the appearance of an independent board and a degree of autonomy which was not constitutionally permitted. Its powers tended to enlarge, and both in fact and in appearance seemed to administer the law at its uncontrolled discretion to such an extent that the control of the Treasury was actually put into abeyance.[26] The lack of control by the Treasury was exacerbated by the nature of the board itself, for the members had equal powers and no one commissioner was responsible for the board's acts.[27]

The Provisional Collection of Taxes Act 1913

The uncontrolled discretion adopted by the revenue boards in the implementation of the tax laws constituted an insidious and pervasive undermining of the safeguard of parliamentary consent. It was able to occur because of failures of bureaucratic structure and political will, and because of the practical demands of tax administration which necessitated a wide discretion. The second principal undermining of the safeguard was both more overt and narrower in scope. Because it came to acquire statutory expression and authority, however, it was an unambiguous undermining, deliberately accepted and afforded parliamentary sanction.

It began as a parliamentary custom permitting taxation by mere resolution rather than by Act of Parliament. This practice had developed as a result of the practical administrative problem which arose from the delay between the government's budget resolutions laying down a new tax or raising the rate of an existing tax and the passing of legislation embodying

---

[24] See generally Chester, *English Administrative System*, pp. 275–81.

[25] See Edward Hughes, *Studies in Administration and Finance 1558–1825* (Manchester University Press, 1934), pp. 279–316.

[26] Twentieth Report of the Commissioners of Inquiry (Excise Establishment), *HCPP* (1836) (22) xxvi 179 at p. 303.

[27] *Ibid.*, p. 307. See too Fourteenth Report of the Commissioners of Inquiry into the Excise Establishment (Paper), *HCPP* (1835) (16) xxxi 159.

those resolutions. Most taxes in the nineteenth century were permanent, imposed by Acts of Parliament of continuous application, but the customs duty on tea and the income tax persisted in retaining their temporary nature. The Acts regulating their collection were framed to expire at the end of each year and the taxes lapsed, necessitating a renewal by Act of Parliament. The fresh Acts imposing taxes or rates for the new fiscal year were generally not passed until after that year had begun, and so the fundamental rule that a tax could only be imposed by Act of Parliament made all such taxes, their rates and their machinery for collection cease with the old fiscal year and any levying of a new tax prior to the new Act technically illegal.[28]

Unless addressed, this legal hiatus between the resolution and the Act implementing it would cause a significant loss of public revenue and considerable inconvenience. In relation to customs duties, any delay at all could lead to forestalling and evasion, with importers knowing the government's intention to impose tax on a commodity and purchasing large quantities either free of duty or at a lower duty before the new tax or rate became legally enforceable. The public revenue would be damaged by upsetting its continuity and consistency; those members of the trading community who had already paid duty on their goods risked being unable to sell them and could face ruin; and the consumer could potentially suffer too. In relation to income tax, it meant that the revenue department of government could not levy the tax itself, nor even proceed with the administrative work such as calling for completed returns of income which necessarily preceded its collection. It was generally agreed that the public interest and the convenience of all taxpayers justified the taking of some action to address the problem.[29] The practice of Parliament was to collect the taxes in question on the authority of the resolutions of the Committee of Ways and Means alone, to be ratified by Act of Parliament in the near future. There was some early precedent in past practice, though not in law,[30] but the practice was believed to have begun in 1830 in relation to the customs,[31] and it was certainly well established by the middle of the

---

[28] See the detailed treatment of the background to this in David W. Williams, 'A Mere Matter of Machinery', unpublished LL.M thesis, University of Wales 1975, pp. 15–23.

[29] See *Parl. Deb.*, vol. 26, ser. 4, col. 467, 28 June 1894 (HC) *per* Sir William Harcourt.

[30] Thomas Babington Macaulay, *The History of England*, 2nd edition, 5 vols. (London: Longman, Brown, Green and Longmans, 1849), vol. i, pp. 454–5; F. W. Maitland, *The Constitutional History of England* (Cambridge University Press, 1926), p. 309; David W. Williams, 'Three Hundred years On: Are our Tax Bills Right Yet?', *BTR* (1989), 370 at 373.

[31] *Parl. Deb.*, vol. 51, ser. 5, col. 886, 7 April 1913 (HC) *per* Felix Cassel.

century. Once the resolution to impose a duty had been passed, explained the Attorney General in a debate on the sugar duties in 1848, it was 'fairly to be presumed' that a bill would be founded upon it, and the practice proceeded upon that assumption. The government would instruct the customs officers to levy, enforce and collect the duty on the basis of the resolution.[32]

It was an invariable practice when Gladstone was Chancellor of the Exchequer. In 1855 Erskine May said it was 'customary' for the government to levy new duties immediately on the basis of the resolutions agreed by the house.[33] In 1860 it was stated in a tax protest meeting that resolutions of the House of Commons for the imposition of new taxes, or the repeal of existing ones, came into immediate operation[34] and in a debate on the new spirit and tobacco duties in 1909, it was called the Treasury's 'established practice'.[35] And so, by the end of the nineteenth century a convention had become established that a procedure which was not strictly legal should be followed. In relation to income tax the practice was not used consistently from 1842 because for nearly twenty years the tax was regularly imposed for three years at a time, and on the few occasions between its reimposition, the Act was nearly always passed in due time. The practice only came into regular use in 1861.[36]

Although the practice was generally recognised as being a dangerous one, it was never tested in a court of law in England during the nineteenth century. It had, however, been adopted in Australia, the free English settlers having brought with them the potent English ideal of taxation only by the vote of a representative legislative body,[37] and there it was made the subject of judicial challenge in 1865.[38] The Legislative Assembly of Victoria passed a resolution imposing customs duties on a number of imported articles, and on the following day the plaintiffs imported a large

---

[32] *Parl. Deb.*, vol. 99, ser. 3, col. 1316, 29 June 1848 (HC) *per* Sir John Jervis.

[33] Thomas Erskine May, *A Practical Treatise on the Law, Privileges, Proceedings and Usage of Parliament*, 3rd edition (London: Butterworths, 1855), p. 425.

[34] *The Times*, 16 May 1860, p. 12 col. b.

[35] *The Times*, 18 May 1909, p. 7 col. c *per* Lord Pentland. See too *Parl. Deb.*, vol. 159, ser. 3, col. 1401, 5 July 1860 (HC) *per* Robert Collier.

[36] T. Gibson Bowles, *Bowles v. The Bank of England: the Proceedings in Court and Official Court Documents* (London: Butterworth & Co, 1914), pp. 76–7.

[37] A. B. Keith, *Responsible Government in the Dominions*, 3 vols. (Oxford: Clarendon Press, 1912), vol. i, p. 7. See too Peter A. Harris, *Metamorphosis of the Australian Income Tax: 1866 to 1922* (Canberra: Australian Tax Research Foundation, Research Study No.37, 2002), pp. 13ff; Stephen Mills, *Taxation in Australia* (London: Macmillan & Co 1925).

[38] *Stevenson* v. *The Queen* (1865) 2 Wyatt, W & A'B 143.

quantity of these articles and paid the duties. The crown argued that the resolution constituted 'an absolute and unconditional grant of the taxes imposed' and that it was the 'practice and universal custom' of the House of Commons.[39] That was somewhat too strongly put for Stawell CJ. 'Without precedent', he said, '– opposed to the opinion of all writers on constitutional law – and in direct violation of the established principle that no tax can be imposed save with the full assent of the three estates of the realm, such a privilege cannot, according to the laws of England, be supported'.[40] The question was raised again in the Supreme Court of New South Wales nearly thirty years later[41] where the Collector of Customs refused to allow certain goods to enter the country until new duties imposed under a resolution of the House of Assembly, though not yet embodied in legislation, had been paid. The court admitted the importers' legal right, but refused to grant them the discretionary writ of mandamus compelling entry on the basis of public policy. The practice was a recognised constitutional principle acted on for many years in order to protect the queen's revenue. To allow the importers to assert their legal right, held Darley CJ, would be to exercise a discretion 'of a most pernicious and mischievous kind, tending to subvert an invariable practice followed by the ablest exponents of our Constitution – a practice based on sound reason and good sense, and devised by able and wise men in the public interests'.[42] The court thus acknowledged that the practice was contrary to the strict legal right of the taxpayer, but accepted it on the basis of public policy. To do otherwise would lead to speculation in the goods in question, to the damage of the interests of the mercantile community and the general good.

Though in England the issue was left judicially unresolved at the end of the Victorian period, from 1870 to 1890 various legislative techniques were adopted purporting to give the practice statutory force. In relation to customs duties, the provisions were effective as the Customs Consolidation Act 1876 made express provision for the validity of the resolution.[43] This was the first reference to resolutions in the statutes, and it was thought that its inclusion suggested a recognition by Parliament of the increasing force and effect of the resolutions of the House of Commons.[44] Again, in relation

---

[39] *Ibid.*, at 146.
[40] *Ibid.*, at 159. In a second action the importers successfully sued the crown for the return of the duties, on the basis of an implied contract: see *Stevenson* v. *The Queen* (1865) 2 Wyatt, W & A'B 176.
[41] *Ex parte Wallace & Co* (1892) 13 NSWLR 1.   [42] *Ibid.*, at 9.
[43] 39 & 40 Vict. c. 36 s. 18. See too 16 & 17 Vict. c. 107 s. 19 (1853).
[44] Gibson Bowles, *Proceedings in Court*, p. 104.

to the customs duties in the Isle of Man, an Act of 1877 provided that any resolution of the Manx legislature relating to customs duties would take effect immediately, subject to the approval of the Treasury, for a period of six months.[45] In these instances, therefore, the legislation expressly recognised resolutions of the House of Commons[46] and when the duty on tea or sugar, for example, was increased, it would be collected at the port on the very next day. In relation to income tax, the first provision was in 1870, to the effect that all the statutory provisions then in force 'shall have full force and effect' with regard to the income tax which may be granted for the coming year, as if it had actually been granted.[47] The provision first appeared at that time because by 1870, even though anti-income tax protests and the movement for its abolition were then at their height, it was clear to the legislators that the tax was permanent in practice, if not in theory. Thereafter, though in increasingly general language, each new Act imposing income tax, culminating in the Customs and Inland Revenue Act 1890,[48] contained a section to the effect that the provisions of all Acts in force on 5 April of the preceding year should apply to the income tax granted by the new Act.[49] Though the editors of *Practical Statutes* in 1870 did not regard it as a development worthy of comment, in the same year one member mildly observed that it was the first time since the income tax had been reintroduced twenty-seven years before that the tax could be levied before the vote.[50] He was correct in his concern, for the provision was sufficiently widely drawn to allow for the collection of the tax itself. However, the objective of the provision, namely to 'ensure the collection in due time' of the income tax granted for the new fiscal year, limited the construction of the widely worded provision to when legally due under the Act. It was ultimately held to apply only so as to allow the preliminary proceedings of income tax assessment, namely the issue of notices and returns, to be undertaken before a vote of Parliament on the tax in order to ensure prompt collection.[51]

An element of the practice was the unwritten understanding that the taxing Act in question would become law in a reasonable time, a point made by the Australian court in 1892. As long as this was so, the practice was convenient and widely accepted. It was whenever greater delays

---

[45] 50 & 51 Vict. c. 5 s. 2 (1887).   [46] 39 & 40 Vict. c. 36 s. 18 (1876).

[47] 33 & 34 Vict. c. 4 s. 1 (1870).   [48] 53 & 54 Vict. c. 8 s. 30.

[49] 34 & 35 Vict. c. 5 s. 1 (1871); 36 & 37 Vict. c. 8 s. 1 (1873); 37 & 38 Vict. c. 16 s. 6 (1874).

[50] *Parl. Deb.*, vol. 199, ser. 3, col. 1731, 10 March 1870 (HC) *per* George Sclater-Booth.

[51] *Bowles* v. *Attorney-General* [1912] 1 Ch 123.

occurred between the resolutions and the enacting legislation[52] that the practice began to show itself inadequate and open to abuse. From 1861 to 1911 the income tax Act was passed in May or June, only exceptionally in August and never beyond September. But in 1911, for no good reason of emergency or urgent business, it was passed in December. The dilatory chancellor was David Lloyd George. The legal position of the income tax was more fragile than that of the customs, and the Victorian practice was soon subjected to judicial scrutiny. Thomas Gibson Bowles MP, 'a purist in matters of Parliamentary etiquette and procedure',[53] and representing nothing less than the liberty of the subject, was the aggrieved taxpayer who first challenged the practice. He was a Victorian John Hampden, 'a most watchful and vigilant guardian of the proprieties of finance'.[54]

Gibson Bowles refused to make a return for the purposes of super-tax, an additional and annual income tax on higher incomes introduced in 1910, on the basis that the revenue department had no authority to demand such a return as no Act had yet been passed imposing the tax for the current financial year. The reliance of the revenue department was not strictly on the parliamentary practice, but on the Act of 1890,[55] arguing successfully that it applied because super-tax was income tax[56] and not 'a new animal in the fiscal menagerie'.[57] Therefore the provisions in force in relation to super-tax on the preceding day had effect with respect to the tax granted just as if it had been imposed by Act of Parliament, and the board's demands for returns were legitimate. The decision in *Bowles v. Attorney General* related only to the board's preliminary administrative activities, not the actual payment of the tax. The legal safeguard of parliamentary consent had been undermined, though legitimately through statutory provision. The judge, however, expressly left open the question whether before the Act was actually passed the board could assess and demand payment of the tax.[58] When the board did indeed purport to do this, Gibson Bowles purchased a quantity of Irish land stock deliberately so as to raise the question of law in the courts and brought a second action in 1913.

In 1912 he had received the dividends net of income tax, the Bank of England having made the deduction despite the Act imposing income tax

[52] For the extent of the delays in each case since 1842, see Williams, 'Mere Matter of Machinery', pp. 217–19.
[53] *Parl. Deb.*, vol. 51, ser. 5, col. 1037, 8 April 1913 (HC) *per* William Joynson-Hicks.
[54] *Parl. Deb.*, vol. 41, ser. 5, col. 1525, 26 July 1912 (HC) *per* Austen Chamberlain.
[55] 53 & 54 Vict. c. 8 s. 30.   [56] 10 Edw. VII c. 8 s. 66 (1910).
[57] *Bowles v. Attorney-General* [1912] 1 Ch 123 at 131.
[58] *Ibid.*, at 137.

for the year having not yet received the royal assent. He maintained the deduction was a 'deliberate, considered, persistent, obstinate'[59] unlawful levy of taxes by a British government resulting in at least £12 million[60] being obtained 'from the ignorance, the fears, and the humility of the taxpayer'.[61] As Hampden had done nearly three hundred years before,[62] he argued on the basis of the long line of statutory authority from Magna Carta which stated unequivocally that no tax could be levied without the consent of Parliament. Erskine May had stated that the practice of relying on a mere resolution was 'not strictly legal',[63] as had the Treasury itself when in 1903 it agreed that it constituted 'an infraction of the Statute'.[64] 'The only taxing power in this realm', insisted Gibson Bowles, 'resides in Parliament. The only authority to levy any tax … is to be found in an Act of Parliament. Where there is no Act there is no taxing authority'.[65] As this was undeniable, the crown maintained the case depended on the construction of the income tax legislation which made the machinery of income tax permanent not only as regards returns, but also as regards assessment and collection. The intention of the legislature was to allow the tax to be levied notwithstanding the Act had not been passed.

Parker J refused to hold that a resolution sufficed to impose a tax on a subject. It was of no legal effect, for a formal Act of Parliament was essential, and 'no practice or custom, however prolonged, or however acquiesced in on the part of the subject, can be relied on by the Crown as justifying any infringement of its provisions'.[66] Neither would he accept that statutory authority existed for deducting the tax before the Act was passed, for the Customs and Inland Revenue Act 1890 tax was limited to keeping the machinery of income tax in force, but not its substance; it gave no authority to demand the tax.[67] Had it intended to impose the tax by mere resolution then the Act would have said so in clear and express terms. The fundamental constitutional principle that the only authority to levy a tax lay in an Act of Parliament was unequivocally reaffirmed.

---

[59] Gibson Bowles, *Proceedings in Court*, p. vii. [60] *Ibid.*, p. ix. [61] *Ibid.*, p. x.
[62] Gibson Bowles drew the comparison himself: Gibson Bowles, *ibid.*, p. xii.
[63] Erskine May, *Parliament*, p. 425.
[64] Fourth Report and Minutes of Evidence before the Public Accounts Committee, *HCPP* (1903) (304) v 21 at pp. xiv and 240; qq. 3479–80.
[65] *Bowles v. Bank of England* [1913] 1 Ch 57 at 71. [66] *Ibid.*, at 84–5.
[67] That was clear from the proviso that nothing in the Act was to be deemed to continue the rate of income tax imposed for the preceding year, for there could not be collection before assessment, there could not be assessment till the rate was known and the rate could not be finally settled by mere resolutions.

When the illegality of the practice was thus confirmed, its necessity was subsequently recognised by giving it formal statutory expression. Since the House of Commons was supreme in matters of taxation, there was no reason why legislation should not be enacted to permit a tax to be levied on the basis of a resolution. Indeed, that had been done in relation to the customs duties, with little opposition. Even before Parker J had delivered his judgment, Lloyd George knew that if the practice were tested in the courts, it would be unlikely to be held to be legal and binding.[68] Accordingly in 1913 he proposed to give it statutory force by providing that a resolution of the Committee of Ways and Means for the imposition of a new tax or the alteration of an existing one, or for the renewal of a temporary tax, should have temporary statutory effect. The proposal gave rise to long and bitter parliamentary debate.

The government argued on the basis of the need to address the illegality the judicial decision had exposed,[69] and on the nature of the proposal in merely regularising and legalising an established and invariable custom.[70] What was clear was that the government had found the safeguard of formal parliamentary authority for taxation irksome, and was prepared to undermine it on the basis of public policy, favouring the public good over the legal rights of individual taxpayers. Opponents rejected the argument that giving the practice statutory form effected no substantial change. Its very nature as mere usage rendered it flexible and adaptable,[71] and since everyone knew it was illegal, it was used cautiously and reasonably by the government. And when the government itself began to abuse it, as a parliamentary custom of however long a standing, it could be challenged in the courts by any aggrieved taxpayer and though it undermined the parliamentary safeguard, it was not final. The usage and the right to challenge it were thus both valuable safeguards to the taxpayer against arbitrary taxation, and the government's proposal significantly undermined the protection of the taxpayer by Parliament. Despite powerful and eloquent opposition, the bill received the royal assent as the Provisional Collection of Taxes Act 1913.[72] It allowed resolutions for the imposition of customs duties and income tax to come into immediate operation, but such taxes

---

[68] *Parl. Deb.*, vol. 41, ser. 5, col. 1522, 26 July 1912 (HC) *per* David Lloyd George.

[69] *Ibid.*, vol. 51, ser. 5, col. 1777, 14 April 1913 (HC) *per* Sir Rufus Isaacs AG; *ibid.*, vol. 51, ser. 5, col. 1838, 15 April 1913 (HC) *per* David Lloyd George; *ibid.*, vol. 51, ser. 5, col. 1840, 15 April 1913 (HC) *per* Sir Rufus Isaacs AG.

[70] *Ibid.*, vol. 51, ser. 5, col. 836, 7 April 1913 (HC) *per* David Lloyd George.

[71] *Parl. Deb.*, vol. 51, ser. 5, cols. 886–8, 7 April 1913 (HC) *per* Felix Cassel.

[72] 3 Geo. V c. 3.

were invalid if not sanctioned by legislation within four months of the resolution. The general consensus was that Gibson Bowles' action had resulted in a much-needed overhaul of parliamentary procedure and in the government having to bring its financial proposals to the house promptly each year, and had placed an accepted practice on a sounder and more secure footing. Although he was incensed at the arrangement for his costs, Gibson Bowles himself was ultimately satisfied with the Act because it limited the exercise of the power and ensured that the Finance Act imposing the income tax for the new fiscal year was passed at the latest by August, and this was a significant improvement on recent practice.[73]

Tensions between the two Houses of Parliament

In his *Treatise upon the Law, Privileges, Proceedings and Usage of Parliament,* first published in 1844, Thomas Erskine May laid down the minutely detailed procedure which money bills had to follow through Parliament in the early Victorian period.[74] It was to ensure that each tax measure was fully discussed by an informed house, and that it received due publicity to enable taxpayers to contact their parliamentary representatives with their concerns and views.[75] A money bill was to be printed and circulated to every member before the crucial second reading, where the government minister explained its merits to his parliamentary colleagues and its principle was fully debated. If it was accepted, the bill was subject to the closest detailed discussion, clause by clause, in committee, a discussion of particular value as members were permitted to speak more than once. After this thorough scrutiny, and any proceedings on report, the bill was reprinted to incorporate the amendments and put to the house at its third reading. The bill then moved for examination by the Lords and finally received the royal assent and became law. Erskine May also reiterated the principles which had long been settled for governing the relationship between the Commons and the Lords with regard to taxation, principles ensuring the supremacy of the former in this respect, and the subservience of the latter.[76] Despite the staunch and long-standing maintenance by the Commons that the Lords could not interfere in any way with a money bill,[77] the Lords refused to acquiesce entirely. Though

---

[73] Gibson Bowles, *Proceedings in Court*, p. xiii.
[74] See Erskine May, *Parliament*, pp. 367–89.
[75] *Parl. Deb.*, vol. 51, ser. 5, col. 940, 7 April 1913 (HC) *per* Sir Frederick Banbury.
[76] *Ibid.*, pp. 420–30.   [77] See above, pp. 18–19.

in practice they had not exercised it for many years, the House of Lords never agreed to relinquish its right to reject such a measure in its entirety.

The Paper Duty Bill 1860

The Lords rarely exercised their power to reject a money bill because it would evidently result in denying supply to the crown. They did purport to exercise it, however, in 1860, an action which gave rise to heated debate in Parliament and which would lead, half a century later, to a constitutional crisis unparalleled since the seventeenth century. The occasion was Gladstone's controversial paper duty repeal bill. He proposed the repeal of the unpopular duty, specifically to reduce the price of newspapers but generally as a step towards tidying and rationalising the fiscal system and redressing the balance between direct and indirect taxation.[78] The House of Commons voted to repeal the duty as an impediment to trade and commerce and a tax on knowledge.[79] As the lessening of that burden on the taxpayer would mean the financial loss would have to be covered, it was proposed to increase the income tax to cover the deficiency. The repeal of the paper duty therefore had to be accorded the same degree of scrutiny as a bill imposing fresh or increased taxation. The social, economic and moral aspects of the proposed repeal were fully discussed, particularly its effect on knowledge and education.

The Conservative opposition ensured the House of Lords rejected the bill. They did so primarily on economic grounds, arguing it was replacing indirect taxation with direct taxation, that a repeal would encourage English paper manufacturers to go abroad, and that the country could not afford to forego this revenue. It was a cheap and easy tax to collect, and the argument that the duty amounted to a tax on knowledge was, said Lord Monteagle, 'threadbare and clap-trap'[80] since most duty was levied on paper for packing rather than printing. The Earl of Derby maintained that a repeal in the current financial, fiscal and political situation was an 'improvident and reckless proposal'.[81] In a measured and scholarly speech Lord Lyndhurst delivered an exposition of the law on the privileges of the

---

[78] See generally T. F. T. Plucknett, *Taswell-Langmead's English Constitutional History*, 11th edition (London: Sweet & Maxwell Ltd, 1960), pp. 548–9. See too H. C. G. Matthew, *Gladstone* (Oxford: Clarendon Press, 1997), pp. 113–14; B. E. V. Sabine, 'Great Budgets: Gladstone's Budget of 1860', *BTR* (1972), 111.

[79] For the arguments of the press against the paper duty see *The Times*, 22 June 1858, p. 8 col. e.

[80] *Parl. Deb.*, vol.158, ser. 3, col. 1490, 21 May 1860 (HL).   [81] *Ibid.*, col. 1530.

Lords in relation to money bills, accepting that they had agreed that they could neither originate nor amend them, but asserting their right to reject them, a right the Commons had never questioned.[82] Indeed the Earl of Aberdeen, when he was Prime Minister in 1853, had stated it, and it was sanctioned by numerous instances in practice.[83] Lord Chelmsford made the point that if the Lords did not exercise their right to reject a money bill in such a clear case as this, they would be mere 'cyphers in the constitution', unable to intervene in a sphere which so closely concerned the public.[84]

The House of Commons was under no illusions as to the constitutional significance and gravity of the Lords' actions. The government did not deny the Lords' strict legal right to reject a money bill in its entirety, but drew a distinction between what was legal and what was constitutional. Despite a clear conflict as to their legal rights in relation to taxation whereby the Commons claimed complete and exclusive power over taxation and the Lords conceded nothing, the two houses had worked in harmony through a tacit understanding that the Commons should have the exclusive right, but that the Lords should have the power to prevent the Commons abusing their power by forcing other measures through under the guise of money bills.[85] In rejecting the paper duty repeal bill, therefore, the Lords had breached this essential understanding. On this basis, the government argued that the Lords could not constitutionally refuse their assent to a money bill which formed an inherent part of the government's whole financial scheme as approved and recommended by the Commons. Such interference with taxation effectively severed taxation from representation and constituted an unprecedented interference with the Commons' exclusive right to regulate taxation, putting its very existence under threat.

Despite strong parliamentary and popular feelings, Lord Palmerston's resolutions affirming the supremacy of the Commons in tax matters were passed unanimously.[86] Though Gladstone had not succeeded in repealing

---

[82] *Ibid.*, cols. 1464–5.   [83] *Parl. Deb.*, vol. 127, ser. 3, col. 670, 27 May 1853 (HL).

[84] *Parl. Deb.*, vol. 158, ser. 3, col. 1507, 21 May 1860 (HL).

[85] *Parl. Deb.*, vol. 159, ser. 3, col. 1434, 5 July 1860 (HC) *per* William Gladstone. This was a reference to the practice of 'tacking', which was long accepted as being both dangerous and unconstitutional: John Hatsell, *Precedents of Proceedings in the House of Commons*, 2nd edition, 4 vols. (London: T. Payne, T. Cadell, W. Davies, 1796), vol. iii, p. 195.

[86] *Parl. Deb.*, vol. 159, ser. 3, col. 1384, 5 July 1860 (HC) *per* Viscount Palmerston. He was severely criticised by his own government colleagues for the weakness of his response: *ibid.*, cols. 1423, 1430, 1461, 1462, 1464, 1471. He was personally opposed to the repeal of the duty: Michael Partridge, *Gladstone* (London: Routledge, 2003), p. 95.

the tax, the Commons had forcibly asserted their rights. The importance of the paper duty bill with regard to the taxpayer's constitutional safeguard of parliamentary consent was its ultimate outcome half a century later. The particular issue of the repeal of the paper duty was dealt with in the following year by Gladstone's scheme of placing all the year's financial proposals, including the paper duty repeal, in one general finance measure, with which the Lords could not interfere without negating all taxation for the entire year and thereby making themselves responsible for bringing the government to a standstill.[87] Apart from the perception that the bill in this consolidated form was a humiliating rebuke to a House of Lords which had acted entirely properly in rejecting the bill in 1860,[88] any decision on the consolidated bill would amount to a vote of confidence in the whole government, and this prevented the Lords from dealing with part of the financial proposals for the year and not all. The power in the Lords to reject money bills still existed in theory, but contemporary commentators understood that in practice it had been effectively denied by the Commons. This paralysing of the Lords constituted, in effect, a distinct undermining of the procedural safeguards of Parliament, for as the Lords could either accept all the financial proposals or reject them all, they clearly would exercise the power only rarely and in cases of real necessity. The Lords believed this was such an occasion in 1909.

The Parliament Act 1911

The relationship between the two houses of Parliament in relation to money bills had been strained throughout Victoria's reign, but it was finally resolved within a decade of the queen's death.[89] Tensions between the Liberal government and the Conservative House of Lords had been growing since 1906, with the rejection by the latter of several Liberal measures of social reform, notably the Education Bill and the Licensing Act. The last straw, however, was the rejection by the Lords of Lloyd George's famous 'People's Budget' in 1909.[90] It was a radical one, aimed at both raising money to address profound social problems and at achieving certain

---

[87] Matthew, *Gladstone*, pp. 113–14. The paper duty was ultimately repealed: *Parl. Deb.*, vol. 162, ser. 3, cols. 587–9, 15 April 1861(HC).

[88] *Parl. Deb.*, vol. 163, ser. 3, col. 88, 27 May 1861 (HC) *per* Edward Horsman; *ibid.*, col. 90 *per* Rainald Knightley; *ibid.*, col. 106 *per* Frederick Lygon; *ibid.*, col. 147 *per* Sir Robert Peel.

[89] See generally Plucknett, *English Constitutional History*, pp. 550–5.

[90] See generally B. E. V. Sabine, 'Lloyd George's Budget of 1909', *BTR* (1975), 114.

non-fiscal social objectives, and considerably affecting property owners. It proposed a rise in income tax on unearned income, the introduction of super-tax on high incomes, an increase in death duties and new taxes on land.[91] The decision to reject the bill was not one taken lightly by the Lords,[92] but they maintained they were legally and constitutionally permitted to do so.[93] The government saw this as yet another act by a partisan House of Lords in its own vested interests[94] to block all Liberal progressive measures. Asquith said it was an intolerable 'indefensible paradox'[95] that an undemocratic hereditary body with no real understanding of the needs and aspirations of ordinary people should be permitted, by rejecting the budget, to control the levying of taxation.[96] What had been an archaic legal survival had been exercised by the upper house contrary to ancient and unwritten usage. He later called it a 'stupendous act of political blindness' amounting to 'political suicide'.[97]

In 1910, and again in 1911, following a general election which Asquith insisted gave his administration a clear mandate to proceed with the limitation of the powers of the House of Lords, he introduced the Parliament Bill. From the point of view of the taxpayer the most significant political objective was to ensure that the House of Lords was prevented from touching the national finance by abolishing its absolute veto over money bills,[98] and making it clear beyond question that it could not 'meddle in any way, to any degree, or for any purpose, with … national finance'.[99] This was achieved by providing that if a money bill, having been passed

---

[91] For the views of a contemporary commentator, see C. F. Bastable, 'The Budget of 1909', *Economic Journal* 19 (1909), 288.

[92] See generally Dennis Morris, ' "A Tax By Any Other Name"; Some Thoughts on Money Bills and Other Taxing Measures', *Statute Law Review* 22 (2001), 211 at 213–16; and 23 (2002), 147.

[93] See Lloyd George's vituperative attack on the House of Lords and his defence of his budget in *The Times*, 22 November 1910, p. 8 col. c.

[94] *Parl. Deb.*, vol. 21, ser. 5, col. 1834, 21 February 1911 (HC) *per* Joseph Pease.

[95] *Parl. Deb.*, vol. 21, ser. 5, col. 1745, 21 February 1911 (HC).

[96] See Asquith's election speech at the Albert Hall in December 1909: *The Times*, 11 December 1909, p. 8 col. a. See too *Parl. Deb.*, ser. 5 vol. 22, col. 283, 28 February 1911 *per* Charles Leach.

[97] *Parl. Deb.* vol. 21, ser. 5, col. 1746, 21 February 1911 (HC) *per* Herbert Asquith.

[98] A money bill was defined as any bill which, in the opinion of the Speaker, contained only provisions dealing with 'the imposition, repeal, remission, alteration, or regulation of taxation; charges on the Consolidated Fund or the provision of money by Parliament; supply; the appropriation, control, or regulation of public money; the raising or guarantee of any loan or the repayment thereof; or matters incidental to those subjects or any of them'.

[99] *The Times*, 11 December 1909, p. 8 col. a.

by the Commons, was sent up to the Lords at least one month before the end of the session, if it were not passed by the Lords, it could nevertheless receive the royal assent and pass into law. The government consistently denied any innovation of any kind and claimed no disturbance to the existing system. It was doing nothing more than giving unambiguous statutory form to the accepted constitutional practice that the Lords could discuss but not amend or reject money bills. The veto was a clear example of a divergence between strict legal right and constitutional practice which developed in an unwritten constitution. Reform was essential now that it was no longer possible to 'trust to the silken threads of unwritten usage'[100] and find the Lords treating their legal rights as constitutional rights.

Parliamentary feelings ran high. The bill was variously called revolutionary, unstatesmanlike, crude, violent, ill-considered, odious, perilous, disastrous, an outrage. 'I believe this to be a bad Bill', said one member, 'introduced for a bad purpose',[101] while another said it was accentuated by malice, and was intended to be 'a Bill of punishment and not a Bill of rights'.[102] The opposition was convinced that the bill was driven entirely by party considerations, by the individual and disparate objectives and values within the Liberal, Labour and Irish Nationalist coalition government under the leadership of Asquith who had united not for the good of the country or because they believed the Parliament Bill was a sound measure, but through self-interest.[103] The Liberals wanted to end the blocking of their progressive social welfare legislation; the Labour party saw it as a step towards single chamber government where the will of the people would be supreme, and the Irish Nationalists – a major force in promoting the bill – saw it as the only way they could secure Home Rule for Ireland. It was 'simply a question of party, party, party'.[104]

A considerable portion of the extensive and bitter debate centred on the innovative clause whereby the powers of the House of Lords with regard to legislation other than money bills were restricted. Therefore though the exercise of the Lords' veto over money bills was the immediate cause of the constitutional crisis, its loss was relatively uncontroversial as the Lords themselves agreed to renounce their rights to reject or amend those

[100] *Parl. Deb.*, vol. 22, ser. 5, col. 59, 27 February 1911 (HC) *per* Richard Haldane.
[101] *Ibid.*, vol. 21, ser. 5, col. 1803, 21 February 1911 (HC) *per* Sir Robert Finlay.
[102] *Ibid.*, vol. 22, ser. 5, col. 250, 28 February 1911 (HC) *per* Sir Gilbert Parker.
[103] See the robust speech of George Sandys in *Parl. Deb.*, vol. 22, ser. 5, cols. 126–33, 27 February 1911 (HC).
[104] *The Times*, 26 May 1911, p. 12 col. f *per* Lord Zouche of Haryngworth.

which were purely financial in character, provided that effectual provision was made against 'tacking',[105] namely the inclusion in a money bill of non-financial elements to ensure their unchecked passage through Parliament. By general consent, therefore, they were to play no constitutional role in relation to money bills. That made the definition of a money bill a question of some moment. Explicit legal tacking of a non-financial element in a finance bill was addressed, but implied tacking, where a bill was in form a money bill, consisting only of clear financial provisions to raise revenue, but where the financial provisions were such as to radically affect the social or political order, was a real danger. The definition was so wide as to allow a single chamber to use taxation to initiate and sustain major social reforms. As the leader of the opposition observed, 'that is neither the old doctrine, nor the constitutional doctrine, nor the right doctrine, nor a rational doctrine', and was, furthermore, one unknown in nearly all other countries.[106] Nevertheless the government refused to amend its definition of a money bill. Its object was to include all those bills over which, by constitutional usage, the Commons had sole authority.[107] The test was whether the main governing purpose of the bill was a financial one.

The tension rose throughout the summer of 1911 at each stage in the parliamentary passage of the bill, with the government conceding nothing, despite the Lords' acceptance of the fundamental principles of the bill with no alteration.[108] All amendments calling for independent scrutiny, further scrutiny, or even merely an interval of time to allow for reflection were dismissed, often sarcastically and contemptuously, by the government. It was unmoved and uncompromising. When it became clear that the Prime Minister had received a guarantee from the king for the creation of sufficient peers to ensure the bill was passed,[109] there was nothing more to be done.[110] Even the leader of the opposition in the upper chamber accepted it, on the basis that '[s]lender opportunities were better than

---

[105] Their lordships also accepted the need to reform themselves to make the house more in touch with popular needs. They embodied their proposals in a Reconstitution Bill, whereby they were to be restructured on the basis of a mixture of hereditary, elected and nominated peers.

[106] *Parl. Deb.*, vol. 24, ser. 5, col. 713, 18 April 1911 (HC) *per* Arthur Balfour.

[107] See the speech of the Prime Minister, *Parl. Deb.*, vol. 24, ser. 5, cols. 257–62, 11 April 1911 (HC).

[108] *The Times*, 21 July 1911, p. 9 col. g; pp. 12–13; *Parl. Deb.*, vol. 28, ser. 5, cols. 1467–84, 24 July 1911 (HC).

[109] *The Times*, 22 July 1911, p. 8 col. a; p. 9 col. c; *ibid.*, 24 July 1911, p. 8 col. a.

[110] *Ibid.*, 28 July 1911, p. 7 col. c.

no opportunities at all'.[111] The result was the Parliament Act 1911.[112] The House of Lords had lost its power, so strongly challenged in 1860, to veto or delay the passage of financial measures. It could not even ensure either that its minimal deliberations would be formally received and considered by the lower house[113] nor that its amendments to deal with clear mistakes or defects in the legislation would be addressed. The only protection the taxpayer was now afforded by the House of Lords was the possibility of a little delay during which he could attempt to rouse public opinion in respect of any new or controversial taxation.

The effect of the parliamentary reforms

Within a dozen years of Victoria's death, therefore, two major reforms of parliamentary process had been effected: the legalising of taxation by resolution and the removal of the House of Lords from any role in relation to money bills. The reforms undermined the taxpayer's parliamentary safeguard in three distinct ways. First, they established the dominance of the House of Commons by effective removal of the second chamber. Secondly, they resulted in a considerable reduction in debate, and thirdly, they led to the dominance of the House of Commons by the executive. In so doing, they went to the very heart of the taxpayer's constitutional safeguard of parliamentary consent.

The dominance of the House of Commons

By paralysing and then negating the role of the House of Lords in tax matters, the House of Commons was unchallenged in its supremacy. It was argued that this was a proper reflection of its constitutional position and a recognition of its democratic structure. The Parliament Act did indeed affirm constitutional usage, but denied the real and important value which lay in the second chamber. Disraeli was one of the few speakers in the paper duty debate in 1860 who not only supported the Lords' action as legally and constitutionally sound,[114] but also addressed the protective function of the Lords' power of critical review and appreciated that

---

[111] *Ibid.*, 29 June 1911, p. 12 col. a. The bill was passed in the House of Lords by a majority of seventeen: see *ibid.*, 11 August 1911, p. 6 col. a; p. 7 col. c. It received the royal assent in the House of Lords, in the absence of all the opposition peers: *ibid.*, 19 August 1911, p. 6 col. g.

[112] 1 & 2 Geo. V c. 13.

[113] *Parl. Deb.*, vol. 23, ser. 5, cols. 2292–3, 5 April 1911 (HC) *per* Winston Churchill.

[114] *Ibid.*, vol. 163, ser. 3, col. 254, 30 May 1861 (HC).

its removal would significantly lessen the constitutional protection of the taxpayer.[115] In their balancing and regulating role the Lords constituted 'the only safeguard against the despotism of democracy'.[116] The removal of this moderating and restraining influence permitted the government to bring about financial changes of real magnitude, or unwise, hasty or harsh measures. There was no longer any check on the taxation measures of the House of Commons, no process whereby a separate chamber could reject a tax measure of which it disapproved, even for the soundest reasons. There was no restraint to prevent the Commons acting autocratically, on a bare majority. 'Taxation', observed Lord Hugh Cecil, 'may be made an instrument of tyranny and often has been so made. To say that a bare majority of a certain partisan assembly is to have this jurisdiction is to set up the apparatus of tyranny in our Constitution'.[117] There was no other second chamber in any major legislature which did not have the right to amend or reject money bills. One safeguard against the imposition of the highest rates of direct and property taxation or the introduction of new forms of taxation had been removed.

The limitation of parliamentary discussion

Both the Parliament Act and the Provisional Collection of Taxes Act severely limited parliamentary discussion. Full debate and critical review of the government's tax measures in Parliament was a major safeguard of the taxpayer, and the procedures of that body had evolved so as to ensure this measure of consideration. Discussion in the house, observed an independent member in 1861, was the principal means whereby the house could guard the freedom of the subject.[118] Parliament's task, and the members' desire, was to test the substance of tax bills and to ensure that they did actually express what Parliament intended. Parliamentary time had been relatively plentiful in the eighteenth century, when legislation was light and mostly straightforward, but by the beginning of the Victorian period it was already under pressure through other political developments.[119] Members were conscious that pressure of time led to hurried measures and inadequate scrutiny. For example one member was

---

[115] *Ibid.*, vol. 159, ser. 3, col. 1498, 5 July 1860 (HC). See too *ibid.*, vol. 163, ser. 3, col. 255, 30 May 1861.

[116] *Ibid.*, vol. 159, ser. 3, col. 1568, 6 July 1860 (HC) *per* Edward Horsman.

[117] *Ibid.*, vol. 23, ser. 5, col. 2079, 4 April 1911 (HC).

[118] *Ibid.*, vol. 163, ser. 3, cols. 71–2, 27 May 1861 (HC) *per* Charles Newdegate.

[119] See generally Chester, *English Administrative System*, pp. 98–122.

aware that the debate on the succession duty bill in 1853 was in danger of being rushed, so he allowed the second reading without opposition, expressly reserving the right to discuss the principle of the bill when the house went into committee.[120] Similarly in 1894 Balfour complained that the discussion of the complicated and controversial finance bill, containing proposals for the new estate duty, was rushed, with only three days for the second reading.[121] However, it was the conflation of the whole year's financial proposals in one bill in 1861 which considerably reduced the extent of free deliberation of taxation measures, for now there could only be one first, second and third reading, one committee, one report, instead of the several which separate consideration of each tax measure would demand. Then the Parliament Act, by imposing a single chamber legislature in relation to taxation, had removed entirely one layer of scrutiny and debate and with it any meaningful opportunity for constructive criticism and scrutiny of legislation in a chamber where debate was particularly free, as party control was not so strong, and particularly valuable, as its members were often experienced and knowledgeable individuals.

The removal of the scrutiny and debate of tax measures by the Lords was compounded by the limitation of the depth and nature of discussion in the Commons which resulted from making statutory the parliamentary practice of levying taxes under the authority of a resolution of the Committee of Ways and Means. The resolutions to which the Act of 1913 gave statutory force were not printed on the order paper of the house, but were hand-written and read out at the end of the day. Notice was minimal, they were widely drafted, and they could be passed at night so that the opposition might only find out about them in the morning. That made criticism of them largely impossible. Subsequent discussion could become merely theoretical with no constitutional force, for it was unlikely that if a tax resolution were passed and became statutory for a certain period, it would be effectively discussed at the end of the period. Potentially the reform allowed for all manner of amendments in taxation to be imposed on the people without the house having the chance to consider them at the report stage. As one member observed, when the unfortunate taxpayer found out about a new or increased tax from his morning newspaper, the revenue authorities would already be empowered to collect it.[122] Taxpayers would not even have the opportunity to lobby their members

---

[120] *Parl. Deb.*, vol. 127, ser. 3, col. 1380, 10 June 1853 (HC) *per* Sir John Pakington.
[121] *Ibid.*, vol. 24, ser. 4, col. 1233, 24 May 1894 (HC) *per* Arthur Balfour.
[122] *Parl. Deb.*, vol. 51, ser. 5, col. 1049, 8 April 1913 (HC) *per* William Fisher.

of Parliament, those 'old constitutional methods of protest',[123] and press for alterations in the proposals. The very meaning of and reason for the resolution, its introduction only by the government, and the processes it had to go through were designed to ensure 'you could not put a tax round the neck of the taxpayer before legislation was passed justifying that particular taxation'.[124] It was widely argued that this instrument of taxpayer protection, deliberately developed to protect a taxpayer against the hasty imposition of a tax, had turned on itself. It now enabled the Treasury to impose taxes more expeditiously and with minimal discussion and debate in the Commons, precluding a thorough investigation of the proposed tax measure and negating true parliamentary consent and disabling the Commons from fulfilling its duty to the taxpaying public.

The power of the executive in the House of Commons

The outcome of the Parliament Act and the Provisional Collection of Taxes Act was to isolate the House of Commons as the only constitutional safeguard lying between the taxpayer and the executive. If then the power of the executive were to increase within the House of Commons, the fundamental safeguard of parliamentary consent would be further eroded. The relationship between the ministers of the crown and the Commons was a subtle one, and there was a clear mutual dependency, but governments with large majorities were able to dominate. The growth of the party system in the latter part of the nineteenth century increased the influence of the government of the day in the Commons and gave ministers greater control over the members of their party in Parliament and thereby over all legislation, including tax measures. The party system dominated from the 1870s, when it was usual to have two parties each of substantial size and acting uniformly in pursuit of their own ideology and policies. One formed the government, the other an increasingly official opposition, with its own leader.[125] The practice of consolidating tax measures in one bill in 1861 overtly increased the power of the government for if the government had a majority in the House of Commons, however slender, a tax measure could be pushed through with minimal discussion, and with the danger that the demands of party loyalty would outweigh a disinterested concern for the safeguarding of taxpayers'

[123] *Ibid.*, col. 1698, 14 April 1913 (HC) *per* Sir Frederick Banbury.
[124] *Ibid.*, col. 872, 7 April 1913 (HC) *per* Sir Alfred Cripps.
[125] M. Sheldon Amos, *Fifty Years of the English Constitution* (London: Longmans, Green and Co. 1880), pp. 340–3, 67–73.

rights. It rendered the Commons less able to deal with taxation in a practical and independent way.

When after the Parliament Act 1911 the only control over tax matters in Parliament lay with the House of Commons, many felt what control they had should be strenuously guarded and not be eroded. Accordingly the Provisional Collection of Taxes Act giving budget resolutions temporary statutory force was widely seen as exacerbating this dominance of the executive, allowing the form, content and ultimately the success of tax measures to be subject to the almost total control of government ministers. The Act and the custom from which it sprang permitting new taxes to be imposed with the Commons hardly noticing, let alone the public, gave the executive excessive and dangerous power. It was generally thought that the Commons had in effect ceded effective control over taxation to the government.[126] An unscrupulous government could propose income tax at a high rate, or a new tax altogether, on a single resolution, with little notice, and early in the year, to be voted on along party lines in the heat of the moment, and would have the force of an Act of Parliament with no discussion until the finance bill later in the year. As a member observed, '[w]e see day by day the rights of the House diminished, while the authority of the Government is becoming more and more accentuated'.[127] This dominance of the executive was condemned as a 'monstrous injustice'.[128] Another saw it as 'another long step towards making the Government of the day independent of Parliamentary control';[129] and yet another said it resulted in the Committee of Ways and Means becoming 'a mere automatic machine for registering and legalising schemes of Treasury officials'.[130] The increasing subservience of the Commons to the executive and its apparent docility before the government were issues of real concern to taxpayers and left them seriously weakened. 'We are not here merely to legislate,' said a member in 1913, 'but to control the Executive by holding the purse strings'.[131] Its effect was to give considerable power to a 'tyrannical oligarchy to tax the subjects of His Majesty without those subjects having that right of safeguarding themselves which they have had certainly for upwards of two centuries'.[132]

[126] *Parl. Deb.*, vol. 51, ser. 5, col. 1036, 8 April 1913 (HC) *per* Sir Alfred Cripps.
[127] *Ibid.*, col. 862, 7 April 1913 (HC) *per* William Fisher. See Ian Ferrier, 'Ship-Money Reconsidered', *BTR* (1984), 227 at 235–6.
[128] *Parl. Deb.*, vol. 51, ser. 5, col. 915, 7 April 1913 (HC) *per* William Joynson-Hicks.
[129] *Ibid.*, col. 880 *per* Lord Hugh Cecil.
[130] *Ibid.*, vol. 51, ser. 5, col. 2162, 17 April 1913 (HC) *per* Ellis Hume-Williams.
[131] *Ibid.*, vol. 51, ser. 5, col. 935, 7 April 1913 (HC) *per* William Joynson-Hicks.
[132] *Ibid.*, vol. 52, ser. 5, col. 67, 21 April 1913 (HC) *per* William Fisher.

The quality of parliamentary scrutiny

The growing impotence of the House of Commons in relation to tax measures resulting from the dominance of the executive was exacerbated by the increasing inability of ordinary members of Parliament effectively to scrutinise and challenge the government's tax measures. This was not just a question of available time but of the quality of their scrutiny. In the eighteenth century Blackstone had described members of Parliament as the guardians of the constitution, 'delegated to watch, to check, and to avert every dangerous innovation',[133] and indeed for much of the nineteenth century tax measures were generally debated at least at considerable length. General themes of fiscal policy were naturally widely discussed, notably the desirability of the taxation of land with its effect on personal wealth and on agriculture, whether graduation was fair, the importance of differentiation between earned and unearned income and the balance between direct and indirect taxation. The succession duty occupied the attention of the House of Commons for some months in 1853, and was actively debated and minutely examined on a number of occasions. The repeal of the paper duty was debated at great length in 1860, and the estate duty was subject to thirty days of discussion in the Commons and Lords, covering nearly 1,900 columns of Hansard.[134]

Nevertheless Blackstone had questioned the quality of the member 'who is a stranger to the text upon which he comments'.[135] The growing complexity of the tax legislation increasingly challenged the effectiveness of the members' scrutiny. This was not the result of any government action, but a natural and inevitable consequence of industrialisation. Tax legislation in the nineteenth century reflected the growing sophistication of its commercial context, and became increasingly complex and technical. So complicated did it become that any permitted parliamentary discussion was itself undermined through the inability of many members of Parliament to master sufficiently the detail of tax legislation so as to debate it effectively. This problem had been growing throughout the century. It was the technical aspects of tax which caused problems to the members of the house. For the most part they were understood in only

---

[133] Sir William Blackstone, *Commentaries on the Laws of England*, 1783 edition printed for W. Strahan and T. Cadell, London and D. Prince, Oxford, 4 vols. (New York: Garland Publishing Inc., 1978), vol. i, p. 9.

[134] Nevertheless Gibson Bowles did not think the issues had been sufficiently discussed in view of the importance of, and complications and queries in, the bill: *Parl. Deb.*, vol. 27, ser. 4, col. 189, 17 July 1894 (HC).

[135] Blackstone, *Commentaries*, vol. i, p. 9.

the most general terms, and they found themselves no match for the government ministers, notably the Chancellor of the Exchequer, who were both knowledgeable in matters of finance and fully briefed by an expert executive. In debating the legislation which imposed the income tax on Ireland for the first time in 1853,[136] one member remarked: 'It was not too much to ask that they should be enabled to understand it. Now he defied any Irish Member to know what he was voting for when he assented to this clause. For himself, he declared solemnly that he did not understand a single word of what he was going to vote for.'[137] In relation to the introduction of estate duty in 1894 there were repeated protests by the members of the house that the provisions of the bill were so technical that only lawyers could understand them and participate in the debate. As one member observed, 'the term "volunteer" was Greek to those who had not studied the question',[138] and Balfour remarked in relation to a particular clause that '[o]ne could hardly read it aloud unless one was unusually articulate and sober ... and [i]f the sub-section were difficult enough to pronounce and understand, it was three times more difficult to understand after it was explained by the Government than it was before'.[139] Indeed one member said that the discussions had been so technical that he had not felt sufficiently competent to participate.[140] Furthermore, not only were the measures themselves often not fully understood, the existing law to be reformed and the practical outcome of the reform were not apparent or accessible. In most cases members could only rely on 'some vague and partial impressions' gleaned from personal experience as lawyers or magistrates or, at best, the oral representations of the proposer of the bill. Without extensive research, which few members had the time or ability to undertake, the impact of a new law on the existing law could not be predicated.[141] As a result of such difficulties, tax measures, especially minor technical ones, had a tendency to be passed too easily. In the 1920s Lord Decies, the director of the Income Taxpayers' Society, complained that they were passed 'practically without discussion'.[142] Major tax measures, on the other hand, sometimes excited the attention of expert members

---

[136] See generally Sir John Sinclair, *The History of the Public Revenue of the British Empire*, The Adam Smith Library, Reprints of Economic Classics, 3rd edition, 1803, 3 vols. (New York: Augustus M. Kelley, 1966), vol. 3, pp. 151–209.

[137] *Parl. Deb.*, vol. 127, ser. 3, col. 733, 27 May 1853 (HC) *per* John Maguire.

[138] *Parl. Deb.*, vol. 25, ser. 4, col. 500, 6 June 1894 (HC) *per* John Lawson.

[139] *Ibid.*, col. 510.   [140] *Ibid.*, col. 521 *per* Sir Donald Macfarlane.

[141] First Report of Mr H. Bellenden Ker on the Proceedings of the Board for the Revision of the Statute Law, *HCPP* (1854) (301) xxiv 153 at p. 223, Appendix 1 *per* George Coode.

[142] *The Times*, 25 May 1927, p. 12 col. d.

on both sides of the house. Despite the problems encountered by some members, and the admittedly complicated nature of the bill, estate duty was subject to a detailed, informed and effective parliamentary debate. In committee, clauses that were too wide, or ambiguous, or frankly incomprehensible, were arrested and addressed, and opposition members were vigilant as to the effect of the words of the legislation. Gibson Bowles was an exceptional and excellent critic in this respect. Having been employed in the legacy duty office of the Inland Revenue, he was knowledgeable as to the law and practice of tax. He clearly mastered the technicalities of the measures before him, and debated knowledgeably and strongly. In the estate duty debate he was thoroughly prepared, understood the issues in their principle and their detail, and was a powerful debater and formidable opponent to Sir William Harcourt.[143] He argued that the new estate duty was imposed on false principles, that it would increase the complexity of the death duties rather than simplify them, that it was administratively unworkable and that it would make dealing with land more difficult.[144] In his parliamentary performance he constituted a real safeguard for the taxpayer.

Conclusion

At the end of the Victorian period the legality of taxation still lay in its foundation in the consent of the taxpayer through representation in Parliament. Traditionally this had always been supported by a number of practical procedural safeguards ensuring comprehensive and free debate in the House of Commons, with full debate in an upper chamber possessing a real power of rejection to be exercised cautiously in general but unhesitatingly in an extreme case. Throughout the nineteenth century, and notably in the first years of the next, the protection given to a taxpayer through these procedures, protection constructed over hundreds of years and at considerable sacrifice, was greatly reduced. This undermining was a consequence of the statutory reforms to the parliamentary process but also of wider economic and social changes consequent on rapid and intensive industrialisation. The public, full and free discussion which had been established as the essential basis of the parliamentary safeguard against autocratic taxation was denied in the second chamber, and could be curtailed in the first. A tax could be passed by a bare majority of one or two,

---

[143] See *Parl. Deb.*, vol. 24, ser. 4, cols. 830–9, 10 May 1894 (HC).
[144] *Ibid.*, col. 831 *per* Thomas Gibson Bowles.

and under the growing influence of party whips and, through them, an increasingly powerful executive. Furthermore, no longer could the House of Lords reject a money bill in its entirety if it felt it was in the public interest to do so, and the Committee of Ways and Means, dominated by an expert and powerful executive, could impose a tax by mere resolution alone, albeit for a limited period. It was not a question merely of procedure, but of real and important substance.

In undermining the parliamentary safeguard of formal consent in this way, legislators were motivated by pragmatic and political considerations. A balance had to be struck between safeguarding the rights of the taxpayer, ensuring the government's financial proposals were passed, and ensuring the Treasury could collect due taxes effectively. The traditional consent of two houses of Parliament, with its integral stages of scrutiny, was perceived as being too restrictive and hindering the raising of the public revenue and the implementation of fiscal policies in the new industrial age. The statutory reforms and the developments in the constitutional relationships between Parliament and the government of the day favoured the interests of the public revenue at the expense of possible harm to the individual taxpayer. Consent to taxation was now solely through representation in the House of Commons on the basis that the house was elective, responsible to the people, familiar with their wishes in matters of taxation and ultimately answerable to them at election.[145] This was a sustainable theory but a nugatory practice which made the levying of taxation in Britain significantly easier than in other countries, notably the USA,[146] and left English taxpayers in a weaker and more vulnerable position than their American or French brethren.

---

[145] This was admitted by the Prime Minister in the debate on the Parliament Bill: *ibid.*, vol. 24, ser. 5, col. 711, 18 April 1911 (HC).

[146] See James Coffield, *A Popular History of Taxation* (Harlow: Longman, 1970), pp. 223–4; Lillian Doris (ed.), *The American Way in Taxation: Internal Revenue, 1862–1963* (Englewood Cliffs, NJ: Prentice-Hall Inc., 1963), p. 5.

3

The administrative safeguard of localism

Introduction

When Sir Robert Peel's second administration was formed in 1841, the established system of tax administration for all the direct taxes was one of localism. Local commissioners made the assessments on the basis of information gathered by their own assessors and collected the tax through their own collectors.[1] It was regarded as of great importance that they be assessed and collected by commissioners who were the representatives of the taxpayers, persons unconnected with and totally independent of central government and so free from its control or influence, and who were furthermore of sufficient personal wealth as not to be open to temptation. Their status held the balance evenly between the state and the taxpayer ensuring, in theory, that the former received and the latter paid no more and no less than each was bound to do by law. Quite apart from the protection which taxpayers derived from the localism inherent in the administrative system, the power they were given to appeal to independent adjudicating commissioners if they were aggrieved by a decision within the assessment process constituted a distinct safeguard. Politicians and civil servants knew that some form of appeal was necessary[2] and it was almost invariably the sole overt formal safeguard against arbitrary fiscal action expressed in the legislation. All parties involved in tax law and practice saw it as the most important and prominent of all the legal safeguards. The right of appeal for aggrieved taxpayers was regarded as a fundamental right of the individual. It also afforded the taxpayer further

---

[1] For the administration of income tax throughout the Victorian period, see *A Guide to the Property Act 46 Geo III* (London: Joyce Gold, 1806), pp. 99–110; Minutes of Evidence before the Select Committee on the Income and Property Tax, *HCPP* (1852) (354) ix 1, qq. 12–177, 1354–69, 2840–2977; CIR Sixth Report, *HCPP* (1862) (3047) xxvii 327 at pp. 349–51; CIR Twenty-eighth Report, *HCPP* (1884–5) (4474) xxii 43 at pp. 118–27.

[2] See, for example, Minutes of Evidence before the Select Committee on Inland Revenue and Customs Establishments, *HCPP* (1862) (370) xii 131, q. 408 *per* Charles Pressly, chairman of the Board of Inland Revenue.

protection of a negative character, because placing the administration of taxes in a specially created local body inevitably meant it was not in the hands of the regular courts and, most significantly, that appellate dispute resolution could avoid them. This constituted a safeguard to the taxpayer in that process in the regular courts was to be avoided if at all possible throughout the eighteenth and most of the nineteenth century. Although the regular courts of law were familiar and authoritative organs of high status, with well established and tested procedures, judges who were learned and independent, as well as being skilled in handling evidence and applying the law, they were neither attractive nor suitable to a taxpayer wishing to appeal against an assessment. There were a number of reasons for this: the judges were felt not to be as sound judges of matters of fact as laymen who understood local values and conditions; litigation was expensive and time-consuming, with technical and complex procedures requiring legal representation; and the courts themselves were dominated by an increasingly rigorous doctrine of judicial precedent and so lacked flexibility. Therefore localism was a fully developed and sophisticated system at the beginning of the Victorian age, and was still valued as the principal formal safeguard for the taxpayer. It continued to apply to the assessed taxes and the land tax and Peel adopted the system when he reintroduced the income tax in 1842. He and his successors maintained the system for the same ideological, political and pragmatic reasons that had moved legislators in the past.

In the Victorian period localism was consistent with prevailing ideologies. Reflecting the wider tradition of amateur participation in local government and the administration of justice, it was the practice of governance and public opinion to have the administration of tax undertaken by a local lay body. The veneration of traditional institutions and the profound importance attached to private property interests all strengthened this principle of local tax administration. It was a system which was peculiarly English, and whose character is revealed when compared with France's highly centralised structures and America's composite system of local and central administration. The French became interested in the English system when, in the nineteenth century, they found their own system of local government somewhat oppressive. Some were mystified by it,[3] others were envious,[4] but all concluded that the fundamental

---

[3] Paul Leroy-Beaulieu, *L'Administration Locale en France et en Angleterre* (Paris: Guillaumin et Cie, 1873), pp. 55–9.
[4] Theodore Zeldin, 'English Ideals in French Politics during the Nineteenth Century', *Historical Journal* 2 (1959), 40.

difference in outlook between the two countries made the English ideal of self-government impossible in France, in the context of taxation or anything else.[5] Whereas in England self-government was engrained in every aspect of life, in society, politics and law, in France the dominant philosophy was one of centralisation.[6] Furthermore, English self-government depended entirely on the Justice of the Peace, a local, unelected and independent landowner who undertook the office through feelings of social and public obligation and was untrammelled by a clear hierarchy of counties, boroughs and parishes. The French system was very different. The local resident landowning aristocracy did not exist,[7] and neither did the concept of unpaid amateurs carrying out a public service.[8] The English system which depended on a man's birth and wealth did not sit comfortably, or indeed at all, with the ideals of the French revolution. So while the Victorian commitment to local autonomy could not resist the imposition of national taxation, which was by its nature the prime and oldest example of central government intervention, it did find expression in the localist system of tax administration.

Peel also found, as had Pitt over forty years before, that localism was such a powerful idea that it was politically necessary to adopt it in order to make taxes acceptable and thereby ensure compliance. Though he made a conscious and considered decision to retain the system on its merits, he was well aware that the machinery of the tax was often 'as vital to the taxpayer as the substantive principles of taxation themselves'.[9] He appreciated the political value of traditional forms and processes, and articulated the principle when adopting it for his income tax in 1842. Even Gladstone, who was critical of the system, considered it politically impossible to abolish it.[10] The political reasoning behind the adoption of the principle of localism in England was not lost on an American commentator looking

---

[5] Michel Chevalier, 'La Constitution de l'Angleterre', *Revue des Deux Mondes* 72 (1867), 529 at 534.

[6] Duc d'Ayen, 'De La Constitution Anglaise et des Conditions du Gouvernement Représentatif', *Revue des Deux Mondes* 39 (1862), 563 at 567.

[7] C. Dupont-White, 'L'Administration Locale en France et en Angleterre', *Revue des Deux Mondes*, 38 (1862), 289 at 323; Leroy-Beaulieu, *L'Administration Locale*, pp. 17–21. See too Hippolyte Taine, *Notes on England*, translated and with introduction by Edward Hyams, 1860–70 (London: Thames and Hudson, 1957), pp. 140–1, 162–3; Duc d'Ayen, 'De La Constitution Anglaise' at 585.

[8] Dupont-White, 'L'Administration Locale en France' at 300.

[9] Minutes of Evidence taken before the Royal Commission on the Income Tax, *HCPP* (1919) (288) xxiii, q. 23,889 *per* Randle Holme, on behalf of the Law Society.

[10] See generally H. C. G. Matthew, *Gladstone* (Oxford: Clarendon Press, 1997), pp. 121–3; B. E. V. Sabine, 'Great Budgets: Gladstone's Budget of 1853', *BTR* (1971), 294.

into the practical workings of the English income tax system on behalf of the Massachusetts Commission on Taxation. He observed perceptively that 'the institution of local commissioners was intended to render the tax less obnoxious to taxpayers by protecting them against the possible rapacity of the Government and furnishing a guarantee that the assessment would not be conducted in an inconsiderate or unduly rigorous manner'.[11] The adoption of the traditional local system of tax administration was thus a political and fiscal necessity because it ensured public co-operation with the payment of tax, and hence determined its success or failure as a fiscal instrument. That localism was highly valued politically is clear from the generosity of appeal provision made in relation to the Irish income tax of 1853, to compensate for the absence of the protection of a localist system. Peel was also undoubtedly aware that not only could acceptable machinery go far to ensure public acquiescence to a tax, it also, when established, contributed significantly to its endurance as it possessed a momentum of its own which drove a tax on. This was partially because of an appreciation that once dismantled, it would be no easy task to re-establish it. So where a system of tax administration existed, or was introduced, the tax it serviced in practice would probably continue. This was recognised in Parliament in 1842 in relation to income tax, and indeed the fears expressed that in practice it would become permanent[12] proved to be well founded.

Local tax administration was also a practical necessity for Peel. That taxes failed for want of adequate administrative machinery was well known. In America one of the principal problems with the introduction of federal income taxes was the lack of machinery to administer them, the difficulty of creating a new infrastructure, and the need to have the machinery working for many years in order for problems to be revealed and addressed, and improvements made. Again, the reason why Ireland did not have to shoulder the burden of income tax until 1853, though it was contemplated before then,[13] was the lack of existing machinery to implement it.[14] It thus made practical sense to superimpose any new tax on the administrative machinery already in existence. It was also a strong response to the concerns about the cost of government which were increasingly expressed throughout the nineteenth century.

---

[11] Joseph A. Hill, *Economic Studies* 4 (1899), 278.
[12] *Parl. Deb.*, vol. 61, ser. 3, col. 1004, 21 March 1842 (HC) *per* Sir George Grey. See too Lord Beaumont at *ibid.*, vol. 64, cols. 304–5, 21 June 1842 (HL).
[13] Report from the Select Committee on Taxation of Ireland, *HCPP* (1864) (513) xv 1, 515, qq. 3804–5 *per* Joseph Napier.
[14] *Parl. Deb.*, vol. 61, ser. 3, col. 445, 11 March 1842 (HC) *per* Sir Robert Peel.

For his income tax, therefore, Peel adopted almost in its entirety the localist machinery created by Pitt in 1799 and refined by Addington in 1803,[15] which in turn was based on the administration of the assessed taxes.[16] The assessments and statements would be collected by the assessors and examined by the commissioners. If they suspected any undercharging they would examine the taxpayer, make general enquiries or require further information, and when they were satisfied they would then make or amend the assessments as appropriate and formally 'allow' them. Appeals would follow. The protective features inherent in localism, and forming its essential raison d'être, remained the same: the commissioners' independence and their local knowledge. The property requirements ensuring their financial independence were unchanged in principle, though now only Additional Commissioners had to be resident in the district.[17] As to functional independence, the Act of 1842 formally confirmed the General Commissioners as ultimately responsible for the assessment of income tax,[18] and their decisions on appeal as final, constituting a forcible expression of the principle of localism.[19] Though the legislation provided that the Board of Inland Revenue had the care and management of the duties,[20] and the surveyor was retained, localism still dominated the process. The interference of central government, though active, was limited to a 'general superintendence'.[21] The American commentator in 1899 noted this independence of the tax commissioners in England, and how they were neither responsible to any higher authority nor owing their offices to their fellow taxpayers, not being elected by them. It struck him forcibly that despite their being themselves property owners and taxpayers in the district for which they were appointed, they did not favour the taxpayer as against the state, and defended the rights of both.[22]

The role of the executive

By statute, the executive had the care and management of the excise, customs, stamps and taxes. Where the taxes were locally administered, the revenue boards were to co-ordinate the various bodies involved in the

---

[15] 39 Geo. III c. 13 (1799); 43 Geo. III c. 122 (1803). See too 46 Geo. III c. 65 (1806); 43 Geo. III c. 99 (1803); B. E. V. Sabine, 'Great Budgets III: Sir Robert Peel's Budget of 1842', *BTR* (1971), 50 at 54–5.

[16] 20 Geo. II c. 3 (1747); 18 Geo. III c. 26 (1778).

[17] 5 & 6 Vict. c. 35 ss. 4, 5, 6, 14, 16 (1842).   [18] *Ibid.*, s. 22.

[19] For appeals to the regular courts of law, see below, pp. 131–9.

[20] See above, p. 49.   [21] *Parl. Deb.*, vol. 61, ser. 3, col. 910, 18 March 1842 (HC).

[22] Hill, *Economic Studies*, 278.

administration and ensure the machinery was consistently applied and the local officials kept fully informed of new legislation and regulations. Its role was essentially one of policy-making, supervision and organisation while the work on the ground, the practical implementation of the legislative regime, was undertaken by the independent local lay commissioners. This central supervision and local administration was a compromise between the government's desire for control and uniformity, and the traditional local demand for self-government. Central to the rationale of localism, therefore, was the presence of the other interested party, the powerful organ of central government with overall responsibility for the public revenue, ensuring that the taxes were efficiently and uniformly levied. The relationship between the taxpayer and the taxing authority of central government was not in legal theory a confrontational one as the fundamental legal principle of taxation was that of consent. This legal principle was reflected in the practical administration of tax, not only through the principle of localism, but equally through an acceptance that any system of tax administration was reliant for its success on the co-operation of the taxpayer. It was accordingly in the interests of central government to maintain, and to be seen to be maintaining, the legal rights of the taxpayer as well as its own right to secure the public revenue. Underlying this pragmatic understanding of the essential consensual nature of taxation was the theory of good government whereby responsible government departments protected the rights of the citizens of the country.

In practice, however, the function of the central government board to exercise executive control over the local implementation of the taxing Acts despite the theoretical and functional independence of the local commissioners and their staff caused considerable tensions which grew throughout the nineteenth century. The central government wanted the tax laws implemented uniformly throughout the country, so that the taxpayers of Wick and Weymouth were treated alike.[23] The strong, focused control that central government sought to achieve was equally the antithesis of the localist system, which embodied independent, and therefore variable, action. The board thus had to organise its central revenue service around a theoretically unmoveable core of local administration, a challenge which introduced a constant tension in its daily operations and its formulation of policy. This tension led the executive into far greater an interference with local administration than the theory of localism

---

[23] Sir Alexander Johnston, *The Inland Revenue* (London: George Allen & Unwin, 1965), p. 43. See too Circular Letter from Tax Office directing Surveyors to make General Survey of Houses and Windows; Treasury Minute, December 1823, *HCPP* (1824) (46) xvii 419.

permitted. It threatened both the protection which was inherent in the principle of localism and that which was integral to good government. In their adherence to localism in tax administration, English governments and taxpayers were engaged in a conflict that came to a head in, and endured throughout, the nineteenth century.

The stamp duties, customs[24] and excise were old and thriving imposts administered entirely by specialist organs of central government. The excise branch of the Inland Revenue was administered by a large salaried staff of officers, appointed by the Treasury and under the board's direct control from 1849.[25] The localism of the direct taxes had no place here. The work of the excise officers demanded far more close contact with the taxpayers than that of the taxes officers, for while in income tax and the assessed taxes there was initial self-assessment, since the taxpayers made their returns which were then checked by the government officers, the excise depended entirely on government officers for its assessment and collection. Excise officers had to make surveys, namely visit traders throughout their district and at frequent intervals to inspect, check or measure beer, spirits, wines, malt and sugar in order to ensure quality and calculate the duty payable.[26] This gauging work was supported by the considerable paperwork which it was also their task to undertake. They had to inspect accounts to ensure duty had been paid on the registration of births or the hire of posthorses for example, that various dealers had purchased their required licences, and were constantly alert to detect any evasion or fraud.[27] Localism was similarly excluded in the administration of the stamp duties, for the board had complete control.[28] The stamp duty was the simplest of all the imposts, since the taxpayers would go to their local stamp office to purchase the stamp they needed on their document, or the stamped paper, or to have a document impressed with a stamp. The

---

[24] For the administration of the customs, see First Report of the Commissioners of Customs, *HCPP* (1857) (2186) iii 301 at pp. 310–22; John W. Hills and E. A. Fellowes, *The Finance of Government*, 2nd edition (London: Philip Allan, 1932), pp. 63–5. See too 16 & 17 Vict. c. 107 (1853) and 39 & 40 Vict c. 36 (1876).

[25] See generally John Torrance, 'Social Class and Bureaucratic Innovation: The Commissioners for Examining the Public Accounts 1780–1787', *Past and Present* (1978), 56 at 62–5.

[26] Minutes of Evidence before the Select Committee on Inland Revenue and Customs Establishments, *HCPP* (1862) (370) xii 131, q. 3271 *per* William Carling, Principal Surveying General Examiner.

[27] For an enjoyable and informative historical description of the daily work of excisemen, see John Pink, *The Excise Officers and their Duties in an English Market Town* (Surbiton: JRP, 1995).

[28] 5 & 6 Will. & M. c. 21 s. 7 (1694).

official distributors simply ensured they provided the stamps the public requested and collected the duties as stamps sold.[29] The far more intricate assessment to the legacy and succession duties[30] and the estate duty was also fully centralised.[31]

The executive and localism

The stamp duties, customs and excise provided a model of centralised tax administration, which showed the executive what it could achieve if it were to acquire total control of all the taxes. The executive saw an efficient, organised, uniform and productive administrative system which involved no element of the localism of the direct taxes.[32] The success of the centralised machinery highlighted the perceived inadequacy of localism and increased latent tensions in this respect between central government and the local commissioners. This was particularly so after 1849, when with the exception of the customs, all the duties were administered under the supervision of the single Board of Inland Revenue.

It has been seen that ideologically, politically and practically localism was essential to central government, but it was also, in some respects, useful. In the 1860s the board maintained that it did not 'at all' wish to dispense with the local commissioners' services,[33] praising them[34] particularly in their appellate capacity. It said it could not 'speak too highly' of the accessible, independent and high-quality adjudication provided by local commissioners.[35] The board also appreciated the protection which localism afforded its own officers in drawing the general and inevitable antipathy to direct taxation onto the commissioners.[36] As a result, the board was careful not to appear to, to encroach on the proper sphere of

---

[29] See CIR Thirteenth Report, *HCPP* (1870) (82, 82–1) xx 193, 377 at pp. 277–8.

[30] Minutes of Evidence before the Select Committee on Inland Revenue and Customs Establishments, *HCPP* (1862) (370) xii 131, qq. 2158–94, 2300–17 *per* Charles Trevor, Comptroller of Legacy and Succession Duties.

[31] *Ibid.*, qq. 3498–3501 *per* R. E. Howard, stamp distributor.

[32] See Henry Parris, *Constitutional Bureaucracy* (London: George Allen & Unwin Ltd, 1969), pp. 22, 32.

[33] Minutes of Evidence before the Select Committee on Income and Property Tax, *HCPP* (1861) (503, 503–1) xvii 1, 339, q. 186 *per* Charles Pressly.

[34] Minutes of Evidence before the Select Committee on Inland Revenue and Customs Establishments, *HCPP* (1862) (370) xii 131, q. 541 *per* Charles Pressly.

[35] In that instance, the Assessed Taxes Commissioners: CIR Sixth Report, *HCPP* (1862) (3047) xxxvii 327 at pp. 346–7. See too *HCPP* (1871) (462) xxxvii 235 at p. 236.

[36] See Minutes of Evidence taken before the Royal Commission on the Income Tax, *HCPP* (1919) (288) xxiii, qq. 553–4.

the local commissioners, and overtly maintained and stressed the distance between the commissioners' responsibility and their own limited powers. Most complaints to the board against alleged over-assessments were met with the response that the taxpayer must appeal to the local commissioners. If a taxpayer had failed to do so, and was now too late, he, or occasionally she, would be told that the board could not interfere.[37] The board also constantly reminded taxpayers that the commissioners' decision was final. Similarly, in replying to a clerk's query as to whether a certain type of security was acceptable from a collector, he was told that it was quite within the discretion of the commissioners whether they accepted it or not. Applications for relief from arrears of income tax were often dismissed when the board 'could see no ground for their interference'. And finally the board refused to supply a commissioners' clerk with a copy of the Property Tax Act and the Guide on the grounds of inconvenience and, it seems, breach of the board's observance of the independence of the local commissioners and their officials.

The attitude of central government to the traditional total division of function inherent in the localist system was, however, fundamentally one of hostility. The surveyor for the City of London, giving evidence before a Select Committee in 1861, was unequivocally opposed to the system and expressed the view of most of the government service when he said he wanted local officials replaced by government commissioners.[38] The board believed a system of local administration by part-time amateur laymen was flawed, careless and inefficient, and increasingly so in an age of growing commercial complexity and sophistication. It maintained the due taxes were not being properly levied and collected, leading to a shortfall in the public revenue and an unequal and unfair sharing of the fiscal burden among taxpayers. It felt the law was not being administered uniformly, as the system both permitted and encouraged local variations. Its experience of the dog licence proved the board correct, as the number of dogs licensed rose by half a million when it took over responsibility for the tax.[39] Gladstone described it as 'an old and somewhat crude system'[40]

---

[37] Minutes of Board of Inland Revenue, 1, 2, 9, 12, 15, 16, 24, 25 January 1849: TNA: PRO: IR 31/141.

[38] Minutes of Evidence before the Select Committee on Income and Property Tax, *HCPP* (1861) (503, 503–1) xvii 1, 339, qq. 2151, 2154, 2160, 2161 *per* Edward Welsh, surveyor for the City of London. See too the leader in *The Times*, 'Income-Tax Administration', 12 September 1928, p. 13 col. c.

[39] See CIR Eleventh Report, *HCPP* (1867) (3927) xxi 503 at pp. 515–16; CIR Twelfth Report, *HCPP* (1869) (4049) xviii 607 at p. 617.

[40] *Parl. Deb.*, vol. 127, ser. 3, col. 813, 30 May 1853 (HC).

in 1853; the board called it 'a vicious organization'[41] in 1861 and an 'antiquated, cumbrous, and inefficient system'[42] in 1869, a view confirmed by the Royal Commission of 1920 which concluded that it had outlived its usefulness.[43] Throughout the nineteenth century the board maintained consistent, trenchant and outspoken attacks on the system of local tax administration and repeatedly demanded that it be replaced.[44] Its reasons were the limited abilities of the local commissioners and the lack of control the board had over them.

The local commissioners

When the income tax was reintroduced in 1842, the localist system was generally accepted as the most appropriate for a temporary tax where local knowledge was the acknowledged basis of assessment. The orthodox view was that this regional and primarily commercial knowledge was necessary to accurate assessment, and provision was made to ensure that the assessing bodies possessed it. The commissioners, as local propertyowners, would be familiar with individual traders, their methods of business and their profits, and everyday mercantile conditions and problems of local commercial life. It has been seen that in the eighteenth century, when commercial activities were mainly, and relatively, small in size, limited in scope and self-contained, such local knowledge was a genuine and valuable aid to correct assessment.[45] For this reason commissioners were usually local businessmen, often retired or active merchants or bankers.

Many commissioners undoubtedly met their statutory responsibilities fully, being proactive and taking care and trouble in examining the returns. Conscientious, and using their commercial expertise and their knowledge of local business conditions and individuals, they arrived at an accurate assessment for each taxpayer.[46] Such assessments of commercial income were the result of a genuine pooling of information from the surveyor, the assessor, the clerk and the Additional Commissioners, all under the authority of the latter, a feature which made them more

---

[41]   CIR Fifth Report, *HCPP* (1861) (2877) xxxi 109 at p. 127.
[42]   CIR Twelfth Report, *HCPP* (1869) (4049) xviii 607 at p. 635.
[43]   Report of the Royal Commission on Income Tax, *HCPP* (1920) (615) xviii 97 at para. 386.
[44]   See, for example, CIR Sixth Report, *HCPP* (1862) (3047) xxvii 327 at pp. 344–5, 351.
[45]   See above, pp. 27–8.
[46]   See evidence of the clerk to the General Commissioners of Income Tax for the City of London in Minutes of Evidence taken before the Select Committee on the Income and Property Tax, *HCPP* (1852) (354) ix 1, q. 2671.

acceptable to the taxpaying public. A striking example of a widespread conscientious and informed approach to the work of the local commissioners was their reaction to the judicial decision in the *Bradley Haverstoe* case which suggested the accepted practice in making assessments to the land tax was wrong.[47] A number of clerks and commissioners read the report of the case in the *Law Times* and contacted the board in some anxiety, seeking advice, instruction and guidance as to whether they should change their current practice in the light of the decision, and stating that to do so would cause considerable inconvenience and expense.[48] Some commissioners even obtained counsel's opinion. In this instance the board insisted that the ruling was 'extrajudicial' and ignored it, but the matter reveals the seriousness with which many local officials regarded their office.

The situation, however, was changing in the Victorian period. The pace, scale and complexity of business, and therefore of tax, were increasing rapidly. Commercial centres were growing in size and trade was becoming national or international in nature.[49] The making of assessments to income tax in particular was becoming more intricate and technical, and to arrive at an accurate assessment of an individual's profits of his trade was not an easy matter. The returns for commercial income tax required by the legislation were simple statements of the profits, unsupported by detailed accounts, and the Additional Commissioners were rarely able or willing to check them adequately. Other than the taxpayer's previous assessments,[50] which could be used by way of comparison,[51] the factual information which was the only just basis for an assessment was not in their own possession. With only a general idea of the likely assessment based on their local commercial knowledge, they did their best to arrive at a just assessment.[52] It was, however, no longer sufficient as it could not give them the intimate knowledge of individuals' trading profits which they needed. The danger was that they would arrive at their assessments on

---

[47] See above, p. 51.
[48] Letters relative to Judgment of Court of Queen's Bench in Case of *Queen* v. *Commissioners of Land Tax for Bradley Haverstoe*, HCPP (1851) (528) xxxi 329 at pp. 329–38.
[49] Minutes of Evidence taken before the Royal Commission on the Income Tax, *HCPP* (1919) (288) xxiii, q. 552.
[50] Minutes of Evidence taken before the Select Committee on the Income and Property Tax, *HCPP* (1852) (354) ix 1, qq. 1529–31, 2675–6.
[51] *Ibid.*, q. 3123.
[52] Where no return had been made, they were empowered to arrive at an assessment 'to the best of their judgment'. See too Assessors' Warrant and Instructions, DRO 337B add 2/ TAXATION/ Income Tax 7.

the basis of mere impression, relying on the style of an individual's life or business and outward appearances. Nevertheless the commissioners were still being drawn from the same class as the Justices of the Peace, propertied men of local status with experience of adjudication and willing to act without remuneration. As a body they were conservative and independent in outlook. Certainly within this group they varied considerably in calibre, competence and interest, but it was generally true that the sheer complexity and intricacy of the law and practice of income tax, as well as the huge growth in volume, made the actual assessing of income beyond their intellectual ability. It was mainly because they were simply not equipped with sufficient commercial or tax knowledge for the task.

The commissioners were also limited in the time they could devote to the process of assessment and their commitment to their office. They met sporadically, and being part-time appointments they were often still active in their own professions. Many were commissioners for more than one of the direct taxes, and were usually also magistrates or held other offices in their localities. They lacked any sophisticated office organisation of their own. If they attempted to examine each of the assessments, the sheer quantity meant they could devote no more than a minute or so to each,[53] so they could rarely look behind the assessment book to the return itself, let alone other more detailed information. It was said in 1873 that in many instances their numbers had dwindled through death or resignation, 'or they shirk the odium and responsibility of their task till the tax becomes a mere voluntary payment at the discretion of the taxpayer'.[54] Their work, it was suggested, was nothing other than a sham.[55] Furthermore, while in practice most commissioners lived in the district to which they were appointed, some did not, and routine business suffered through want of regular attendance. The clerk in Stafford, for example, complained in 1860 that he could not get any papers signed on non-meeting days, for of his eight commissioners three resided in Scotland or abroad, two at some distance from Leek and could rarely act, and the remaining three were aged over seventy and could not easily act.[56] Many commissioners were directors of public companies and their attendance at those meetings, a surveyor cynically observed in 1861, was remunerated, and their tax

[53] Minutes of Evidence taken before the Royal Commission on the Income Tax, *HCPP* (1919) (288) xxiii, qq. 21,664–76.
[54] *The Times*, 27 January 1873, p. 12 col. b.
[55] Minutes of Evidence taken before the Royal Commission on the Income Tax, *HCPP* (1919) (288) xxiii, qq. 23,971–5.
[56] TNA:PRO IR 40/1052.

duties inevitably suffered.[57] There were difficulties where commissioners had to be resident, because businessmen in industrial centres were abandoning the traditional practice of living at their place of business.

While the overall calibre of the commissioners was generally high, and their inefficiency was mainly due to circumstances outside their control rather than any inherent lack of education or probity, that was not the case with their subordinate officers appointed to carry out the practical task of assessment and collection. It was left to the commissioners themselves to ensure the ability and integrity of their subordinate officials, for the legislation required no formal qualifications, merely that they be 'able and sufficient', fit and responsible.[58] Though some were conscientious and able, often retired tradesmen, many assessors and collectors were not of the highest calibre, especially in the country districts. Their limited competence and lack of any sense of responsibility towards the exchequer was a constant source of complaint by the board who maintained that many were illiterate, incapable and even corrupt.[59] It quoted numerous examples, such as a local assessor, a butcher by trade, who had declined to charge a taxpayer on his horse and carriage because if he had done so he would have lost his custom.[60] It believed they were too lenient in the administration of taxes, and were capricious in those whom they favoured.[61] It was also not unusual for them to have more than one employment and assessors were commonly collectors too. As to the clerks, although a surveyor complained to *The Times* in 1873 that they were 'functionaries wholly useless' who often discharged their duties in a 'slipshod and irregular manner',[62] they were in practice solicitors[63] and most were responsible and able individuals. While the clerk continued to be the individual responsible for the administrative side of the commissioners' work, he had evolved from a purely ministerial creature into their

---

[57] Minutes of Evidence before the Select Committee on Income and Property Tax, *HCPP* (1861) (503, 503–1) xvii 1, 339, qq. 2150, 2155, 2159 *per* Edward Welsh.

[58] 38 Geo. III c. 5 s. 19 (1797) (land tax); 43 Geo. III c. 99 s. 9 (1803); 43 & 44 Vict. c. 19 s. 41 (1880) (assessed taxes, income tax).

[59] CIR Sixth Report, *HCPP* (1862) (3047) xxvii 327 at pp. 344–5; CIR Thirteenth Report, *HCPP* (1870) (82) xx 193 at p. 207.

[60] CIR Twelfth Report, *HCPP* (1869) (4049) xviii 607 at p. 635.

[61] CIR Sixth Report, *HCPP* (1862) (3047) xxvii 327 at p. 352.

[62] *The Times*, 27 January 1873, p. 12 col. b.

[63] Minutes of Evidence before the Select Committee on Inland Revenue and Customs Establishments, *HCPP* (1862) (370) xii 131, q. 184 *per* Charles Pressly. Legal qualifications were not required by law, though there were demands for reform in this respect: see Minutes of Evidence taken before the Royal Commission on the Income Tax, *HCPP* (1919) (288) xxiii, q. 23,892 *per* Randle Holme.

principal legal adviser and a key force in the working of the tribunal. The commissioners looked to him for substantive legal advice as to the rules of law applicable in individual cases, the correct procedures to be followed, and the drafting of the stated cases.[64] An efficient clerk was essential to the smooth operation of the localist system, and indeed when commissioners had a competent clerk the taxpayer benefited, for the clerk would often ensure on appeal that the taxpayer's view was put to the tribunal.[65] Furthermore, most clerks built up a wide experience through acting for more than one board of commissioners, notably those of the land tax, assessed taxes and income tax, while many held other public and private posts too.[66]

Control by the Board of Inland Revenue

In practice the relationship between the central and local administration was 'close and direct',[67] with clerks constantly writing to the board for advice and guidance on behalf of their commissioners and the board issuing instructions to the local officials explaining their duties. Such matters covered every aspect of all the taxes, for example the correct valuation of land subject to income tax, the status of interest paid to friendly societies, and the estimation of income with respect to tithes commuted into a rentcharge.[68] Many local commissioners carried on their work in harmony with the board and made full use of the support it offered. The board, however, had no formal control over the local commissioners or their clerks, assessors or collectors, other than with regard to receipts and the accountability of taxes. Neither the commissioners nor their clerks, assessors and collectors were answerable to the board. If they abused their position and absconded with the tax receipts or overcharged individual taxpayers, or even simply refused to co-operate with proposed reforms, the board was powerless. This was despite its statutory duty to supervise the administration of the revenue and that most of the local commissioners' subordinate officers were remunerated out of public funds. It could not dismiss incompetent or even dishonest assessors,

---

[64] C. Stebbings, 'The Clerk to the General Commissioners of Income Tax', *BTR* (1994), 61.

[65] Minutes of Evidence taken before the Royal Commission on the Income Tax, *HCPP* (1919) (288) xxiii, q. 23,872 *per* John Budd, on behalf of the Law Society.

[66] For example, one commissioners' clerk was also a coroner for Middlesex: Minutes of Evidence before the Select Committee on Inland Revenue and Customs Establishments, *HCPP* (1862) (370) xii 131, q. 2443 *per* Edward Welsh.

[67] B. E. V. Sabine, 'The General Commissioners', *BTR* (1968), 18 at 28.

[68] Minutes of Board of Inland Revenue, 2, 8, 11 January 1849: TNA: PRO: IR 31/141.

collectors or clerks, nor order them to co-operate with any government initiative. A famous example was the case of the clerk at Louth in
Lincolnshire, who refused to discharge his commissioners' assessment
on a railway company when requested to do so by the board, the company having been assessed at its head office in London. The clerk, the
board reported, 'observed no measure in his hostility and resistance to
[its] authority'[69] and he refused to co-operate for several years, despite a
ruling by the Attorney General. Again, when in 1860 the quarterly collection of income tax was introduced to replace the old half-yearly collec-
tions, the board knew the collectors could refuse to co-operate and that
legislation would be necessary.[70] Similarly, in relation to the administration of the land tax, the local commissioners ignored the board's requests
to make an annual assessment of the land according to its value, as the
legislation required, rather than merely permit the same assessment to
stand unchanged.[71] A lack of co-operation could be relatively minor, as
when clerks refused to use the official forms provided by the board and
printed their own.

Defalcations by subordinate local officials undoubtedly occurred.[72] In
1860 the board maintained they were common and a return of the number
of defalcations by parochial collectors of taxes shows a loss to the revenue
of nearly £20,000 over twenty years.[73] Among the clerks, assessors and
collectors whose remuneration was by poundage and so directly linked
to the quantum of the tax assessed, the dangers were all too clear. The
temptation to fraud was significant for such remuneration could be very
considerable. Clerks were entitled to 2d in the £ in relation to income tax,
and the same rate applied to the assessed taxes. A single clerk in the 1860s
received some £6,000.[74] Some collectors too did very well indeed. The

[69] CIR Sixth Report, *HCPP* (1862) (3047) xxvii 327 at p. 353.
[70] CIR Fifth Report, *HCPP* (1861) (2877) xxxi 109 at pp. 126–8.
[71] CIR Fifteenth Report, *HCPP* (1872) (646) xviii 259 at pp. 299–300; CIR Sixteenth Report,
    HCPP (1873) (844) xxi 651 at p. 682; CIR Seventeenth Report, *HCPP* (1874) (1098) xv 673
    at pp. 697–8.
[72] It has been cogently argued that these frauds were symptomatic of the growing tension
    between the state and civil society: see Robert Colley, 'The Shoreditch tax frauds: a study
    of the relationship between the state and civil society in 1860', *Historical Research* 78
    (2005), 540.
[73] See Return of the number of defalcations by parochial collectors of taxes from 1847–67,
    HCPP (1867) (546) 757. For an example of a defaulting collector in Manchester, see Sabine,
    'General Commissioners', 18.
[74] The surveyor of the clerk's division maintained he had received £7,194 6s, while the clerk
    said he had received only £5,757 7s 8d: Minutes of Evidence before the Select Committee
    on Inland Revenue and Customs Establishments, *HCPP* (1863) (424) vi 303, q. 812.

collector for the ward of Broad Street was one of the most highly remunerated, receiving £922 in poundage in 1861.[75] Defalcations ranged from
the unlawful selling of income tax returns as waste paper from the clerk's
office,[76] to the orchestrated forging of signatures on a certificate for the
redemption of land tax.[77] Many frauds were possible because of the common practice of appointing the same person as assessor and collector.[78]

The board considered that its negligible degree of control over local officials rendered them unreliable[79] and constituted a serious handicap to the
efficient administration of taxes. It constantly expressed its concern and
exasperation in this respect. It believed that it was the lack of central control which permitted defalcations in subordinate officers and incompetent
administration by the commissioners. As one surveyor observed, if he sent
for any of these local officials, 'they come or not, as they please, and I am
quite at their mercy as to the information they afford'.[80] The board thought
it was 'a great misfortune', 'a very anomalous state of things',[81] and that the
surveyors could not form an adequate check so as to prevent frauds by the
assessors and collectors. Indeed, it felt it was 'an almost incredible absurdity' that officials appointed to assist in collecting the public revenue should,
through their method of appointment, be able to disrupt the very task they
were appointed to undertake.[82] The board had a duty to the public revenue,
and to have to act through the agency of independent officials who could
resist its orders and undermine the intentions of Parliament was 'highly
objectionable'.[83] In a hand-written memorandum of 1906 relating to amal-
gamating collection with local authorities and making the surveyor the
assessor, it was stated that 'The state cannot take into its service persons it
does not appoint; and the clerks are not in the same boat as the assessors.
The Clerks are never whole-timers and always agitate as trustees of public
in interest of local authorities (their patronage)'.[84]

[75] Minutes of Evidence before the Select Committee on Inland Revenue and Customs
Establishments, *HCPP* (1862) (370) xii 131, q. 2441 *per* Edward Welsh.
[76] *Ibid.*, qq. 2414–21.   [77] Colley, 'Shoreditch Tax Frauds', 540.
[78] *Ibid.* See too Stephen Matthews, 'A Chester Scandal of 1854: A Study in Administrative
Failure', *BTR* (2000), 154.
[79] CIR Sixth Report, *HCPP* (1862) (3047) xxvii 327 at p. 345.
[80] Minutes of Evidence before the Select Committee on Income and Property Tax, *HCPP*
(1861) (503, 503–1) xvii 1, 339, q. 2161 *per* Edward Welsh.
[81] Minutes of Evidence before the Select Committee on Inland Revenue and Customs
Establishments, *HCPP* (1862) (370) xii 131, qq. 1508, 1514 *per* Thomas Dobson, Principal
Secretary, Board of Inland Revenue.
[82] CIR Sixth Report, *HCPP* (1862) (3047) xxvii 327 at p. 354.
[83] CIR Fifth Report, *HCPP* (1861) (2877) xxxi 109 at p. 127.
[84] TNA: PRO IR 74/20 (1906).

The board was not entirely powerless in relation to local officials, but, as it observed in relation to the clerk at Louth, the remedies were cumbersome, slow and unreliable.[85] It had, however, other means at its disposal. In one instance a clerk was found to have allowed the duplicates of the first assessments to income tax to be made out by the collectors and the supplementary assessments to be made out by the surveyor, instead of doing it himself as the legislation required, and had permitted the collectors to be remunerated out of the surplus land tax raised beyond the statutory quota. The board expressed its 'discontent' at his conduct, strongly reprehending these 'great irregularities' and was determined to make an example of him. Despite the clerk's exemplary conduct for many years in all other respects and his adherence to a long-established practice, as well as an assurance that he had 'no corrupt motive' and that the practice would cease immediately, the board withheld his poundage for nearly three years, impervious to the clerk's despairing requests.[86] This reveals that despite its limited statutory authority over the local commissioners' officials, and their theoretical independence, in practice the board could exercise a degree of effective and, in this case somewhat harsh, control.

It was consistent with, and a consequence of, the principle of localism, that the taxpayers should take responsibility for the defaults of the officials their representatives had appointed. The protection afforded by the law to the taxpayer against defalcations was for the commissioners to demand security from the collector on his appointment, but this was by no means a universal practice. Some lost tax might then be recovered from the collector's sureties or the sale of his effects, but in many cases it was not and in consequence the taxpayers of the parish would have to pay the tax twice over. They would feel a defalcation keenly. They could apply for relief from the Treasury on the grounds of the hardship a re-assessment would entail, and in practice some settlement was often arrived at, but this was entirely discretionary.

The tensions which arose between the board and local commissioners were predictably considerable. It was said in 1906 that from as early as 1842 the government 'fretted and strained at the gentle check and restraint imposed by the wisdom of those who devised' the localist system.[87] By the

---

[85] CIR Sixth Report, *HCPP* (1862) (3047) xxvii 327 at p. 354. See Minutes of Board of Inland Revenue, 2 January 1849: TNA: PRO: IR 31/141 where the board ordered the discharge of a double assessment.

[86] Correspondence respecting Frauds in Collection of Taxes and Conduct of Inspectors of Taxes in Kensington Division, *HCPP* (1823) (371) xiv 495.

[87] TNA: PRO IR 74/20 (1906).

last quarter of the nineteenth century, efficient assessment by competent local commissioners and their staff had become the exception rather than the rule. This, along with the realisation that income tax was taking on a far from temporary character through regular renewals, led the board increasingly to doubt the suitability of the local system for its long-term administration.[88] As a result, it made numerous attempts throughout the nineteenth century to assume the duties of the local administrative bodies and to take complete control of the assessment and collection of the direct taxes. Their attempts were both formal and informal.

The assault on localism

Formal incursions

The revenue boards had always had statutory authority to appoint a staff to undertake the practical administrative work, and that staff embodied the power and control of the executive. In 1851 the total staff of the Board of Inland Revenue amounted to some 5,000, mainly excise officers, rising to over 6,000 in 1884.[89] From the early days of the reintroduced income tax the board took the view that the tax would be far more accurately and efficiently assessed and collected if local assessors and collectors could be replaced with these crown-appointed officers.[90] Indeed the first formal incursion of the revenue boards had been through the introduction of the central government surveyor to ensure the hearth, window and inhabited house duties were efficiently administered and surveyors were given extensive powers to examine and amend assessed taxes returns in 1810. The assessment of all the direct taxes by its own officers would, the board argued, be efficient for three reasons.

First, unlike local officials, they were full-time appointments. It was clear that officers who devoted their whole time to their duties would be more efficient than those who combined them with other employment.

Secondly, they were experts in the law and practice of taxation, being generally highly trained officers. The board required an 'intimate and

---

[88] Minutes of Evidence before the Select Committee on Inland Revenue and Customs Establishments, *HCPP* (1862) (370) xii 131, q. 472 *per* Charles Pressly.

[89] See Wyn Griffith, *A Hundred Years, The Board of Inland Revenue 1849–1949* (London: Inland Revenue, 1949), pp. 26–7.

[90] Minutes of Evidence before the Select Committee on Inland Revenue and Customs Establishments, *HCPP* (1862) (370) xii 131, q. 199 *per* Charles Pressly; Martin Daunton, *Trusting Leviathan: the Politics of Taxation in Britain, 1799–1914* (Cambridge University Press, 2001), pp. 194–7.

accurate knowledge' of tax in its officers in all the branches[91] and all had to undergo extensive training. Customs officers had to pass tests of competence from 1700,[92] and entry to the central department of the excise was by examination long before it was adopted for the whole service.[93] Indeed it was the revenue boards which led the civil service in appointing its staff through competitive examination, and this ensured that tax officers were among the most highly skilled and competent members of the service. Excise officers needed special training to acquire a thorough understanding of the manufacturing processes under their control, and they enjoyed a clear career structure based on a demanding combination of formal examination and practical experience.[94] Senior excisemen acquired a profound knowledge of the working of every branch of the excise, and were in close touch with the board with regard to the organisation of the staff, the problems raised by the practical administration of the law and the concerns of the trading community. In the taxes, the examinations and training to become a surveyor were demanding and wide-ranging.[95] Not only did he have to master the law and practice of taxation, but also the principles of accountancy and commercial practice, as well as management skills and qualities of diplomacy, negotiation and, to some extent, advocacy. The task of the surveyor became more burdensome as the nineteenth century progressed. It increased in complexity, technicality and volume, and in practice went far beyond the statutory duty to supervise. The board and its staff had to deal with a fourfold growth in the number of taxpayers. As the rates of income tax increased, so businessmen took the tax into account to a greater degree than before, and that demanded new skills of the board's staff. With their training and the extensive support of the board, the surveyors met the challenge where local commissioners

---

[91] CIR Fourth Report, *HCPP* (1860) (2735) xxiii 235 at p. 258.

[92] Sir John Craig, *A History of Red Tape* (London: Macdonald & Evans Ltd, 1955), p. 96. For the training of customs officers, see First Report of the Commissioners of Customs, *HCPP* (1857) (2186) iii 301 at Appendix D, pp. 394–9.

[93] CIR First Report, *HCPP* (1857) (2199) iv 65 at p. 116. For the qualifications and training of excise officers, see generally John Owens, *Plain Papers relating to the Excise Branch of the Inland Revenue Department* (Linlithgow, 1879), pp. 110–20; G. E. Aylmer, 'From Office-Holding to Civil Service: The Genesis of Modern Bureaucracy', *Transactions of the Royal Historical Society*, 30 (1980), 91.

[94] For the duties of the various officers of the excise see Minutes of Evidence before the Select Committee on Inland Revenue and Customs Establishments, *HCPP* (1862) (370) xii 131, qq. 1564–1616; Graham Smith, *Something to Declare* (London: Harrap, 1980), pp. 85, 116–22.

[95] For the recruitment and training of surveyors, see David Williams, 'Masters of All they Surveyed: 1900–1914' *BTR* (2005), 142 at 144–7.

did not. They were, even in this new climate, powerful, organised and well trained, and possessed in addition as much local knowledge as the assessor,[96] and their quality was generally both praised and appreciated. They were described as 'most efficient officers',[97] tactful and conciliatory in their dealings with taxpayers,[98] discharging their duties with intelligence, discretion and 'perfect fairness'.[99] In this they constituted a valuable protection to the taxpayer, in that he was equipped to detect incorrect assessments by the commissioners and other breaches the latter might make through their own lack of knowledge.

Thirdly, the Board of Inland Revenue, like the Board of Excise before it, could ensure that all its officers implemented the taxes in question uniformly and according to its wishes, for they were subject to the board's instructions as to how to administer the tax and its close control.[100] The overarching duty of any central tax official in the field, whatever duty he was responsible for, was to protect the interests of the crown in the administration of the revenue, just as the local commissioners for the direct taxes protected the interests of the taxpayer. His allegiance was entirely to the board and not to his district, and his duty was to ensure that all taxpayers who were liable to pay a tax did so, did so promptly, and the tax collected. The disciplinary structure within which he worked allowed him none of the latitude adopted by some local officials, a latitude which, if he adopted it, would 'bring down a storm of indignation' upon the board.[101] It was this control the board enjoyed over its own officers which would ensure the efficient administration of the public revenue.

The control of the board over its officers was close, direct and often personal. It covered many aspects of their working and personal lives, including their marital status,[102] residence,[103] place of work, their conduct both in and out of working hours and, above all, the carrying out of their

---

[96] TNA: PRO IR 74/20 (1906).

[97] CIR Third Report, *HCPP* (1859) (2535) xiv 451 at p. 480.

[98] Minutes of Evidence taken before the Royal Commission on the Income Tax, *HCPP* (1919) (288) xxiii, q. 23,871 *per* John Budd.

[99] Minutes of Evidence before the Select Committee on Inland Revenue and Customs Establishments, *HCPP* (1862) (370) xii 131, qq. 4608–9 *per* Lord Belhaven, Vice-Lieutenant and Convener of the Commissioners of Supply for the County of Lanark.

[100] See, for example, Pink, *Excise Officers*, pp. 23, 25; David Williams, 'Surveying Taxes', *BTR* (2005), 222.

[101] CIR Sixth Report, *HCPP* (1862) (3047) xxvii 327 at p. 352.

[102] For the anti-marriage ordinance for excise officers, see Owens, *Plain Papers*, pp. 51–2.

[103] The board in 1849 noted the 'inexpediency' of allowing a surveyor to live far from his office: Minutes of Board of Inland Revenue, 8 January 1849: TNA: PRO: IR 31/141.

professional duties. The orders, regulations and circulars instructing tax officers how to administer the taxes in their charge were voluminous, constant and detailed. Officers were told what to do and how to do it, and if they fell short of the board's expected standards the board would and could take action.

The board first introduced various strategies to ensure the good conduct of its officers. All the boards took care in their choice of individual appointees, required them to take oaths swearing to take only their official remuneration and to pay over their receipts to the proper authority, subject to a penalty. Surveyors were generally salaried, but they were occasionally remunerated by poundage and where an official's remuneration was directly linked to the quantum of the tax he assessed in this way, the dangers to the impartiality and independence of tax assessment were all too clear and well known.[104] Despite this, poundage was not abolished until 1891.[105] Furthermore, the board took steps to ensure that officers should not become too entrenched in local life and thereby lay themselves open to political, social or commercial influence. Excise officers were transferred to another district every few years under the established yet notorious system of 'removes'.[106] Again in the excise the legislature imposed clear divisions of function between assessment and collection and tried to ensure no close personal connections were formed between assessors and collectors. In the case of income tax, however, the delineation was clear only in theory, since in practice the lay assessors were also appointed collectors. The board was vigilant in ensuring its officers maintained the high standards of the service, and in 1856 periodical inspections were introduced for surveyors of taxes, since they had been subject to less supervision than their colleagues in the excise. These inspections, the board reported in 1858, had been successful since there had been a decline in the number of cases of misconduct reported to it,[107] though for most of the nineteenth century inspectors remained very few in number.

Despite these various precautions, misconduct by government officials did occur, and there were regular complaints about individual surveyors,

---

[104] Minutes of Evidence before the Select Committee on Inland Revenue and Customs Establishments, *HCPP* (1862) (370) xii 131, qq. 4614–16; 4619 *per* Lord Belhaven.

[105] 54 & 55 Vict. c. 13.

[106] Twentieth Report of the Commissioners of Inquiry (Excise Establishment), *HCPP* 1836 (22) xxvi 179, at p. 529, Appendix 73 *per* Charles Browne, Under-Secretary. See too Williams, 'Masters', 149–51; Owens, *Plain Papers*, pp. 410–15.

[107] CIR Second Report, *HCPP* (1857–8) (2387) xxv 477 at p. 510.

ranging from a 'want of courtesy'[108] to 'vexatious conduct'[109] and out-right fraud. Complaints about surveyors' surcharges were commonplace, and in some instances were well founded. The boards took all complaints very seriously indeed[110] and laid down detailed procedures to investigate even the most minor misdemeanour.[111] Orders admonishing officers for undesirable behaviour were commonplace, while slackness and inefficiency were reprimanded with a demand for 'more attention and punctuality in the discharge of [the] duties'.[112] In 1849 the taxpayers of Lichfield complained of the conduct of the surveyor, which was investigated by the board and resulted in his removal to another district and his demotion to a lower class.[113] There were statutory controls where the misconduct was serious, as where a surveyor made a false or vexatious charge, was guilty of any fraudulent, corrupt or illegal practice, or failed to charge someone to tax who should have been charged. In such instances he was liable to a penalty of £100 and the discharge from his office after a full internal inquiry.[114] In 1849 the surveyor at Welshpool had, because of his long-standing 'pressing embarrassments', engaged in various pecuniary transactions which the board drew short of calling fraudulent, but which threw the tax affairs of his district into disarray.[115] He had been imprisoned for debt, and the board concluded that he was not a fit person to continue in office, and dismissed him. The forging of the signature on a land tax redemption certificate by a local official in Shoreditch was part of a long-standing fraud which involved not only the clerk, assessors and collectors, but also the surveyor himself.[116] The board naturally wished to ensure beyond doubt that an officer was guilty of misconduct before dismissing him, but the detailed procedures in place to ensure that this could be done contributed to the protection of the taxpayer against dishonest crown officials. Where the officer's misconduct amounted to a criminal offence, the punishment could be severe. One excise officer caught stealing the revenue was punished in 1834 by transportation, and his punishment was read out to excise officers all over the country every year for ten years by order of the Commissioners of Excise in an attempt to act as a deterrent to others who might have been tempted to follow his example.[117]

[108] Minutes of Board of Inland Revenue, 20 January 1849: TNA: PRO: IR 31/141.
[109] *Ibid.*, 14 February 1849.   [110] Owens, *Plain Papers*, pp. 123–4, 151.
[111] Minutes of Board of Inland Revenue, 20 January 1849: TNA: PRO: IR 31/141.
[112] *Ibid.*, 22 January 1849.   [113] *Ibid.*, 14 March 1849.
[114] CIR Second Report, *HCPP* (1857–8) (2387) xxv 477 at p. 511.
[115] Minutes of Board of Inland Revenue, 31 January 1849: TNA: PRO: IR 31/141.
[116] Colley, 'The Shoreditch Tax Frauds'. See too Matthews, 'A Chester Scandal'.
[117] Pink, *Excise Officers*, p. 38.

For some offences, the ultimate penalty was exacted. When in 1831 a clerk in the Stamp Office was found guilty of using spoilt stamps for fraudulent purposes, it was a capital offence.[118]

One infamous and fully documented incident concerned a fraud by George White, the surveyor of the Kensington Division, with respect to the collection of the land and assessed taxes in 1823. In 1818, fifty-six inhabitants of Chelsea complained of his unlawful and vexatious exactions. He had charged taxpayers for more servants than they kept, more horses than they owned and more windows than their houses enjoyed. He had charged business carts as pleasure carriages and imposed excessive valuations on houses. In all these instances he had obliged the taxpayers to appeal, with the inconvenience and worry that entailed, and even then he often ignored the commissioners' rulings. Furthermore, his behaviour towards taxpayers and the commissioners was threatening, insulting and disrespectful. The surveyor denied the charges and alleged revenge on the part of the taxpayers for having imposed legitimate surcharges, and on the part of the commissioners for having revealed their procedural irregularities. After a full and lengthy inquiry, revealing not only that all the accusations were well founded but that the surveyor had fraudulently evaded his own full tax liability, the board dismissed him, conscious that the episode had brought all government officials into 'hatred and contempt' and '[excited] a disgust … many fold against the revenue'.[119]

By law, the surveyor was constrained in the role he could play. His duty was to supervise the administration of the taxes, to ensure that the local assessors and collectors of the direct taxes were properly appointed by the local commissioners, that they arrived at their assessments correctly in accordance with the policy of the board, and that they accounted for their receipts to the proper authorities. In view of this vague though undoubtedly limited statutory authority, and despite the term 'supervision' being loosely interpreted by the board, any transfer of assessing powers to the surveyor could only be achieved by express statutory provision. Accordingly the board began a sustained and unequivocal policy formally to undermine local tax administration in this way, a policy it promoted throughout the Victorian period and beyond. This would not of itself ensure that defalcations would never occur, for there were dishonest surveyors as much as there were dishonest lay tax officials, but it would ensure some degree of formal control and supervision, and of

---

[118]   R. v. *Smith* (1831) 5 Car & P 107.
[119]   Correspondence respecting Frauds in Collection of Taxes and Conduct of Inspectors of Taxes in Kensington Division, *HCPP* (1823) (371) xiv 495.

disciplinary proceedings and increased security for the taxpayer if it were to occur. It had the added advantage of saving money, since it was shown to be cheaper to administer the tax by government officers earning a salary than local officials remunerated by poundage.

Assessment by government officers was not unknown, and was particularly prevalent in Scotland, where the paucity of the poundage had made it impossible to find any local assessors to act. As early as 1805 an Act addressed these 'inconveniences', and the power of making assessments to the assessed taxes was given to the surveyor in all cases where the local commissioners had failed to appoint an assessor.[120] This proved both popular and efficient, and from that time onwards the assessed taxes in Scotland were assessed by the officers of central government.[121] The local commissioners' role was limited to hearing and determining any appeal against this assessment. In relation to the land tax and the income tax, however, the system of local administration was adopted and retained though not, in the case of income tax, consistently. In 1862 in some nineteen districts in Scotland the local commissioners voluntarily appointed the surveyors to make the assessments to income tax[122] because of a difficulty in finding local assessors to serve, the Scots not feeling the same degree of attachment to the principle of localism.[123] On the basis of this experience it was thought it would give 'no discontent whatever to the taxpayers' for the entirely centralised system of assessment to the assessed taxes to be adopted for the income tax. Local assessors were 'an obstruction',[124] and taxpayers greatly preferred dealing with a trained and expert official, even a government one, who understood their private tax affairs rather than with a local officer who was largely untrained and might even be a rival in trade. Indeed it seems that the Scots were far less sensitive about the issue of disclosure to either local officials or surveyors than the English. What they wanted above all was competent and accurate assessment. Appeals against income tax assessments were few, and most were settled out of court by the surveyor and the appellant. But even when the case went to appeal, it was felt that the public had confidence in the commissioners and were 'perfectly protected' by the system.[125]

---

[120] 45 Geo. III c. 95 s. 1 (1805).
[121] Minutes of Evidence before the Select Committee on Inland Revenue and Customs Establishments, *HCPP* (1862) (370) xii 131, qq. 3001–9, 3090–1 *per* Angus Fletcher, Comptroller General and Solicitor for the Inland Revenue in Scotland.
[122] *Ibid.*, q. 3072.   [123] *Ibid.*, q. 1640 *per* Thomas Dobson.
[124] *Ibid.*, q. 3071 *per* Angus Fletcher.
[125] *Ibid.*, q. 4625 *per* Lord Belhaven. See too *ibid.*, qq. 4627, 4629.

The system worked 'most harmoniously'.[126] In Ireland too the board had control over the assessment to tax, and even more comprehensively than in Scotland. When the income tax was extended to Ireland in 1853, as there was no machinery of assessed taxes an entirely new system had to be constructed. In accordance with the preference of the board, the surveyors were made the assessors.[127]

The board in London looked to Scotland as the prime example of what could be achieved were local administration to be replaced. In 1860 it issued a circular to all the local commissioners in England to ascertain their views on the giving of greater assessing and collecting powers to the surveyor.[128] The board proposed bringing collection entirely within its control, though leaving untouched the appellate functions of the local commissioners. The commissioners who responded were unanimous in rejecting in the strongest terms any interference with their powers of assessment,[129] and clearly there was to be no assistance from that quarter in altering the English system of tax administration. The strength of feeling overall was such that the proposal was dropped. The statutory provision for centralised assessment continued, but did so slowly and piecemeal: the abolition of the assessed taxes in 1869 by their conversion into excise licences effected a change of administration from local commissioners to the board[130] and legislation of 1873[131] and 1874[132] provided that surveyors were to assess Schedule A and B income tax and the inhabited house duty. When in 1915 it was suggested that certain weekly wage earners should be assessed by the surveyor, the proposal was viewed with considerable concern as denying the protection of an impartial and independent local body standing between them and the crown to particularly vulnerable taxpayers who were generally unable to obtain or afford expert technical advice.[133] Nevertheless it was accepted, but only because it was essential in order to make a large number of new assessments immediately,[134] and

---

[126] *Ibid.*, q. 3160 *per* Angus Fletcher.
[127] *Ibid.*, q. 2465 *per* Edward Welsh. The surveyors made the assessments under all the schedules of charge: 16 & 17 Vict. c. 34 ss. 16, 20.
[128] *HCPP* (1871) (462) xxxvii 235.
[129] Though there was some support for the central appointment of collectors: Minutes of Evidence before the Select Committee on Inland Revenue and Customs Establishments, *HCPP* (1862) (370) xii 131, q. 286 *per* Charles Pressly.
[130] CIR Fifteenth Report, *HCPP* (1872) (646) xviii 259 at p. 286.
[131] 36 & 37 Vict. c. 8 s. 2 (1873).   [132] 37 & 38 Vict. c. 16 (1874).
[133] *Parl. Deb.*, vol. 76, ser. 5, cols. 1098–1129, 6 December 1915 (HC). See too *The Times*, 25 October 1915, p. 9 col. e; *ibid.*, 30 October 1915, p. 9 col. f.
[134] The board had felt confident of success since it had already, albeit provisionally, advertised for extra staff: see *The Times*, 26 October 1915, p. 10 col. b.

because it was the outcome of an agreement with the representatives of the local commissioners,[135] and taxpayers would continue to be protected through their right of appeal to the General Commissioners.[136]

Just as inaccurate assessment led the board to place the assessing function in its surveyors whenever it could, so the loss to the public revenue through the defalcations of local officials, and the inability of the board to prevent them, led it to take every opportunity to centralise collection. It began by taking to itself the power to select the lay collectors. When in 1854 the rate of income tax was doubled as a result of the war with Russia and temptation to fraud grew, the question of collectors' security became more pressing. An Act of 1854 provided that if local collectors did not give security for the due payment of the money collected, the board could appoint a collector itself.[137] It was intended to address the consequences of defalcations, namely the problem of the security not being consistently required of the local collectors, but it attacked local collection by making it attractive to allow the board to appoint the collector: it provided that the parish would be absolved from all responsibility in case of a defalcation.[138] An Act of 1879 permitted local collectors of income tax, inhabited house duty and the land tax to refuse appointment, and provided that if no appointment were made, the power to appoint a local collector should vest in the board.[139] The success of this inroad into pure localism led the board to seek to put collection into the hands not merely of lay collectors of its own appointing, but of its own official collectors. In 1881 it experimented with formal centralised collection in England and selected Hull and Hereford for the collection of Schedule D and E income tax.[140] So successful was this experiment that the board extended it to Blackburn and Bradford, and reported that it worked 'admirably'.[141] By 1886 it was in force in most of the major towns in England.[142] The board could not

---

[135]   *Parl. Deb.*, vol. 76, ser. 5, col. 1110, 6 December 1915 (HC) *per* Reginald McKenna.
[136]   Although this was thought to be unrealistic in relation to 'the simple working man who is being taxed for the first time': *ibid.*, col. 1118 *per* George Barnes.
[137]   17 & 18 Vict. c. 85 s. 2.
[138]   *Ibid.*, s. 5. The board reported that in its first year of operation, it was asked to select and appoint collectors for 900 parishes, a number which revealed the extent of the grievance felt by the public: CIR Twenty-third Report, (1881) (2770) xxxix 89 at p. 135. Indeed by 1862 there had been no losses from defalcations in those districts enjoying a centrally appointed collector: Minutes of Evidence before the Select Committee on Inland Revenue and Customs Establishments, *HCPP* (1862) (370) xii 131, q. 2463 *per* Edward Welsh.
[139]   42 & 43 Vict. c. 21, s. 23 (1879).
[140]   CIR Twenty-fourth Report, (1881) (2967) xxix 181 at pp. 243–5.
[141]   CIR Twenty-fifth Report, (1882) (3325) xxi 275 at p. 344.
[142]   CIR Twenty-ninth Report, (1886) (4816) xx 279 at pp. 324–5.

resist observing that its success proved their long-held view that taxpayers preferred paying their income tax to government officials. The movement was unrelenting and to some degree successful. Although attempts to introduce central collectors failed in 1883[143] and 1887 due to popular resistance, an Act of 1890 provided the board was to appoint any collector not required to be appointed by another authority[144] and the assessment of weekly wage earners by the surveyor in 1915 also authorised the collection of the tax by the board.

The informal erosion of localism

The appointment by the board of its own officers as assessors and collectors was a formal and overt incursion into local tax administration achieved through express legislation. It was also, because of the principle's entrenched legal and political position, piecemeal and relatively minor in its overall effect. Of far more potency and effectiveness in this respect was the informal and insidious undermining achieved through naturally occurring changes in practice arising from the growing sophistication and momentum of the central revenue boards. The development of tax law and practice, and its inevitable increase in complexity and technicality reflecting a rapidly expanding commercial life, was the principal instrument for the erosion of localism in tax administration. It found expression in the increasing dominance of the surveyor.[145] The part-time, amateur, unpaid lay commissioners who were motivated by their commitment to civic duty and entirely dependent on their sometimes imperfect and anecdotal local knowledge, struggled to maintain their position and influence in the face of the professional tax officer of central government.

As an expert in tax administration, a master of both the law and practice, and able to devote his entire time to his duties, the surveyor of taxes outstripped virtually any lay commissioner in terms of knowledge and understanding. He also had the ability to acquire far more extensive and accurate information about individual taxpayers in his district. He was already an integral and powerful part of the administrative process and was involved in some way at nearly every stage, checking the assessments to satisfy himself they were correct and examining all claims for

---

[143] *Parl. Deb.*, vol. 279, ser. 3, cols. 488–506, 10 May 1883 (HC). See too Sabine, 'General Commissioners' at 30–1.

[144] 53 & 54 Vict. c. 21 s. 4.

[145] See generally Robert Colley, 'The Arabian Bird: A Study of Income Tax Evasion in Mid-Victorian Britain', *BTR* (2001), 207; Sabine, 'General Commissioners'.

abatement and exemption.[146] His enquiries were conducted through correspondence, calls for accounts, interviews with taxpayers and meetings with the local assessor. He had a knowledge of earlier assessments, of the individual's style of living and of the state of his business, as well as the board's own table of trading and professional profits. The commissioners reviewed the assessments, with greater or lesser care, heard the surveyor's views on each and decided on the assessment. It was inevitable in the light of the surveyor's superior knowledge that the commissioners would listen to him, accept his advice and his figures and sign the assessment book with little or no real enquiry. The extent of the surveyor's influence in arriving at assessments of commercial income varied considerably throughout the country. Where the attention of the commissioners was 'meagre and haphazard',[147] he would be the only one with an accurate idea of what the assessment should be. For the same reason of expertise the surveyor began to dominate the appellate hearings of the lay commissioners, which he would attend to put the case for the crown, though to a lesser extent than the ministerial assessment stage prior to appeal. It was in appeal hearings that often intense tensions arose between the expert professional surveyor knowing the law and practice of tax, and the amateur local commissioners wanting, at best, to proceed along the lines of common sense in the context of a real local knowledge, at worst being uninterested and incompetent.

It is clear that the commissioners' assessing functions were being insidiously eroded in the course of the practical daily tax administration. A clear movement is discernible whereby tacitly the commissioners were allowing the surveyor to take control. As early as the 1850s in places, and more generally by the 1870s, the real responsibility, if not the theoretical one, for making the assessments lay with the surveyor. He guided the commissioners because he had the knowledge and expertise they lacked, and through this he emerged as the real power in the process. However necessary and however much his expert supervision afforded the individual taxpayer an added element of protection where the amateur localist system may have failed him, to allow the surveyor to become the key official in the administration of tax was, quite apart from its infringement of the principle of localism, an undermining of the passive supervisory role which he was given by the legislation. The concept of assessment by an independent

---

[146] For a detailed account of the work of the surveyor in relation to income tax in the years before the First World War, see Williams, 'Surveying Taxes' at 227–34.

[147] Report of the Royal Commission on the Income Tax, *HCPP* (1920) (615) xviii 97 at para. 352.

representative of the taxpaying public was rendered almost nugatory and so mere lip service was paid to the principle of localism. In 1853 Gladstone acknowledged that the assessment was in reality made by the surveyors and not the local commissioners,[148] and indeed, necessarily so.

Finally, it appeared that towards the end of the period the board adopted a longer-term policy of 'peaceful penetration'[149] and more covert attempts to gain jurisdiction, though this was the view of the public and was coloured by both journalistic licence and vested interests. The board was accused of denying improvements to those elements of the local system with which it had some influence, notably by refusing the reorganisation that assessors and collectors had long demanded, permanent appointments, fixed salaries and superannuation. As this would inevitably reduce the efficiency of the local system, the president of the national association of assessors and collectors was reported as having accused the board of adopting a 'policy of attrition' to strengthen its claim that the work of the assessors was of such 'minor quality and quantity that in the interests of efficiency and economy their office should be abolished'.[150]

Government alternatives to localism: the Special Commissioners of Income Tax

The formal and informal attempts to bring assessment and collection into the hands of the board were deliberate incursions into the principle of local tax administration. Other initiatives of central government, however, introduced with different objectives, potentially had the same effect. These were the introduction of its own alternatives to the administration of taxes, particularly the hearing of appeals, by the local institutions. Appeals to the central revenue boards had always been a natural feature of the centralised customs, excise and stamp duties, and this continued after the amalgamations of the early nineteenth century. The Board of Inland Revenue's minute books reveal that from its earliest days it was deluged with applications of various kinds concerning the centralised taxes, the assessed taxes and the income tax. Most applications were minor, comprising complaints, memorials, petitions, inquiries and appeals from individual taxpayers covering every aspect of tax law and administration relating to all the taxes in the board's charge. They ranged from formal legal appeals, to informal applications for relief, requests for the return of

[148] *Parl. Deb.*, vol. 127, ser. 3, col. 819, 30 May 1853 (HC).
[149] *The Times*, 29 June 1927, p. 17 col. b.
[150] *Ibid.*, 'Income-Tax Administration', 12 September 1928, p. 13 col. c.

overpayments of tax and complaints about decisions taken.[151] Similarly, as the revenue boards were theoretically subordinate to the Treasury, there was an equally established practice of aggrieved taxpayers appealing to the Treasury. The practice was seen in relation to the customs,[152] the excise,[153] the legacy and succession duties,[154] and in relation to locally administered taxes. The applications were of various kinds, such as requests for discretionary relief for a parish from the hardship of a reassessment.[155]

Adjudication by officers of the central government departments charged with the administration of taxes was familiar in other more specialist forms. It was integral to the administration of the excise in London, where minor breaches of the excise laws which were not thought by the central excise board to be sufficiently important to go before the Court of Exchequer were tried before a specialist bureaucratic court known as the Excise Court of Summary Jurisdiction.[156] Its jurisdiction consisted of proceedings for the recovery of penalties, for double duty as a means of securing the payment of the single duty, and for complaints.[157] Appeal lay to the Court of Excise Commissioners of Appeal.[158] While this specialist bureaucratic adjudication was perceived as natural in a centralised tax such as the excise, and was accepted by the public, it did not sit comfortably with the entrenched localism of the income tax. Furthermore, the excise courts were anomalous among bureaucratic tax tribunals in that they exercised a criminal jurisdiction, which raised considerable problems of independence. The Irish excise courts, described as 'courts formed by a meeting of Revenue officers, who act alternately as prosecutors, witnesses

---

[151] See, for example, the applications for the repayment of sums paid in error for armorial bearings, and overpayments in respect of a dog and a game certificate: Minutes of Board of Inland Revenue, 1 January 1849: TNA: PRO: IR 31/141. See too Minutes of Evidence before the Select Committee on Inland Revenue and Customs Establishments, *HCPP* (1862) (370) xii 131, qq. 1361–3 *per* Thomas Dobson.

[152] Chester, *English Administrative System*, p. 226.

[153] Twentieth Report of the Commissioners of Inquiry (Excise Establishment), *HCPP* (1836) (22) xxvi 179 at pp. 535, 597, Appendix 73.

[154] CIR Ninth Report, *HCPP* (1865) (3550) xxvii 105 at p. 122.

[155] Minutes of Evidence before the Select Committee on Inland Revenue and Customs Establishments, *HCPP* (1862) (370) xii 131, qq. 2425, 2427 *per* Edward Welsh.

[156] It was first established in 1660: 12 Car. II c. 24 s. 45. See 7 & 8 Geo. IV c. 53 s. 65 (1827); 4 & 5 Will. IV c. 51 (1834). In the rest of the country excise cases were tried by Justices of the Peace at Petty Sessions with appeals lying to Quarter Sessions.

[157] Some 148 parishes and 25,000 traders came within its authority in 1833. See Third Report of the Commissioners of Inquiry into the Excise Establishment: Summary Jurisdiction, *HCPP* (1834) (3) xxiv 87, p. 138, Appendix 7 *per* P. W. Mayow.

[158] 7 & 8 Geo. IV c. 53 ss. 81, 82 (1827). The appeal court was abolished by 4 & 5 Vict. c. 20 s. 25 (1841) and by s. 26 gave the power of appeal to a Baron of the Exchequer.

and judges',[159] were condemned as 'in theory and principle, indefensible'.[160] It was therefore of striking significance when Peel introduced a bureaucratic alternative to the General Commissioners of Income Tax.

The Special Commissioners of Income Tax had been created in 1805 with limited and purely administrative duties, primarily concerning charities' claims to tax exemptions,[161] and Peel transformed them into a tribunal for the assessment of commercial income.[162] Taxpayers were given the option of being assessed by the Special Commissioners on the basis of their returns and the surveyor's inquiries. However it was the extension of the Special Commissioners' appellate jurisdiction which was particularly significant to localism, because it ultimately came to dominate their work. A taxpayer who had been assessed to income tax on any commercial income could elect to appeal against the assessment to the Special Commissioners. Peel extended the Special Commissioners' jurisdiction in this way not in order to undermine the local apparatus, but to address a feature of that system which was deplored by the very great majority of taxpayers and which was threatening his ability effectively to tax the commercial wealth of the increasingly industrialised economy: publicity. Publicity was the price which the taxpayer had to pay for the safeguard of non-governmental tax administration, but for commercial taxpayers in particular it was too high a price. And Peel needed to ensure that every facility was given to the tax-paying public to make certain that all incomes were returned and fully and properly charged to the tax.

No taxpayers liked divulging personal financial affairs to local tax commissioners who were men they often knew, especially when they believed that it was practically impossible to avoid publicity.[163] When assessors and collectors were all local residents, with often annual

---

[159] Ninth Report of the Commissioners of Inquiry into the Collection and Management of the Revenue arising in Ireland and Scotland, *HCPP* (1824) (340) xi 305 at p. 310.

[160] *Ibid.*, p. 312 *per* John Foster. See too Third Report of the Commissioners of Inquiry into the Excise Establishment: Summary Jurisdiction, *HCPP* (1834) (3) xxiv 87 at p. 96. Despite repeated recommendations for its abolition, it was not until 1890 that the power of the excise commissioners in the Summary Court to hear and determine informations for penalties was abolished.

[161] 45 Geo. III c. 49 ss. 30, 37, 73–85. See A. Hope-Jones, *Income Tax in the Napoleonic Wars* (Cambridge University Press, 1939), pp. 23–8; A. Farnsworth, 'The Income Tax Commissioners', *Law Quarterly Review* 64 (1948), 372. For a comprehensive account of the functions of the Special Commissioners, see J. Avery Jones, 'The Special Commissioners from Trafalgar to Waterloo', *BTR* (2005), 40 and J. Avery Jones, 'The Special Commissioners after 1842: from Administrative to Judicial Tribunal', *BTR* (2005), 80.

[162] 5 & 6 Vict. c. 35 ss. 130, 131 (1842).

[163] *Parliamentary History*, vol. 34, col. 89, 14 December 1798 *per* Michael Taylor.

periods of office, it would not be long before most of the inhabitants of the parish would be familiar with the private financial affairs of a significant proportion of their neighbours.[164] Disclosure of such information was of particular importance to the business community. The local commissioners who were in receipt of the financial details of their fellow taxpayers' businesses would inevitably be placed in a situation of suspicion in relation to those taxpayers who were their competitors in trade. This was a recurrent source of national complaint, and was something which was acknowledged by the board as being undesirable.[165] It was partly a question of distaste, but also a genuine fear that the information could be used to their commercial disadvantage. There was no real evidence of any deliberate disclosure of confidential information, though enough of careless or inadvertent exposure to make taxpayers persistently suspicious.[166] There was little faith in the efficacy of the statutory procedures for ensuring the integrity of the local commissioners and the security of financial information, namely the property qualifications, the oaths of secrecy and the provisions for hearing appeals in private. The granting of assessment and adjudicatory powers to the Special Commissioners addressed these problems directly, for they constituted a central tribunal based in London composed of full-time paid and pensionable civil servants appointed by the Treasury. They were generally experienced tax officials or men with legal training or political expertise, and were entirely under the control of the board. In this they were utterly different in character from all other bodies of tax commissioners other than the excise court. They were entirely independent of any local interests, and were bound by the same rules of secrecy as all other officials involved in the administration of the income tax.

Although the Special Commissioners were not extensively used in their assessing function,[167] by the end of the nineteenth century it was widely accepted that the quality of their adjudication was significantly higher than that of the local commissioners, and any important, difficult

---

[164] *Cobbett's Political Register*, vols. ix–x, cols. 751, 754–5, Letter from 'A Northern Freeholder', 3 May 1806.

[165] Minutes of Evidence before the Select Committee on Inland Revenue and Customs Establishments, *HCPP* (1862) (370) xii 131, qq. 2396, 2411–12 *per* Edward Welsh.

[166] See, for example, *Parl. Deb.*, vol. 33, ser. 1, cols. 26–7, 30–1, 7 March 1816 (HC); *ibid.*, vol. 61, ser. 3, cols. 1272–3, 4 April 1842 (HC). See too the comments made in the context of a local rebellion against income tax in Devon, as reported in the *Exeter and Plymouth Gazette*, 13 January 1871 and 1 December 1871.

[167] Returns relating to the Special Commissioners, *HCPP* (1863) (528) xxxi 607.

or technical tax appeal would be far better resolved by them.[168] They were a highly respected tax tribunal among those taxpayers aware of their existence[169] and their use increased steadily throughout the nineteenth century. In one sense they did not undermine localism because they were merely an alternative tribunal to the local commissioners, not a mandatory one, and operated in the very limited sphere of commercial income. They could be viewed as constituting not so much a breach of the principle of localism but rather a support of the principle of privacy in income taxation by providing a choice to taxpayers reluctant to expose their commercial affairs to their neighbours. But they were unambiguously an arm of the executive and as much a creature of central government as the surveyor who appeared before them in appeal hearings, and as such they directly and fundamentally challenged the principle of localism. They provided, more insidiously, expert and efficient tax adjudication at the heart of an administrative system which was legally locally based, with the considerable financial and intellectual resources of central government behind them. They provided adjudication of a quality and authority the local commissioners could not begin to withstand.

The various instances of bureaucratic adjudication, namely the Special Commissioners of Income Tax, the Excise Court of Summary Jurisdiction, appeals to the central boards and to the Treasury, were yet further, and potent, examples of the growing authority of the executive in tax matters. Furthermore they brought with them clear conflicts of interest and the danger of bias.[170] This absence of independence was, in general, outweighed by the advantages of expert adjudication in the eyes of both executive and taxpayer, but they were legally anomalous and open to justified criticism in this respect.

Conclusion

From the beginning of Victoria's reign, central government had understood that the traditional system of local tax administration was no longer

---

[168] Minutes of Evidence before the Royal Commission on the Income Tax, *HCPP* (1919) (288) xxiii, q. 15,921 *per* A. M. Bremner, barrister, on behalf of the General Council of the Bar of England.

[169] See the evidence of G. O. Parsons, the secretary to the Income Tax Reform League, who said in 1919 that he felt the taxpayer received 'the best of treatment': *ibid.*, q. 1,853. This confidence proved to be enduring: see Report of the Committee on Ministers' Powers, *HCPP* (1931–2) (4060) xii 341 at pp. 432–3.

[170] See the concerns raised in Minutes of Evidence before the Royal Commission on the Income Tax, *HCPP* (1919) (288) xxiii, q. 23,898 *per* Randle Holme.

appropriate or effective, and that its inadequacies would only increase as the economy continued to grow in strength and sophistication. The fiscal and administrative demands of central government, themselves the result of a radically transformed economy, rendered local tax officials physically and intellectually unable or unwilling to undertake the task of tax administration. This was particularly evident in relation to the income tax of 1842, its inquisitorial and confrontational nature revealing more than ever before the inherent weaknesses of the localist system. The anachronistic safeguard of local tax administration hindered the government's efficient collection of the public revenue. Government found it irksome, and the forces of its hostility, coupled with its growing power and with a changing society in which national identity was coming to dominate local allegiances, made it difficult for localism to maintain its place in the new order. But while central government was impelled to undermine the traditional legal safeguard of localism, political and pragmatic forces rendered it incapable of undertaking the sweeping legislative reforms that were needed, and it had to resort to piecemeal or informal measures. The result was a century of continuous and increasing tension between taxpayer and taxing authority, between tax law and tax practice. Ultimately it was a battle won by central government and the clear yet delicate balance of localism and centralism that had been a central feature of the administration of all taxes and had been so highly valued by Pitt, Peel and, to some extent, Gladstone, was upset in the relentless tide of centralism. By the start of the Great War 36 per cent of the income tax was assessed by Inland Revenue officials and 64 per cent was collected by them,[171] and by the middle of the twentieth century the local tax officials had been entirely stripped of their assessing powers. Nevertheless localism robustly maintained a place as the taxpayers' 'natural safeguard',[172] albeit in the considerably diminished form of a purely appellate jurisdiction. As late as the 1920s the commissioners entrusted with the administration of income tax and their officials were variously described as trustees for their fellow taxpayers,[173] 'the bulwark and protection of the taxpayer against the executive',[174] and 'the sole guardians of the taxpayer's interests'.[175]

---

[171] The figures are those of the financial secretary to the Treasury, in the debate on the Finance (No. 3) Bill in 1915: *Parl. Deb.*, vol. 76, ser. 5, cols. 1123–4, 6 December 1915 (HC).

[172] Report of the Royal Commission on the Income Tax, *HCPP* (1920) (615) xviii 97 at para. 344.

[173] *The Times*, 20 April 1921, p. 11 col. f; TNA: PRO IR 74/20 (1906).

[174] *The Times*, 28 May 1923, p. 8 col. e.   [175] *Ibid.*, 1 July 1927, p. 12 col. c.

4

Judicial safeguards

Introduction

The law provided a threefold judicial safeguard for taxpayers against arbitrary taxation by the state: the strict interpretation of taxing Acts which generally worked to their advantage because it was inherently a limiting and restrictive construction of the legislation; a degree of appeal to the regular courts of law, though not a general right; and the theoretical existence of the judicial review of erroneous adjudicative determinations. These three protective elements of the law applied in principle to all the taxes, direct and indirect. It has been seen that in practice the role of the judges in constituting a safeguard was potentially of considerable value to the taxpayer, but was of limited application at the beginning of Victoria's reign. The nineteenth century was to see an inconsistent attitude to the role of the judiciary in tax matters, with considerable tensions between the public policy considerations of the government and legislature, and the judges' own views of their role in the English legal system.

The interpretation of tax statutes

The literal approach maintained

The principle of consent demanded that a tax be imposed with the agreement of Parliament, and that authority to tax was expressed through the wording of the tax legislation. Its scope had then necessarily to be established, and that task fell to the judges. It was for them to read the statute put before them to find its correct meaning and to ascertain whether it applied to the taxpayer's situation. In this way, though Parliament was pre-eminent in making tax law, the judges had a crucial part to play in expounding it. Their interpretation of statutes constituted a central part of the legal process. The strict adherence to a literal approach to the interpretation of statutes, established as the traditional English approach in

111

the eighteenth century,[1] was increasingly criticised in the nineteenth in relation to non-fiscal legislation.[2] One lawyer said that 'a mere lexigraphical judgment as to what may be the verbal effect of the terms of a detached or isolated provision, is not even a lawyerlike interpretation, still less a judicial enunciation of the law'.[3] Certainly the taxing authorities found it unduly restrictive. In 1919 Arthur Ereaut, a former surveyor, told the Royal Commission on the Income Tax that the rule was 'unfortunate', since it led taxpayers to believe that they were 'entitled to pay – not their fair share according to the spirit of the Acts and intention of the Legislature – but as little as the letter of the law demands'.[4] It had led to increased and avoidable litigation and to a greater use of tax experts to exploit weaknesses in the law. The letter, he said, kills. His solution was for the courts to apply a purposive approach and interpret the Acts according to their spirit rather than their letter. Such a view was perhaps not surprising emanating from a dedicated public servant, but was not one which the judiciary was prepared to adopt. The application of the literal approach in tax was not only rigorously maintained by the judges throughout the Victorian period, but was perceived by contemporary commentators as being intensified.[5]

The Victorian judges inherited a strict and literal approach to the interpretation of tax statutes, whereby the words of the statute constituted the entire scope and delineation of the charge to tax.[6] They saw in it a clear constitutional provenance as a support for, and natural consequence of, the fundamental safeguard of parliamentary consent. It ensured taxpayers were taxed only by the express words of the statute, as they were entitled to be, for as Earl Cairns remarked in 1879 'there was not any *a priori* liability in a subject to pay any particular tax'.[7] As a

---

[1] See above, pp. 31–3.

[2] See 'Editor's Notes', in *Law Quarterly Review* 9 (1893), 106 *per* Sir Frederick Pollock.

[3] First Report of Mr H. Bellenden Ker on the Proceedings of the Board for the Revision of the Statute Law, *HCPP* 1854 (301) xxiv 153 at p. 224, Appendix 1 *per* George Coode.

[4] Minutes of Evidence taken before the Royal Commission on the Income Tax, *HCPP* (1919) (288) xxiii, q. 4817.

[5] Report and Minutes of Evidence before the Select Committee on Means of Improving Manner and Language of Current Legislation, *HCPP* (1875) (280) viii 213, qq. 1636, 1640, 1694 *per* Sir Henry Thring, parliamentary draftsman. But see the comments of Sir Thomas Archibald, judge of the Court of Common Pleas at *ibid.*, q. 1982.

[6] See generally A. H. Manchester, *A Modern Legal History of England and Wales 1750–1950* (London: Butterworths, 1980), pp. 33–6; Vinelott J, 'Interpretation of Fiscal Statutes', *Statute Law Review* 3 (1982), 78. For the construction of tax legislation in nineteenth-century America, see Thomas M. Cooley, *A Treatise on the Law of Taxation*, 2nd edition (Chicago: Callaghan and Co, 1886), pp. 263–73.

[7] *Pryce* v. *Monmouthshire Canal and Railway Companies* (1879) 4 App Cas 197 at 202.

subject could only be taxed with the consent of Parliament, it followed that to ensure that was so, the words of the taxing statutes had to be clear and unequivocal and given only their natural, ordinary and literal meaning. They were to be understood by the judges as they were in 'the common language of mankind',[8] in their 'popular use',[9] 'according to [their] natural construction'.[10] The importance of taxation to the public revenue and common weal was recognised, but policy considerations of state and concerns for the public purse were overshadowed by the importance of protecting the taxpayer's constitutional right only to be taxed by clear words in the taxing Act.

The literal approach to the interpretation of tax legislation constituted a safeguard to individual taxpayers against the state which on the whole served them well. It was an essentially narrow approach which excluded any charge to tax on the basis of the spirit or purpose of a statutory provision and accepted only taxation by clear words.[11] The degree of protection was relative. The literal approach protected his fundamental rights more effectively than the more liberal purposive rules of interpretation because it ensured a greater degree of certainty and predictability in the charge to tax. It also, of course, resulted in a narrow and rigid code of tax law, a strictness which the doctrine of judicial precedent only served to increase[12] and which on occasion perpetuated the harsh or inequitable treatment of taxpayers.

The Victorian law reports abound with the judicial reiteration of the application of the literal rule to the interpretation of tax legislation.[13] The fundamental constitutional right of taxation by parliamentary consent was consistently reiterated, promoted and favoured as the conscious underpinning of their approach. Lord Westbury said it was a 'great rule in the construction of fiscal laws that they are not to be extended by any

---

8 *R* v. *Winstanley* (1831) 1 C & J 434 at 444 *per* Lord Tenterden.
9 *Braybrooke* v. *Attorney-General* (1861) 9 HLC 150 at 165 *per* Lord Campbell LC.
10 *Re Micklethwait* (1855) 11 Exch 452 at 456 *per* Parke B.
11 Robert Stevens, *Law and Politics: the House of Lords as a Judicial Body, 1800–1976* (London: Weidenfeld and Nicolson, 1979), pp. 170–6; 264.
12 See *Gresham Life Assurance Society* v. *Styles* (1890) 2 TC 633 at 640 *per* Lord Esher MR, where he held himself bound by an earlier construction of the term 'profits and gains' under Schedule D income tax.
13 *Clifford* v. *CIR* [1896] 2 QB 187 at 192–3 *per* Pollock B; *IRC* v. *Tod* [1898] AC 399 at 414 *per* Lord Herschell; *Swayne* v. *IRC* [1899] 1 QB 335 at 344 *per* Wills J; *AG* v. *Carlton Bank* [1899] 2 QB 158 at 164 *per* Lord Russell; *Simpson* v. *Teignmouth and Shaldon Bridge Co* [1903] 1 KB 405 at 411–13 *per* Lord Halsbury; *Horan* v. *Hayhoe* [1904] 1 KB 288 at 290–1 *per* Lord Alverstone; *Whiteley* v. *Burns* [1908] 1 KB 705 at 709 *per* Lord Alverstone.

laboured construction',[14] Lord Cairns observed in 1878 that a tax Act 'must be construed strictly: you must find words to impose the tax, and if words are not found which impose the tax, it is not to be imposed',[15] and in 1891 Lindley LJ expressed it thus: '[a]ll … taxing Acts … are to be read strictly; that is to say, they are not to be extended so as to have the effect of imposing on the subject a tax which Parliament has not clearly made him pay'.[16] When in 1844 the Lord Chancellor said a provision for a reduced railway toll should be given its widest interpretation, as that would be the most beneficial to the public,[17] Lord Brougham observed that '*in dubio*, you are always to lean against the construction which imposes a burthen on the subject. The meaning of the Legislature to tax him must be clear'.[18] To the same end the judges continued to interpret exemptions in taxing Acts liberally to favour the taxpayer.[19]

In 1869 in the case of *Partington* v. *AG*, Lord Cairns laid down the classic statement of the basis of the Victorian approach: 'If the person sought to be taxed comes within the letter of the law', he said,

> he must be taxed, however great the hardship may appear to the judicial mind to be. On the other hand, if the Crown, seeking to recover the tax, cannot bring the subject within the letter of the law, the subject is free, however apparently within the spirit of the law the case might otherwise appear to be. In other words, if there be admissible, in any statute, what is called an equitable construction, certainly such a construction is not admissible in a taxing statute, where you can simply adhere to the words of the statute.[20]

The point was forcibly made in relation to the Inland Revenue's attempt to charge the Earl of Sefton with succession duty in 1865. When the earl inherited land which was neither marketable as building land nor cultivable, the board agreed it would not be subject to the tax, though sought to tax it some years later when it was profitably sold. In narrowly construing the words 'annual value' which was the basis of valuation, the court held that the object of the Act was to tax the value of the succession, not that of

---

[14] *Dickson* v. *R.* (1865) 11 HLC 175 at 184 *per* Lord Westbury.
[15] *Cox* v. *Rabbits* (1878) 3 App Cas 473 at 478 *per* Lord Cairns.
[16] *Re J Thorley* [1891] 2 Ch 613 at 623 *per* Lindley LJ.
[17] *Stockton and Darlington Railway* v. *Barrett* (1844) 11 Cl & Fin 590 at 601 *per* Lord Lyndhurst.
[18] *Ibid.*, at 607 *per* Lord Brougham. See too *Ryder* v. *Mills* (1849) 3 Exch 853 at 869 *per* Parke B; *Wroughton* v. *Turtle* (1843) 11 M & W 561 at 567 *per* Parke B.
[19] See, for example, *Stockton and Darlington Railway* v. *Barrett* (1844) 11 Cl & Fin 590; *R.* v. *Special Commissioners of Income Tax* (1888) 2 TC 332 at 336 *per* Grantham J.
[20] *Partington* v. *AG* (1869) LR 4 HL 100 at 122 *per* Lord Cairns.

the property,[21] and furthermore that there was nothing in the language to permit a valuation which included future expectations, nor had machinery been provided to do so.[22] Similarly in *Bowles* v. *Bank of England* in 1913 Parker J construed the Customs and Inland Revenue Act 1890 strictly and narrowly, observing that if the legislature had intended the executive to levy a tax on the basis of a mere resolution of the Committee of Ways and Means, contrary to the Bill of Rights, it undoubtedly would have said so expressly.[23]

The judges were thus not prepared to strain the language to enlarge the scope of a taxing Act in order to bring a taxpayer into charge. A literal meaning, however, came at a price, for if the construction were clear, any hardship on the taxpayer was immaterial. The approach left no room for flexibility, implication or equity in taxation, and the personal views of a judge were irrelevant. When Lord Wynford observed in 1831 that there was no injustice in his finding that certain property was not subject to auction duty, he added that the judges were not 'sitting judicially, to be led away by the equities of any case', but were to 'administer the law, whatever it may be'.[24] And as Lopes LJ remarked in 1894, 'we have nothing to do with whether the law may press hardly in certain cases, what we have to do is to administer the law as we find it'.[25] In Rowlatt J's pithy aphorism in 1921, there was no equity about a tax.[26]

Looking to the literal meaning of the words did not necessarily ensure that there was only one meaning. When faced with an ambiguous term with several meanings, the judges had to decide which to adopt, an approach which called for a wider consideration. In *AG* v *Hallett*,[27] for example, the court had to decide whether the words 'competent to dispose of by will' in the Succession Duty Act 1853 referred to the successor's interest in the property to be disposed of or his personal capacity. The latter construction would mean that a successor incompetent by reason of lunacy or coverture would not be liable to the duty. In finding for the crown, Pollock CB held that the word 'competent' here referred to the power to make a will by reason of having sufficient interest in property, and assuming

[21] *AG* v. *Earl of Sefton* (1863) 2 H & C 362 at 371 *per* Wilde B. Affirmed by the House of Lords: *AG* v. *Earl of Sefton* (1865) 11 HLC 257.

[22] *AG* v. *Earl of Sefton* (1863) 2 H & C 362 at 372 *per* Wilde B.

[23] *Bowles* v. *Bank of England* [1913] 1 Ch 57 at 87 *per* Parker J.

[24] *R.* v. *Winstanley* (1831) 1 C & J 434 at 440 *per* Lord Wynford. He added that if they felt the law produced an injustice, they could, in their legislative capacity, alter it: *ibid.*, at 442.

[25] *Grainger and Son* v. *Gough* (1894) 3 TC 311 at 321 *per* Lopes LJ.

[26] Rowlatt J in *Cape Brandy Syndicate* v. *IRC* [1921] 1 KB 64 at 71.

[27] *AG* v. *Hallett* (1857) 2 H & N 368.

the capacity to make one. All the judges agreed that the rule of construction was one of common sense. '[E]very one who hears language uttered is continually correcting its imperfections and removing its ambiguity by the mere exercise of ordinary good sense', said Pollock CB.

> If one meaning only can be applied to certain words, it must be presumed that that was the meaning intended; but where the words admit of several meanings, whether in an act of parliament or any other instrument, if one of them leads to a manifest absurdity, we are bound to adopt that meaning which does not.[28]

All the judges agreed that it was absurd to suppose that Parliament intended that succession duty not be paid by the insane. Similarly, the force of common sense made itself felt in holding that a resident superintendent of an asylum should be exempt from inhabited house duty because although the house was separate, it did form part of the asylum.[29]

If a judge, after careful examination of the Act, was in reasonable doubt as to the meaning of a provision, he would give the taxpayer the benefit of the doubt,[30] as, for example, when in 1831 Lord Tenterden construed a statute giving a dock company the right to impose a duty on ships in such a way as to ensure the burden of dock duties was not geographically extended.[31] This was partly the result of the constitutional importance of taxation and its impact on the subject, and showed an appreciation of the weaker position of the individual taxpayer in relation to the crown. It was also the result of the judges' perception of taxing Acts as penal enactments.[32] Lord Esher MR frequently condemned the taxing Acts as tyrannical and viewed them as penal statutes.[33] Certainly taxing Acts were analogous to penal Acts, not because the rates of tax in the nineteenth century were high but because they imposed some charge on the subject and often contained severe penalties for non-compliance, and it had always been the case that a penalty should only be imposed by clear words.[34] Furthermore tax Acts almost inevitably potentially imposed some hardship on the taxpayer. The judges also never forgot that it was the

---

[28] *Ibid.*, at 375 *per* Pollock CB.   [29] *Jepson* v. *Gribble* (1876) 1 TC 78.
[30] *Wilcox* v. *Smith* (1857) 4 Drew 40 at 49 *per* Sir R. T. Kindersley.
[31] *Kingston upon Hull Dock Company* v. *Browne* (1831) 2 B & Ad 43.
[32] See, for example, Grantham J in *R.* v. *Special Commissioners of Income Tax* (1888) 2 TC 332 at 336; *Scruton* v. *Snaith* (1832) 8 Bing 146 at 152 *per* Park J.
[33] *Gresham Life Assurance Society* v. *Styles* (1890) 2 TC 633 at 639; *Grainger and Son* v. *Gough* (1894) 3 TC 311 at 318.
[34] It has been suggested that the literal interpretation of penal statutes revealed a degree of judicial humanitarianism: Manchester, *Modern Legal History*, p. 34.

responsibility of the taxing authorities to ensure the Acts were properly drafted so as to make the charge to tax clear and plain. If they failed to do so, it was not for the taxpayers to suffer, and they should be given the benefit of the doubt. 'It is not the subject who makes the law', said Lord Wynford in 1831 in relation to auction duty, 'it is the Crown who proposes the law, and by whom the law is prepared; and if there be any ambiguity, let the Crown suffer, and not the subject'.[35] The judges were, furthermore, always conscious that the taxing authority had the opportunity every year to amend tax legislation as it wished.

In interpreting ambiguous and obscure words, the judges would gener-ally have no option but to attempt to read them to promote what they con-sidered to be the intention of Parliament. In such cases, therefore, there was necessarily a degree of flexibility introduced into their approach to the construction of taxing Acts. Though as their tax expertise grew, the judges became more confident in seeking the intention behind the tax-ing Acts, it was an approach which was adopted with considerable cau-tion and recognised as a hazardous and unpredictable enterprise. As Lord Cranworth observed in 1852, when a judge departed from 'the great car-dinal rule' of literal construction, he was 'launched into a sea of difficul-ties which it is difficult to fathom',[36] and Baron Branwell agreed that it was far better to be 'accused of a narrow prejudice for the letter of the law than set up, or sanction vague claims to disregard it in favour of some higher interpretation, more consonant with the supposed intention of the fram-ers or the spirit which ought to have animated them'.[37] Lord Halsbury was particularly cautious. '[I]n a Taxing Act', he remarked in 1892, it is impos-sible … to assume any intention, any governing purpose in the Act, to do more than take such tax as the statute imposes'.[38] And five years later, he said he looked for 'a plain interpretation to be put upon plain words'.[39] There was, in his view, 'no governing principle' to assist a judge in con-struing a taxing Act, simply the Act itself.

In looking to the intention of the Act before them, the judges were con-siderably limited in their tools, for they did not allow themselves to stray outside the boundaries of the statute itself and use extrinsic evidence. They were not permitted to use copies of bills at any stage in their passage through Parliament, nor the reports of the debates on a bill either in the

[35] See *R. v. Winstanley* (1831) 1 C & J 434 at 442.
[36] *Gundy* v. *Pinniger* (1852) 1 D G M & G 502 at 505.
[37] *AG* v. *Sillem* (1863) 2 H & C 431 at 537.
[38] *Tennant* v. *Smith* (1892) 3 TC 158 at 163.
[39] *Lord Advocate* v. *Fleming* [1897] AC 145 at 151.

house or in committee,[40] partly because they were regarded as unreliable and unsafe.[41] This was so even when the Chancellor of the Exchequer, the Prime Minister or even the draftsman himself had clearly said what the meaning of a statute was intended to be. A frequent suggestion in this respect was to insert an objects clause into the Act. In relation to the Succession Duty Act 1853, for example, a member of Parliament proposed 'a simple controlling definition of the principle of the tax', the aim being to exclude subsequent disputes as to construction, but this was rejected as unacceptably dangerous.[42] Though the overall intention of the Act would always be explained by counsel in the course of judicial proceedings,[43] judges tended not to seek the 'general purview'[44] of an Act, but instead sought intention in the context of previous and subsequent provisions, something they often described as the 'scheme' of the Act.[45] A vague and indefinite phrase in the Income Tax Act 1842 was construed by looking at the other provisions, a divided Divisional Court[46] holding that a commercial taxpayer given the right to claim repayment of income tax if 'at the end of the year' overpayment could be proved, a 'reasonable construction' was that the phrase meant 'reasonable diligence after the end of the year'.[47] The Court of Appeal agreed the words could not mean the very moment the year ended and looked to the commercial context of the provision for a construction which would allow it to apply 'in a reasonable business-like manner'.[48] To that end Esher MR concluded that it meant 'in as short a time as in the particular case, by exertion the party can fairly be said to have found out and to have proved'.[49]

[40] See Willes J in *Millar* v. *Taylor* (1769) 4 Burr 2303 at 2332.
[41] For a full discussion of the nature and origins of the rule, see Michael Rawlinson, 'Tax Legislation and the Hansard Rule', *BTR* (1983), 274.
[42] *Parl. Deb.*, vol. 129, ser. 3, cols. 206–9, 14 July 1853 (HC) *per* James Freshfield. See Arthur Ereaut's similar suggestion in Minutes of Evidence taken before the Royal Commission on the Income Tax, *HCPP* (1919) (288) xxiii, q. 4817.
[43] See Report and Minutes of Evidence before the Select Committee on Means of Improving Manner and Language of Current Legislation, *HCPP* (1875) (280) viii 213, q. 1955 *per* Edward Bouverie MP.
[44] *Ibid.*, q. 1637 *per* Sir Henry Thring, parliamentary draftsman.
[45] See *IRC* v. *Priestley* [1901] AC 208 at 213 *per* Lord Halsbury. This contextual approach was sometimes adopted even in cases where the meaning was clear: *IRC* v. *Herbert* [1913] AC 326 at 332 *per* Lord Haldane. See too *AG* v. *Heywood* (1887) 19 QBD 326 at 331 *per* Stephen J.
[46] Grantham J and Cave J disagreed upon the construction of the phrase, and so, as junior judge, Grantham withdrew his judgment.
[47] *R.* v. *Special Commissioners of Income Tax* (1888) 2 TC 332 at 346 *per* Cave J.
[48] *Ibid.* at 349 *per* Lord Esher MR.   [49] *Ibid.*, at 350.

The judges had more difficulty in rationalising their strict approach when the adoption of the ordinary meaning of the words led to an absurd or unreasonable outcome. In *Warburton* v. *Loveland* in 1828,[50] a case not on tax but on the construction of the Irish Register Act,[51] Burton J laid down the rule of the construction of written instruments in words which were often cited thereafter with approval in the English courts.[52] He was faced with words in the statute which were clear and unambiguous, namely that all unregistered deeds were fraudulent and void, and he refused to limit their meaning. He said that the generality of the words could 'properly be restrained within the limits of the declared or implied policy of the statute' if the orthodox construction gave rise to repugnance or inconsistency within the statute. This was to be undertaken with caution, however, within the statute itself and not upon 'merely speculative grounds', for that approach to construction 'incurs the hazard, and has, perhaps, in some instances, produced the effect of legislating in the form of exposition'.[53] This preamble served to limit his later statement of the rule, which, standing alone, suggested more latitude than he intended. 'I apprehend', he said,

> it is a rule in the construction of statutes, that, in the first instance, the grammatical sense of the words is to be adhered to. If that is contrary to, or inconsistent with any expressed intention, or any declared purpose of the statute; or if it would involve any absurdity, repugnance, or inconsistency in its different provisions, the grammatical sense must then be modified, extended, or abridged, so far as to avoid such an inconvenience, but no farther.[54]

The Court of Exchequer Chamber of ten judges was equally divided,[55] and the case went to the House of Lords.[56] Lord Tindal CJ held that where the language of a statute was clear and explicit, the courts had to give effect to it whatever the consequences might be 'for in that case the words of the statute speak the intention of the Legislature',[57] but where the words were doubtful, the court had to address that doubt 'by discovering the

---

[50] *Warburton* v. *Loveland* (1828) 1 Hud & Br 623.   [51] 6 Anne c. 2.
[52] For example by Lord Wensleydale in *Grey* v. *Pearson* (1857) 6 HLC 61 at 106.
[53] *Warburton* v. *Loveland* (1828) 1 Hud & Br 623 at 636–7.   [54] *Ibid.*, at 648.
[55] The courts below, namely the Court of King's Bench and the Court of Exchequer, had themselves reached conflicting decisions.
[56] *Warburton* v. *Loveland* (1832) 11 Dow & Cl 480. Surprisingly in view of the history of the case their Lordships were unanimous in their decision to affirm the decision of the Court of Exchequer Chamber.
[57] *Ibid.*, at 489.

object which the Legislature intended to accomplish by passing the Act'.[58] To do this he was prepared to be wider ranging in his approach to construction, looking closely at the words of the statute, but also at the mischief the legislature sought to suppress. He looked at the preamble of the statute, and the other clauses in order to ascertain the intention of the legislature.[59] Concluding that the object of the statute was to prevent fraudulent conveyances of land by registration, he gave the clause in question a wide meaning.

In 1857 Lord Wensleydale praised the wisdom of the courts in anxiously adhering to the express words of an instrument and giving them their ordinary meaning, and said that where an adherence to the ordinary sense of the words gave rise to an absurdity or inconsistency with the rest of the instrument, the sense of the words could be modified to avoid such a result.[60] In 1859 he expressly approved the rule as stated by Burton J, saying it was 'universally adopted in Westminster Hall'.[61] This slight relaxation of the rigidity of the literal interpretation of statutes was generally adhered to by the judges, and since they frequently reiterated that taxing Acts were no different in this respect from other Acts,[62] it followed that this approach was equally applicable.

And so when in *Colquhoun* v. *Brooks*[63] in 1889 the court was faced with a provision which had a clear literal meaning which was unreasonable in its operation, the judges looked to the Act as a whole in order to arrive at a correct construction. The provision in question was section 2 of the Income and Property Taxes Act 1853[64] which, in the broadest and most comprehensive language, imposed the charge to income tax. The taxpayer was resident in England and was a partner in an Australian firm. He made considerable profits from his Australian enterprise, but received in England only a small proportion of the total profits made. The question was whether he should be taxed on the whole profits or just those he actually received. There was no doubt that he would be liable to income tax on all the profits of his business in Australia, whether or not he received them in the United Kingdom if the words of the section were given their natural meaning. However, Lord Fitzgerald found 'insuperable difficulties in giving full effect to the universal language' of the provision, and said that the scope of the provision must be controlled.[65] Lord Herschell accepted

[58] *Ibid.*   [59] *Ibid.*, at 489–94.   [60] *Grey* v. *Pearson* (1857) 6 HLC 61 at 106.
[61] *Thellusson* v. *Rendlesham* (1859) 7 HLC 429 at 519.
[62] *Mersey Docks and Harbour Board* v. *Lucas* (1881) 51 LJ QB 114 at 118 *per* Brett LJ.
[63] *Colquhoun* v. *Brooks* (1889) 2 TC 490.
[64] 16 & 17 Vict. c. 34.   [65] *Colquhoun* v. *Brooks* (1889) 2 TC 490 at 497.

that the natural meaning of the words, though clear, would lead to anomalies and inconsistencies within the Act, and it was legitimate to consider the rest of the Act to 'throw light upon the intention of the Legislature'. He concluded that as the Act did not provide the machinery necessary to assess trading profits arising and remaining abroad, it strongly suggested that it did not intend to tax such profits.[66] Turning instead to the fifth case of Schedule D he arrived at a legitimate and sensible construction which was in accordance with the intention of the legislature as seen from the scheme of the entire Act.[67] The judges were prepared to go even further, though only when absolutely necessary,[68] as when in 1915 they were prepared to pare down or even contradict the statutory language where the Act's 'scheme and its machinery and … manifest purpose'[69] suggested that it should be done.[70]

In interpreting the tax legislation the different techniques the judges adopted and the factors they took into account depended to a large degree on their personal values and experience.[71] Some contemporary commentators believed that the literal approach to statutory interpretation, in tax and other fields, revealed the judges' inability to address principles.[72] In many instances they interpreted taxing Acts with a mixture of common sense, commercial practice such as they understood it, traditional notions of property law and, above all, a not insignificant self-confidence.[73] They were not entirely deficient in specialist tax knowledge, for while appeals to the regular courts in tax matters were relatively rare, they were certainly not unknown. From the seventeenth century they had regularly been involved in litigation over the stamp duty Acts – though primarily

[66] *Ibid.*, at 501.
[67] See too *Clerical, Medical, and General Life Assurance Society* v. *Carter* (1889) 2 TC 437; *Leeds Permanent Benefit Building Society* v. *Mallandaine* (1897) 3 TC 577.
[68] *Drummond* v. *Collins* [1915] AC 1011 at 1018 *per* Lord Loreburn.
[69] *Ibid.*, at 1017.
[70] It has been shown that the judges in the late nineteenth and early twentieth century were willing to relax the literal approach to favour the taxpayer in some tax avoidance cases: see Assaf Likhovski, 'Formalism and Israeli Anti-Avoidance Doctrines in the 1950s and 1960s', in John Tiley (ed.), *Studies in the History of Tax Law* (Oxford and Portland, Oreg: Hart Publishing, 2004), pp. 339–44.
[71] See W. R. Cornish and G. de N. Clark, *Law and Society in England 1750–1950* (London: Sweet & Maxwell, 1989), pp. 21–3.
[72] Manchester, *Modern Legal History*, p. 33.
[73] R. Cocks, 'Victorian Barristers, Judges and Taxation: A Study in the Expansion of Legal Work', in G. R. Rubin and David Sugarman (eds.), *Law, Economy and Society, 1750–1914: Essays in the History of English Law* (Abingdon: Professional Books Ltd, 1984), pp. 445–69 at p. 449 and notes 11 and 12.

to decide whether a document had been properly stamped so as to be admissible in evidence[74] – the excise Acts and occasionally the land tax Acts, and appeals to the courts had been permitted for the assessed taxes throughout the eighteenth century. They also had experience of tax legislation through the exercise of their supervisory jurisdiction. A number of factors led the judges to favour the formalistic approach to the interpretation of tax statutes: the relative unfamiliarity of tax matters, the absence of principle in the legislation, the perception of taxing Acts as penal statutes, the importance accorded in English law to instruments under seal,[75] a veneration of the common law, contemporary views on the judges as mere interpreters of the law rather than as law-makers, and their respect, as a class, for private property. A formal approach concentrating on the words of the statute met all the needs and concerns of the judges, and was consonant with a training where central importance was given to the written word, its accuracy and rigour. Furthermore, in most instances this ordinary literal reading gave rise to the reasonable outcome intended by Parliament.[76] In terms of safeguarding the taxpayer, it established a firm if restrictive base of statutory interpretation which provided some rigour in the protection of his fundamental rights in individual instances.

The nature of tax legislation

By modern standards, nineteenth-century taxing Acts were relatively simple and short, and were generally confined to the raising of revenue rather than any wider, and possibly hidden, social or economic objective.[77] Rates of tax were low, and tax avoidance had not yet become an issue of popular or judicial importance. Some tax Acts were highly regarded. Despite a great deal of challenging litigation on the Succession Duty Act 1853,[78] Lord Wensleydale called it 'well-drawn',[79] a point echoed by other

---

[74] See generally R. S. Nock, '1694 And All That', *BTR* (1994), 432.

[75] D. J. Llewelyn Davies, 'The Interpretation of Statutes in the Light of their Policy by the English Courts', *Columbia Law Review* 35 (1935), 519 at 522.

[76] As in *Re Micklethwait* (1855) 11 Exch 452, where the court, giving the word 'property' its natural meaning, held that it included the benefit of a covenant. See too *Lord Advocate* v. *Fleming* [1897] AC 145.

[77] See *Coltness Iron Company* v. *Black* (1881) 1 TC 287.

[78] See, for example, the cases reported in the CIR Sixth Report, *HCPP* (1862) (3047) xxvii 327 at pp. 383–8, and the numerous cases on foreign domicil in CIR Sixteenth Report, *HCPP* (1873) (844) xxi 651.

[79] *Braybrooke* v. *Attorney General* (1861) 9 HLC 150 at 173 *per* Lord Wensleydale.

judges, members of Parliament and the draftsman himself.[80] However, overall the standard of legislative drafting was low in the nineteenth century, with a lack of principle, uniformity and consistency which was the subject of considerable contemporary criticism.[81] The words had to be clear and state Parliament's intention,[82] for as was remarked in the course of the estate duty debate in 1894, '[t]he Courts of Law must decide, not according to what we mean, but to what we say'.[83] Accustomed as the judges were to complex and technical legislation, they complained emphatically about 'the vast heap of undigested matter which is cast down before them to digest into some rational shape',[84] and were justified in so doing. Indeed, their tone was 'sometimes not very respectful to the wisdom of Parliament'.[85] Though the situation was improving by 1875, with the introduction of the parliamentary draftsman,[86] a better style of drafting, clearer arrangement of clauses and the subdivision of bills into parts,[87] the quality of the tax legislation was problematic for the judges, just as it was for members of Parliament and the taxpaying public. It necessarily affected their ability to safeguard the taxpayer's constitutional right to be taxed only with the consent of Parliament. Where the taxing provision was obscure, litigation, with all its expense and difficulty, was the taxpayers' only recourse, and they were accordingly at the mercy of poor and inaccurate drafting.[88] The interpretative safeguard of the taxpayer was thus undermined by the nature and bulk of Victorian tax legislation.[89]

---

[80] *AG v. Earl of Sefton* (1863) 2 H & C 362 at 375 *per* Wilde B; *Parl. Deb.*, vol. 25, ser. 4, col. 1420, 18 June 1894 (HC) *per* Robert Reid; Minutes of Evidence before the Select Committee on Means of Improving Manner and Language of Current Legislation, *HCPP* (1875) (280) viii 213, qq. 1700, 1703 *per* Sir Henry Thring.

[81] See generally Manchester, *Modern Legal History*, pp. 36–7.

[82] *Parl. Deb.*, vol. 25, ser. 4, cols. 1247–9, 15 June 1894 (HC); *ibid.*, col. 1359, 18 June 1894.

[83] *Ibid.*, vol. 27, ser. 4, col. 186 , 17 July 1894 (HC) *per* Sir J. Lubbock.

[84] Minutes of Evidence before the Select Committee on Means of Improving Manner and Language of Current Legislation, *HCPP* (1875) (280) viii 213, q. 1946 *per* Edward Bouverie MP.

[85] *Ibid.*, q. 214 *per* Sir Thomas Erskine May, clerk to the House of Commons.

[86] See Manchester, *Modern Legal History*, pp. 36–7.

[87] Minutes of Evidence before the Select Committee on Means of Improving Manner and Language of Current Legislation, *HCPP* (1875) (280) viii 213 at pp. 216, 218 and qq. 1345–7 *per* Sir C. Hall, Vice Chancellor.

[88] See, for example, John Prebble, 'Why is Tax Law incomprehensible?', *BTR* (1994), 380 at 383.

[89] For the amount of statute law in general, see Minutes of Evidence before the Select Committee on Means of Improving Manner and Language of Current Legislation, *HCPP* (1875) (280) viii 213, qq. 1811–2 *per* Robert Wright, barrister.

The drafting of tax statutes to be clear and accurate yet as brief as possible was no easy task. It was 'a very rare accomplishment'[90] and required, said the Attorney General in 1894, 'the utmost patience, time, and trouble to get things well together'.[91] It had to satisfy the demands of the parliamentary process and the public revenue, and these affected the character of the legislation. Tax Acts were, by their nature, notoriously complex[92] and technical, dealing with a specialised field of activity in an increasingly commercial society. And the legislation was complicated whether the tax raised £15 million or £15,000.[93] The rules laid down had to apply to diverse and often complicated circumstances. The Succession Duty Act 1853, for instance, aimed to affect all the various ways in which property could be disposed of or could devolve by operation of law, and was inherently intricate. Although it was clear that complicated statutes caused problems in the collection of the revenue, it was also clear that if the wording of a tax Act permitted a taxpayer to fall outside the charge, that taxpayer, or his advisers, would argue his exclusion robustly and often with considerable ingenuity.[94] The taxing authorities wished to ensure that the provisions applied to all situations they had envisaged, and others they had not, and they wished to address loopholes in the law which had been revealed in earlier implementation.[95] To this end their provisions were as detailed, precise, certain and prescient as the draftsman could make them. As Stephen J observed in 1891, 'it is not enough to attain to a degree of precision which a person reading in good faith can understand; but it is necessary to attain if possible to a degree of precision which a person reading in bad faith cannot misunderstand'.[96] As rates rose and became progressive, taxpayers had an increasing incentive to exclude themselves from the statutory provisions by close scrutiny of the language used and imaginative interpretation. Draftsmen responded with renewed effort to ensure that taxing Acts contained no such ambiguity or lacunae, and tax Acts became ever-longer, detailed and complex.

This complexity was compounded by the distinctive characteristics of the legislation's expression resulting from the highly formalised

<hr>

[90] *Ibid.*, q. 1903 *per* Edward P. Bouverie MP.
[91] *Parl. Deb.*, vol. 25, ser. 4, col. 1384, 18 June 1894 (HC) *per* Sir John Rigby AG.
[92] For another perspective on the complexity of taxing Acts see Prebble, 'Tax Law', 380.
[93] CIR Fifth Report, *HCPP* (1861) (2877) xxxi 109 at p. 125.
[94] Social, economic and legal conditions were such in the nineteenth century that the very great majority of taxpayers were men.
[95] See generally John Clark, 'Statutory Drafting', at 327–8.
[96] *Re Castioni* [1891] 1 QB 149 at 167 *per* Stephen J.

parliamentary process for the imposition of taxation, itself the consequence of its constitutional and political importance. It has been seen that
the opportunities for debate, both in substance and in time, were increasingly limited throughout the nineteenth century. This had a twofold effect.
First, the conditions under which financial legislation was debated in the
House of Commons made rushed, infelicitous and inaccurate drafting
almost inevitable.[97] The constitutional position of the House of Lords in
relation to money bills meant that any imperfections noted after their passage through the Commons could not be rectified, and it was feared this
would get worse after the passing of the Parliament Act 1911, when the
House of Lords could no longer even point out a drafting error. Secondly, it
led to a drafting practice which aimed at clauses which were as unequivocal and precise as possible, even if they were complex, so as to ensure that
amendments and the consequent debate would be kept to a minimum. It
was, however, suggested that bills were deliberately unintelligible in order
to ensure they succeeded in their passage through Parliament in a reasonable time. As Lord Hewart somewhat cynically observed in 1929, 'to be
intelligible is to be found out, and to be found out is to be defeated'.[98] A tax
barrister had similarly observed in 1919 that more revenue was obtained
when the tax legislation was left obscure, for then only experienced tax
officials would understand it.[99] The outcome was a detail and length of
statutory provision rarely found in other forms of legislation.

Above all, the complexity of tax Acts was the result of the common and
increasing practice of legislation by reference, a problem in all legislation
but one of particular aggravation in tax. It was the practice whereby an
amending statute was passed containing a provision that it was to be construed with a number of other Acts as far as they were consistent. So the
income tax of 1842 was subject to the Taxes Management Acts of 1803,[100]
1808[101] and 1810[102] which were expressly incorporated by reference into
the substantive Act. Those Acts in turn referred to a number of earlier
Acts. Furthermore, the Act provided that the powers and provisions
of 'any other Acts relating to the Duties of Assessed Taxes' were to be
included.[103] This meant that for nearly all the principal taxes a number of

[97] *Parl. Deb.*, vol. 24, ser. 5, col. 320, 11 April 1911 (HC) *per* Herbert Nield.
[98] Lord Hewart, *The New Despotism* (London: Ernest Benn Ltd, 1929), p. 77.
[99] Minutes of Evidence taken before the Royal Commission on the Income Tax, *HCPP* (1919) (288) xxiii, q. 15,991 *per* A. M. Bremner, barrister, on behalf of the General Council of the Bar of England.
[100] 43 Geo. III c. 99.   [101] 48 Geo. III c. 141.   [102] 50 Geo. III c. 105.
[103] 5 & 6 Vict. c. 35 s. 3 (1842).

Acts had to be construed together as one,[104] and this caused immense difficulties for the judges. 'It requires great pains', observed a judge in 1875, to ascertain what are the exact provisions that you have to construe'.[105] In 1897 Grantham J complained that he had 'to go back from page to page, and then go on to certain other pages and then come back again, so that it has been almost impossible to follow this case without a great deal of difficulty'.[106] It was described as 'very objectionable' by an experienced draftsman[107] and 'dreadful' by a Queen's Counsel who once, having had to advise as to the legal protection afforded to a tax collector, found a provision to the effect that all statutory provisions relating to the assessed taxes, whether repealed or not, were to be in force for that purpose, at which point he 'gave up the search as hopeless'.[108] Sir George Jessel MR, who called it a Chinese Puzzle, believed the practice stemmed from the parliamentary process, in that it ensured that the bill was as short as possible and as such more likely to be passed.[109]

The complexity and bulk of the tax legislation were compounded by its literal interpretation by the judges. This was not peculiar to England, for tax legislation was as strictly construed in America, and there the application of the strict literal approach was believed by some commentators to have 'defeated the plain and manifest purpose in enacting the laws'.[110] This gave the law of each tax a character all of its own. The relationship between taxing Acts and the judges was, however, a circular one, since the complexity of the former was due to a considerable extent to the attitude adopted by the latter. The draftsman had to make the provisions as comprehensive as possible and to address as many situations as could be foreseen. He could not do so through broad and simple language, because if he did not expressly provide for a wide range of situations, he knew he could not rely on the judges to construe the language to achieve his aims. His response, therefore, was to draft lengthy and detailed provisions expressly addressing as many foreseeable situations as possible.[111] Furthermore, as has been

[104] D. de M Carey, 'On Construing "As One With"', *BTR* (1975), 260.
[105] Minutes of Evidence before the Select Committee on Means of Improving Manner and Language of Current Legislation, *HCPP* (1875) (280) viii 213, q. 1969 *per* Sir Thomas Archibald.
[106] *Leeds Permanent Benefit Building Society* v. *Mallandaine* (1897) 3 TC 577 at 587.
[107] Minutes of Evidence before the Select Committee on Means of Improving Manner and Language of Current Legislation, *HCPP* (1875) (280) viii 213, q. 1350 *per* Sir C. Hall VC.
[108] *Ibid.*, qq. 712–3 *per* Joseph Brown QC.   [109] *Ibid.*, q. 1165.
[110] Cooley, *Law of Taxation*, p. 263.
[111] Third Report of Mr H. Bellenden Ker on the Proceedings of the Board for the Revision of the Statute Law, *HCPP* (1854) (302–1) xxiv 407 at p. 412.

seen, taxing Acts occupied a special position in statute law. Their virtually exclusive ministerial provenance, their regularity and frequency, and the uncommonness of delegated legislation, were all well known to the judges, and coloured their attitudes to this form of legislation.[112]

Not only did the pressures of Parliament, the executive, the taxpayer and the judges result in a detailed, complex and often obscure law, they also resulted in a law which had no real coherence, either physically or intellectually. It grew by degrees, amendment upon amendment, through the successive annual Finance Acts. The English part of the bill introducing the new estate duty in 1894, for example, consisted of 497 lines, to which 360 were added in committee and on report.[113] And though the bulk of tax legislation grew inexorably, attempts at the consolidation of taxing Acts were sporadic. The outcome was a large body of legislation which had grown piecemeal, addressing a number of different taxes, some ancient and some new, each with their own distinctive features expressed. Within each specific tax regime, the number of statutes was generally large. This was particularly so in the excise, where each commodity subject to the duty was invariably regulated by several Acts. If any principle existed at all, it was hard to discern.[114] The judges were thus presented with a hotch-potch of unrelated imposts with no overall rationality and little internal principle.[115] In many cases the main concepts underlying a tax were left undefined by the legislators, the prime example being income tax, where notions such as income, residence, trade and profits[116] were left entirely to the judges to address. Lord Esher MR observed in 1889 that the arguments put to him about the Income and Property Taxes Act 1853 were 'enough to puzzle one's head off nearly'.[117] That legislation was described in Parliament as 'slovenly and disgraceful',[118] and apparently the judges had maintained

---

[112] David W. Williams, 'Taxing Statutes are Taxing Statutes: The Interpretation of Revenue Legislation', *Modern Law Review* 41 (1978), 404 at 404–8.

[113] *Parl. Deb.*, vol. 27, ser. 4, col. 190, 17 July 1894 (HC) *per* Thomas Gibson Bowles.

[114] The situation continued far into the twentieth century: see G. S. A. Wheatcroft, 'The Present State of the Tax Statute Law', *BTR* (1968), 377.

[115] See Vinelott J, 'Interpretation of Fiscal Statutes', *Statute Law Review* 3 (1982), 78 at 79.

[116] For the absence of any definition of 'profits and gains' in the Income Tax Act 1918 see Minutes of Evidence taken before the Royal Commission on the Income Tax, *HCPP* (1919) (288) xxiii, qq. 15,940–47 *per* A. M. Bremner. See generally A. Farnsworth, 'The Income Tax Act, 1842 – A Century of Judicial Interpretation', *Law Quarterly Review* 58 (1942), 314; Martin Daunton, *Trusting Leviathan: the Politics of Taxation in Britain, 1799–1914'* (Cambridge University Press, 2001), pp. 204–10; Williams, 'Taxing Statutes', 407–8.

[117] *Clerical, Medical, and General Life Assurance Society* v. *Carter* (1889) 2 TC 437 at 442.

[118] *Parl. Deb.*, vol.127, ser. 3, col. 725, 27 May 1853 (HC) *per* John Phillimore.

that it was 'not framed as an Act of Parliament should be'.[119] The stamp duty Acts were notoriously obscure, and even provisions in fundamental procedural Acts were sometimes flawed. In 1898 a provision in the Taxes Management Act 1880 was judicially described as 'a little elliptical'.[120] Even the Finance Act 1894, introducing estate duty at the end of the Victorian period, was not a success in this respect. Gibson Bowles, remarking on the 'extraordinary complications' of the bill,[121] criticised the draftsman, saying that it was 'grossly and shamefully prepared'.[122] Lord Macnaghten called one section 'one of the least intelligible sections in an Act of Parliament not remarkable for perspicuity'.[123] Wills J expressed the general judicial view of tax litigation in relation to a case in 1897, which he said 'taxes all one's ingenuity and all one's power of understanding to see what the Legislature have meant'.[124] Even the central boards sympathised with the judges in this respect. One distributor of stamps in Manchester said that the Stamp Acts were complex and difficult to read, and that the Succession Duty Act was difficult to interpret,[125] and the Comptroller General and Solicitor for the Inland Revenue in Scotland said in 1862 that the Succession Duty Act had been found challenging by lawyers and law officers of the crown.[126]

The interpretation of statutes by the executive

The efficacy of the safeguard inherent in a strict approach to the interpretation of tax Acts was undermined directly by poor drafting and complex legislation. It was, however, undermined in another more fundamental way when it was bypassed entirely, namely when tax legislation was interpreted by a body other than the judiciary, one not constitutionally permitted to undertake the task, and that interpretation was acted upon by the taxpaying public. As part of its statutory duty to manage the income tax, excise duties and stamps, the Board of Inland Revenue necessarily interpreted the tax legislation on a daily basis in its practical implementation

---

[119] *Parl. Deb.*, vol. 127, ser. 3, col. 723, 27 May 1853 (HC) *per* John Bright.
[120] *Lord Advocate* v. *AB* (1898) 3 TC 617. See I. J. Ghosh, 'The Construction of Fiscal Legislation', *BTR* (1994), 126 at 131.
[121] *Parl. Deb.*, vol. 27, ser. 4, col. 189, 17 July 1894 (HC).   [122] *Ibid.*, col. 191.
[123] *AG* v. *Duke of Richmond* [1909] AC 466 at 470. See William Phillips, 'Three Score Years and Ten', *BTR* (1964), 152.
[124] *Leeds Permanent Benefit Building Society* v. *Mallandaine* (1897) 3 TC 577 at 584.
[125] Minutes of Evidence before the Select Committee on Inland Revenue and Customs Establishments, *HCPP* (1862) (370) xii 131, q. 3570 *per* R. E. Howard, stamp distributor; *ibid.*, q. 2894 *per* Thomas Stannus, stamp distributor.
[126] *Ibid.*, q. 3060 *per* Angus Fletcher, Comptroller General and Solicitor for the Inland Revenue in Scotland.

of its provisions. The board's duty was to administer the law enacted by Parliament and not to amend it in any way. In some instances the meaning was clear and evident; in many others it was obscure and doubtful, as for example in the absence of any clear definition of what constituted paper for the purpose of levying the paper duty, a duty the board condemned as untenable for that reason. The task of interpretation in such instances inevitably fell on the executive[127] and the board had to arrive at its own construction as a prerequisite to the execution of the legislation. This was all the more significant and important due to the nature of the main income tax Acts, for the Act of 1803 which formed the basis of subsequent Acts left terms of fundamental importance undefined.[128] The judges would eventually construct a body of case law defining these concepts, but until then it fell to the revenue boards. The boards, which had been intimately involved in the drafting of the legislation itself, confidently interpreted it entirely as they saw fit, in consultation with their own solicitor and his supporting legal staff.[129] So, for example, the Board of Inland Revenue interpreted the Act subjecting every horse running for any kind of prize to an excise duty as a racehorse 'in its spirit rather than in its letter', and exempted all horses running for farmers' and yeomanry plates, or those who were merely hunters, and again the board drew its own distinction between a gardener and an under-gardener in relation to the assessed tax on servants.[130] Again, the board, albeit with the permission of the Chancellor of the Exchequer, adopted a liberal construction of the income tax legislation in relation to allowances for wear and tear of implements.[131]

The board ensured its own interpretation of the legislation was disseminated throughout the service, through the circulars and instructions that all boards had published from their earliest days.[132] They issued in copious numbers from London throughout the nineteenth century, to be adopted and applied by the board's officers all over the country. They kept the practice of the department up to date, for every new law, every new situation, commercial development or legal decision necessitated a new communication from the board. Crucially, though, it ensured a uniformity

[127] See Sir Maurice Sheldon Amos, 'The Interpretation of Statutes', *Cambridge Law Journal* 5 (1934), 163.
[128] See Wheatcroft, 'Tax Statute Law' at 385.
[129] See Minutes of Evidence before the Select Committee on Inland Revenue and Customs Establishments, *HCPP* (1862) (370) xii 131, q. 2200 *per* Charles Trevor, Comptroller of Legacy and Succession Duties.
[130] CIR Thirteenth Report, *HCPP* (1870) (82, 82–1) xx 193 at pp. 255, 323.
[131] CIR Twenty-first Report, *HCPP* (1878) (2158) xxvi 717 at p. 780.
[132] 12 & 13 Vict. c. 1 s. 3 (1849).

of implementation of the law in accordance with its views. Above all the board was determined to ensure that its officers did not interpret legislation according to their own personal, and necessarily variable, view.[133] The opinion of the board on a question of law was conclusive for their officers and, indeed, for the local commissioners.[134] Above and beyond these formal circulars, points of the interpretation of terms in the legislation constantly arose, and necessitated correspondence with the board in London for clarification and guidance, both from their own officers and the local commissioners.

The taxpayer was in a weak position in relation to the board's view of legislation. Its self-imposed duty to interpret tax legislation inevitably placed a wide discretion in the executive. The paper duty interpretation, and many others like it, constituted examples of the board making arbitrary decisions, though having no choice in view of a lacuna in the legislation. If the board's interpretation of a relieving section was restrictive, or that of a charging section wide, it could impose obligations on a taxpayer and thereby constitute taxation by the executive and not by Parliament.[135] Though they could and did materially affect the fiscal situation of individual taxpayers, the circulars were not subject to the scrutiny of Parliament, and for tax to be imposed by executive action was contrary to the fundamental constitutional principles of taxation and had no legal basis. Not being bound by strict judicial approaches demanding adherence to the words of the statute alone, there was the clear danger that the board might, when a provision was unclear or ambiguous, incline to an interpretation which favoured its own convenience at the expense of the taxpayer. With their specialist expertise of tax administration it was almost inevitable that its interpretation would be coloured by an appreciation of the practical implications of any interpretation.[136] Indeed it has been argued that this is what occurred throughout the nineteenth and twentieth centuries,

---

[133] Ninth Report of the Commissioners of Inquiry into the Collection and Management of the Revenue arising in Ireland and Scotland, *HCPP* (1824) (340) xi 305 at p. 342, Appendix 4 *per* Thomas Carr, Solicitor of Excise.

[134] Minutes of Evidence before the Select Committee on the Income and Property Tax, *HCPP* (1852) (354) ix 1, qq. 2469–73 *per* George Offor, Chairman of Commissioners for Tower Hamlets.

[135] There was the underlying point that the accountability to Parliament of the board was not robust: John Booth, *The Inland Revenue … Saint or Sinner?* (Lymington: Coracle Publishing, 2002), p. xii.

[136] See generally H. Wade MacLauchlan, 'Judicial Review of Administrative Interpretations of Law: How Much Formalism Can We Reasonably Bear?', *University of Toronto Law Journal* 36 (1986), 343 at 344–63.

and, moreover, that it became enshrined in the statutes themselves and the practices of the board.[137]

Furthermore, while the board was quite aware its interpretation was not legally binding, taxpayers were in all practical ways subject to it until it was challenged. If they did not agree with it their only recourse was to appeal, a course of action which would put them to inconvenience, anxiety and considerable expense. The board had plentiful resources with which to pursue its interpretation of the legislation through the courts, resources far greater than those available to the majority of taxpayers. And as its own interpretation enjoyed an authority of experience, it was often generally accepted, even though it was understood that the law could only be authoritatively interpreted by the courts. With this monopoly on the initial interpretation of tax legislation, the persistent complexity of the legislation served to increase the influence of the executive.

Appeals to the courts

Attitudes to tax appeals

The strict approach to the interpretation of statutes was regarded by the judges as the natural consequence and support of the fundamental safeguard of parliamentary consent. Appeal to the regular courts of law going to the merits of the decision itself, addressing potentially issues of both law and fact, and enabling the superior court to replace the tribunal's decision with its own, was seen as a clear and discrete safeguard in its own right.[138] Nevertheless, the prevailing view of appellate provision in tax matters was well established by the beginning of the reign, and was restrictive; there was either no appeal allowed at all, or else one only on a point of law. Of the two major direct taxes in force in 1837, one enjoyed a power of appeal to the courts of law, the other did not. The assessed taxes retained their statutory right of appeal by the surveyor or the taxpayer from the decision of the local commissioners to the superior courts of law by way of case stated. The power was consistently though not excessively used, the Board of Inland Revenue recording thirty-nine appeals in 1858,[139] and thirty-five in 1859.[140] Within the land tax administrative

---

[137] Booth, *The Inland Revenue*, p. xiii.

[138] *Allen* v. *Sharp* (1848) 2 Exch 352 at 367 *per* Platt B.

[139] CIR Third Report, *HCPP* (1859) (2535 sess. 2) xiv 451 at pp. 513–21.

[140] CIR Fourth Report, *HCPP* (1860) (2735) xxiii 235 at pp. 283–90. A surveyor observed in 1852 that he did not take out an appeal once in five years: Minutes of Evidence before the

structure, on the other hand, no appeal to the courts of law was permitted at all, on either law or fact, and so the traditional provisions for finality of the commissioners' determinations took full effect. As to the indirect taxes, the Commissioners of Excise Appeal or the Justices of the Peace at Quarter Sessions who heard the initial appeals in excise matters could, at their discretion, state a case for the opinion of the Court of Exchequer.[141] In relation to the stamp duty, where the commissioners gave their opinion on the duty chargeable on an instrument, appeal was permitted to the Court of Exchequer by case stated.[142] Indeed, the case of *Partington* v. *AG* was an example of a special case for the opinion of the court in a stamp duty matter.[143]

In view of the state of tax legislation in the nineteenth century and the undermining of the localist safeguard as well as the inadequacies of that system, allied to the growth of the power of the executive,[144] the need for increased appeal provision to the regular courts was a matter of some moment. As rates rose and commerce expanded, it became urgent. By the end of the Victorian period, thousands of pounds, sometimes hundreds of thousands, could depend on the outcome of an income tax appeal, and assessments to estate duty could be very considerable indeed. There were, however, strong public policy and pragmatic reasons for Victorian legislators to maintain the status quo and restrict appeals to the regular courts. To allow appeals on questions of fact was still perceived as both unnecessary and undesirable.[145] First, it would cause a delay in the collection of the public revenue and interrupt its flow. The object of any tax was to raise revenue, and to do so quickly and consistently. An appeal to the regular courts would prolong litigation and so hinder the implementation of the tax Act in that particular instance. It could delay it to a considerable degree since an appeal could entail proceedings before the lowest tier of

Select Committee on the Income and Property Tax, *HCPP* (1852) (354) ix 1, q. 1559, and see too q. 1555. For examples of such cases, see Return of Cases determined on Appeal in England relating to Assessed Taxes, *HCPP* (1831–2) (87) xliv 1.

[141] 7 & 8 Geo. IV c. 53 s. 84 (1827). And there was the further possibility of the writ of error to the Exchequer Chamber and then to the House of Lords.

[142] 33 & 34 Vict. c. 97 ss. 18(1), 19(1) (1870).

[143] *Partington* v. *AG* (1869) LR 4 HL 100.

[144] As Farwell J remarked in 1911, 'the Courts are the only defence of the liberty of the subject against departmental aggression': *Dyson* v. *AG* [1911] 1 KB 410 at 424.

[145] Minutes of Evidence to Second Report of the Judicature Commissioners', *HCPP* (1872) (631) xx 245, Answers to Questions 23–28. See too Report of the Royal Commission on the Income Tax, *HCPP* (1920) (615) xviii 97 at para. 590; Minutes of Evidence to Third Report of the Judicature Commissioners, *HCPP* (1874) (957–1) xxiv 13, Answers to Questions 14–15.

the superior courts and another two stages to the appropriate court of appeal and thence to the House of Lords. This delay was unacceptable to any government, and it would obviously be exacerbated if there were a large number of appeals. In 1848 Parke B observed in relation to a tax on horse dealers that if the right of appeal were not limited, there would be a 'flood of litigation'. 'Actions would be innumerable', he continued, 'juries would have to decide on facts without end, judges on law, and cases would be carried to the highest tribunal, when the exigencies of the state required a speedy determination'.[146] The legislators were justified in their fears, in that the quantity of litigation pending under the Succession Duty Act 1853 was partly responsible for a marked absence of any increase in the receipts from the death duties.[147] Where a tax was particularly unpopular, as with the income tax in 1842, there was a clear danger that any right of appeal would be extensively used, possibly simply to delay payment of the tax in question, a concern underlying the proposal in 1894 that the estate duty be paid before allowing any appeal to the High Court against the valuation of the estate. Though this might be balanced to some extent by the pacifying effect of the right of appeal, it could not outweigh it. The assessed taxes had been equally unpopular, but they were in essence voluntary, and could be avoided by not purchasing the items subject to the tax; the income tax was mandatory, and as an appeal would offer the only legitimate means of escaping liability, it was not unreasonable to think it might be abused. It was clearly not in the state's interests to allow appeals to the regular courts from the determinations of the tax tribunals.

Secondly, the widespread provision for tax appeals could work against the interests of the legal system as a whole. By the middle of the nineteenth century there was a clear movement for the legislative reform of the courts of law. It was recognised that legal processes were too slow, formal and expensive. The procedures of the common law courts and then of the Court of Chancery were reformed, and improvements in personnel achieved. The Judicature Commissioners reviewed the state of the entire legal system and made recommendations for reform. In such a climate it was clear that the notion of a large number of new appeals, generally small-scale and factual and tending to clog an already overburdened legal system, would not find favour.

---

[146] *Allen* v. *Sharpe* (1848) 2 Exch 352 at 363. This was particularly important in tax matters, where the executive would pursue a case to the highest court where a matter of principle was involved: see Report of the Royal Commission on Income Tax, *HCPP* (1920) (615) xviii 97 at para. 594.

[147] CIR Second Report, *HCPP* (1857–8) (2387) xxv 477 at p. 501.

Thirdly, appeals to the regular courts were unnecessary because appeals were comprehensively permitted within the localist system, and indeed were integral to it. The legislation provided a swift, inexpensive and independent settlement of disputes where the parties could have their cases fully heard and argued. Furthermore, these lay adjudicators possessed the requisite local knowledge to determine facts and settle disputes, a specialist knowledge the regular courts lacked. The introduction of appeals to the courts of law would complicate the system for taxpayers and cause them undesirable publicity. It would also burden them with considerable expense arising from court fees and the danger of costs, and most of all the unavoidable and considerable expense of professional legal representation. These were expenses most individual taxpayers, unlike the revenue boards, would find hard to bear.

There were, however, equally cogent arguments in favour of extending the right of appeal to the regular courts. First, all the local commissioners administering the direct taxes, with the exception of the Special Commissioners of Income Tax, did indeed possess specialist knowledge of a local nature which orthodox fiscal thinking promoted as necessary for accurate assessment. But it has been seen that in the course of the nineteenth century it became apparent that this specialist knowledge was insufficient.[148] It was arguable that an appeal to a court of law, composed of trained and able lawyers albeit ones not possessing specialist tax or local knowledge, would be an even greater necessity than before and beneficial to the taxpayer. Secondly, the very qualities which distinguished the tax tribunals and ensured swift, informal and inexpensive determination of tax disputes rendered them vulnerable to error, ignorance, mismanagement and slackness and made appeal powers desirable.

Nevertheless, taxpayers were not forceful in calling for wider appellate powers. Though in general they respected and trusted the judges, and acknowledged the appeal to the courts of law as the ultimate safeguard against any abuses by the executive, the expense and duration of litigation meant that in general they feared and avoided it. Only where questions of law were concerned, or where large sums were in question, was the demand for appellate powers more insistent. It was the revenue boards in particular who pressed for the right to appeal to the regular courts, especially from the decisions of the General Commissioners. They knew that those determinations were not always sound, and that if a revenue officer felt the decision was contrary to law, he could do

---

[148] See above, pp. 87–8.

nothing about it.[149] The boards believed the right of appeal to the regular courts would make the commissioners more careful and considered in their determinations.[150] Such demands, however, were motivated primarily by a dissatisfaction with the localist system of tax administration rather than a belief in the desirability of appeals as such. Their preference was to abolish localism and retain a restrictive approach to appeals to the courts. As one commentator remarked in 1824, 'it is better to have a very good tribunal without an appeal, rather than a less good tribunal with an appeal from it'.[151]

The judges too saw some merit in permitting appeals, at least on points of law. They agreed that the tax commissioners were the bodies best suited to decide questions of fact, but felt that an appeal on questions of law was necessary to guarantee the law remained correct and consistently applied, to ensure their authority over the tribunals and to protect the liberties of the subject.[152] Indeed the need for the superior courts of law to supervise and control the decisions of inferior courts was described in 1854 as 'so great and so obvious', in order 'that the law in its principles and practice may flow in an uniform and continuous channel from the fountain head'.[153]

The extension of the right of appeal

Reluctant as the legislature was to grant full appeal rights in tax disputes, it appreciated the contribution which appeal provisions made to the popular acceptance of both the substance of taxation and its machinery. It also felt some disinclination expressly to deny access to the courts of law to the parties to enforce their rights. Furthermore, the reforms in legal process throughout the nineteenth century were undermining the

---

[149] Minutes of Evidence before the Select Committee on the Income and Property Tax, *HCPP* (1852) (354) ix 1, q. 1548.

[150] See, for example, *ibid.*, q. 1556.

[151] Ninth Report of the Commissioners of Inquiry into the Collection and Management of the Revenue arising in Ireland and Scotland, *HCPP* (1824) (340) xi 305, at p. 333 *per* John Foster, counsel to the revenue board.

[152] Though such considerations were mentioned in the nineteenth century, as in Minutes of Evidence before the Select Committee on the Income and Property Tax, *HCPP* (1852) (354) ix 1, qq. 1556–7, they became particularly important in the twentieth century: Minutes of Evidence before the Committee on Administrative Tribunals and Enquiries, *HCPP* (1956) (218) viii 1 at p. 194 para. 14, p. 678 para. 11(e). See Bowen LJ in *R. v. Justices of County of London and London County Council* [1893] 2 QB 476 at 492.

[153] Report of the Royal Commission on Bankruptcy, *HCPP* (1854) (1770) xxiii 1 at p. 38.

culture of restraint in appeal provision within the wider legal system. The Judicature Act 1873 provided that an appeal was to lie from every judgment and order of the High Court,[154] and new and wide powers of appeal from inferior courts of law, notably the county courts and Quarter Sessions, were granted. This made the pressure to allow appeals from the tax tribunals irresistible, particularly since the sums in question were often considerably greater than in the regular inferior courts. And so although new taxes were few in the nineteenth century, appeal provision was cautiously increased.

When the income tax was extended to Ireland in 1853, appeals to the regular courts were permitted, in striking contrast to the tax in England. Doubtless this was as compensation for the absence of any localist safeguard in that country, but nevertheless it involved the regular courts in tax matters. Taxpayers dissatisfied with the assessment could appeal to the Assistant Barrister of the district in which they were assessed, an appeal which was by way of re-hearing and was private.[155] The Assistant Barrister, a judge with a local and limited jurisdiction, was given the same powers in relation to the assessment and the appeal as the Special Commissioners would have, and his determination was to be final. Of some 2,500 income tax appeals in Ireland in 1854, in seventy-seven cases notice of appeal to the Assistant Barrister was given.[156] When the succession duty was introduced in the same year, the Act gave taxpayers dissatisfied with their assessment the right to appeal by petition to the Court of Exchequer or, if the sum in dispute did not exceed £50, to the County Court.[157] The Board of Inland Revenue complained in 1857 that litigation under the Act had been 'most unscrupulous and incessant', with 'extravagant objections',[158] and took the view that in many cases it was with the intention of postponing the payment of the duty, rather than with any strong belief that the claims of the board were unfounded. The board took particular objection to the litigation in *Wilcox* v. *Smith*,[159] describing it as 'a point which it was painful to see submitted to a Court of Justice as one of doubt'.[160]

It was in the field of income tax that the reluctance to grant powers of appeal was most persistent. When the first opportunity arose to permit

---

[154] 36 & 37 Vict. c. 66 s. 19. See too First Report of the Judicature Commissioners, *HCPP* (1868–9) (4130) xxv 1 at p. 20.

[155] 16 & 17 Vict. c. 34 s. 22 (1853).   [156] *HCPP* (1854) (471) lviii 373 at p. 374.

[157] 16 & 17 Vict. c. 51 s. 50 (1853).

[158] CIR Second Report, *HCPP* (1857–8) (2387) xxv 477 at p. 501.

[159] *Wilcox* v. *Smith* (1857) 4 Drew 40.

[160] CIR Second Report, *HCPP* (1857–8) (2387) xxv 477 at p. 501.

appeals for the newly revived income tax in 1842, the finality clauses of the original income tax were retained unaltered, with no provision for allowing the opinion of the judges to be taken. Similarly, where an appeal was allowed to the Special Commissioners under Schedule D, the determination of that tribunal was expressly 'final and conclusive in the matter'.[161]

However, the pressure to allow an appeal to the regular courts became irresistible and the legislature, taking a pragmatic and politically expedient view, finally permitted it in 1874, though it was a cautious reform. The compromise was adopted of extending the traditional appeal in tax matters on questions of law alone, which was still regarded as the proper province of the judges, and for which recognised machinery existed. The appeal by way of case stated had been developed in tax matters on the basis of the common law special case procedure and had been in use since the eighteenth century in relation to the assessed taxes. Lord Wynford even recommended it for use in the new county courts.[162] Thirty years later the Judicature Commissioners said it 'affords the opportunity of precisely and distinctly stating the point in dispute unincumbered by irrelevant matter'.[163] To allow appeals to the courts on questions of law alone would overcome the problems of excessive and expensive litigation before a court deemed unsuitable, would ensure that the law itself remained consistent, and would address any weakness in the concept of a lay bench. Accordingly in 1874 the right was given to the crown and the taxpayer to require the income tax commissioners to state a case for the opinion of the Exchequer Division of the High Court, on the grounds that their decision had been erroneous in point of law.[164] The procedure differed slightly from that in operation in the assessed taxes, in that legal argument was allowed, and reasons for the ultimate decision expected. The court would hear and determine the question of law and could reverse, affirm or amend the original determination. It was a clear and unambiguous strengthening of the judicial safeguard of appeal. Some four years

---

[161] 5 & 6 Vict. c. 35 s. 130 (1842).

[162] *Parl. Deb.*, vol. 65, ser. 3, col. 238, 18 July 1842 (HL).

[163] Minutes of Evidence, Second Report of the Judicature Commissioners, *HCPP* (1872) (631) xx 245 at p. 273, Answers to Questions *per* William Raines, judge.

[164] 37 & 38 Vict. c. 16 ss. 8, 9 (1874); 43 & 44 Vict. c. 19 s. 59 (1880). The procedure was founded on the Queen's Remembrancer's Act 1859, 22 & 23 Vict. c. 21 s. 10. See generally W. A. Wilson, 'The Theory of the Case Stated', *BTR* (1969), 230; C. Stebbings, 'The Appeal by way of Case Stated from the Determinations of General Commissioners of Income Tax: An Historical Perspective', *BTR* (1996), 611. There existed a precedent for the use of the case stated procedure within the internal income tax structure itself: *ibid.*, at p. 617.

later the appeal provision was further extended, in the interest of the taxpayer and the revenue, to the Court of Appeal and thence to the House of Lords,[165] thereby bringing tax appeals into line with other litigation.

The board remained aware of the difficulties of granting the right of appeal. It believed the number of appeals would be substantial but not excessive. It could not of course control the number of appeals initiated by the taxpayer, but it was careful not to appeal unnecessarily itself, and would not let any appeal go forward without its sanction. It wished to guard against proceeding with 'frivolous or vexatious' cases. As a result, the number of appeals was less than the number of the expressions of dissatisfaction. The board regarded the power as 'convenient' and 'very acceptable to the public'.[166] Although it was, in income tax terms, a development of real importance for all the parties and for tax law itself, opening the era of case law in that field, it excited remarkably little public discussion.

There were undoubtedly some problems with the appeal by way of case stated. Other than some procedural requirements which could bear heavily on a taxpayer,[167] where a judge entertained doubts as to the findings of fact, he was powerless for he could not stray outside the four corners of the case stated whose facts were conclusive. It was said that in some such instances 'the case stated the appellant out of Court'.[168] This, along with the difficulties posed by mixed questions of law and fact, resulted in some calls for a power of appeal on questions of both law and fact[169] such as the death duties enjoyed. There were, however, practical problems with allowing appeals on questions of fact. The appeal could only be by re-trial or by examining the shorthand notes of the hearing before the commissioners. The former would give rise to considerable expense, and would undermine those very features of cheapness, speed and informality for which the General and indeed Special Commissioners and other tax tribunals had been created. A reliance on the shorthand notes of the evidence would require a profound change in both practice and culture, certainly among local commissioners, for evidence was very rarely recorded, the clerk almost invariably merely noting the decision. On the whole, however, it

---

[165] 41 & 42 Vict. c. 15 s. 15 (1878).
[166] CIR Seventeenth Report, *HCPP* (1874) (1098) xv 673 at p. 712.
[167] See Minutes of Evidence before the Royal Commission on the Income Tax, *HCPP* (1919) (288) xxiii, q. 23,895 *per* Randle Holme.
[168] *Ibid.*, q. 15,935.
[169] *Parl. Deb.*, vol. 11, ser. 5, cols. 1619–21, 1 October 1909 (HC) *per* Sir Archibald Williamson; *ibid.*, cols. 1622–3 *per* Sir Edward Carson.

seems that the executive and the taxpayer were broadly satisfied with the scope of the appellate powers. A leading tax barrister said the view of the bar was that the right of appeal from the decisions of the income tax commissioners should not be extended to questions of fact, but should remain restricted to questions of law.[170] In relation to the new estate duty appeal was allowed to the High Court only on the question of the valuation of the estate,[171] and demands for a wider power on all points of dispute were rejected as ridiculous, potentially leading to a mass of questions of no practical importance coming before the courts.[172] Similarly the Royal Commission on the Income Tax in 1920 expressed concern at the 'alarming extension of the field of litigation'[173] were appeals on points of fact to be allowed. Accordingly, the orthodox position remained fundamentally unaltered. As late as 1915, and speaking of the income tax, Lord Reading reiterated the superior ability of local tribunals to determine questions of fact, their accessibility and their finality, with the ultimate safeguard of review on points of law.[174]

The supervisory safeguard strengthened: the growth of certiorari

The third and last element of the judicial safeguard was the supervisory jurisdiction of the superior courts of law. It has been seen[175] that the power of the superior courts of law to control the exercise of jurisdiction in courts of inferior jurisdiction was well established and understood. The juridical basis of this control was the royal prerogative,[176] and it was exercised through the writ of error, and the prerogative writs of prohibition, certiorari and mandamus. The judges' legal powers of review addressed the jurisdiction and proceedings of inferior courts, embracing the extent and exercise of their powers and procedures. Arguably such control was necessary, since the tax system was dominated by statutory tax tribunals, either lay or bureaucratic, lacking the general legal knowledge and skills which were deemed indispensable in the regular legal system. They also

---

[170] Minutes of Evidence before the Royal Commission on the Income Tax, *HCPP* (1919) (288) xxiii, qq. 15,929–37 *per* A. M. Bremner.

[171] 57 & 58 Vict. c. 30 s.10 (1894), or the County Court if the estate was valued at less than £10,000: s. 10 (5).

[172] *Parl. Deb.*, vol. 25, ser. 4, cols. 1383–4, 18 June 1894 (HC).

[173] Report of the Royal Commission on the Income Tax, *HCPP* (1920) (615) xviii 97 at para. 590.

[174] *R. v. Commissioners of Taxes for St Giles and St George, Bloomsbury* (1915) 7 TC 59 at 65.

[175] See above, pp. 35–9.

[176] *Mayor and Aldermen of City of London* v. *Cox* (1867) LR 2 HL 239 at 254 *per* Willes J.

had unclear jurisdictions and informal processes which could rarely be described as robust. Review by the superior courts could, by ensuring the tribunals abided by the accepted norms of judicial conduct in their adjudicatory role, constitute a powerful safeguard to the taxpayer against mismanagement, incompetence or error.[177]

The writ of mandamus had always been applicable to tax tribunals, and continued to be so used in the Victorian period, for example in relation to the Special Commissioners of Income Tax to compel them to issue orders for repayment of sums which the General Commissioners had certified had been overpaid by the taxpayers.[178] Though theoretical difficulties existed in relation to the application of prohibition, they were rarely raised and the writ was frequently employed.[179] It was the application of certiorari to the tax tribunals which was particularly problematic. Though there had been considerable progress in legal theory in the eighteenth century whereby the first two legal obstacles to the application of certiorari to tax tribunals had been overcome,[180] the third and last, namely the need for the commissioners to constitute a court, was still a material difficulty. Since the tax tribunals were not, in juridical terms, courts at all, the application of the writ to the tax tribunals was not legally possible in 1837.

The bureaucratic excise tribunals, exercising a wide criminal jurisdiction, were more obviously courts, but even the lay tribunals for the direct taxes possessed some of the usual characteristics of a court of law, such as the power to administer oaths, and an obligation to observe the rules of natural justice. They were also empowered to impose penalties for the making of false statements and their decisions were expressed to be final. Furthermore their determinations undoubtedly affected the rights of individuals. In other ways, however, they were clearly not a court. They were not presided over by a legally qualified person, their procedures were not fixed and their hearings were often private. Above all, their overall and dominant function was clearly administrative in nature. They were

---

[177] For example, taxpayers were entitled to be heard in good faith and fairly: *Wood* v. *Woad* (1874) LR 9 Ex 190 at 196 *per* Kelly CB; *Cooper* v. *Wandsworth Board of Works* (1863) 14 CB NS 180 at 194 *per* Byles J; *ibid* at 190 *per* Willes J; *Hopkins* v. *Smethwick Local Board of Health* (1890) 24 QBD 712 at 714–5 *per* Wills J.

[178] *R.* v. *Special Commissioners of Income Tax* (1888) 2 TC 332.

[179] *R.* v. *General Commissioners of Taxes for the District of Clerkenwell* [1901] 2 KB 879; *R.* v. *Commissioners for the General Purposes of the Income Tax for Kensington* [1913] 3 KB 870; *R.* v. *Swansea Income Tax Commissioners* (1925) 9 TC 437. See, however, *Chabot* v. *Lord Morpeth* (1844) 15 QB 446.

[180] See above, pp. 38–9.

appointed under statutes for the management and regulation of taxes in order to execute the substantive tax legislation. Their primary function in so doing was to take responsibility for the assessment and collection of tax, an undoubtedly administrative function. For most of the nineteenth century this function prevailed over their judicial function of hearing and determining appeals against assessments. That was understood as nothing more than the final step in the administrative procedure of assessment, and indeed there was never any clear delineation between the two functions of making the original assessment and hearing an appeal, and the determination of any appeal could legitimately be said to constitute the making of the assessment. As an administrative body with merely incidental judicial powers, they were not exercising the judicial power of the state, so they were not courts and could not be constituents of the judicial system. Context was everything. The law reflected this: income tax assessments had to be 'allowed and confirmed' by the commissioners, and assessments which were subject to an appeal could only be allowed once the appeal had been heard.[181] It followed that there was no *lis* in any appeal before the commissioners, for they were mere valuers.[182] It had long been settled that certiorari would not lie in relation to acts which were purely ministerial in nature,[183] and this principle had been established in relation to Justices of the Peace when they were exercising their licensing powers[184] and Assessment Committees exercising their statutory duty to hear and determine objections to valuation lists for the purposes of rating.[185] In all such cases the bodies in question were not courts giving judgment in litigation in the traditional sense.

This lack of status as a traditional court was potentially fatal to the application of certiorari to the various bodies of tax commissioners. Only if the strict traditional insistence on excluding administrative acts could be breached, or else the definition of a court widened, could the taxpayer

---

[181] 8 & 9 Geo. V c. 40 ss. 122, 123 (1918). This was finally abolished by 5 & 6 Geo. VI c. 21 Schedule 10 paras. 3, 4 (1942).

[182] See generally C. Stebbings, 'The General Commissioners of Income Tax: Assessors or Adjudicators?', *BTR* (1993), 52.

[183] *Re Constables of Hipperholme* (1847) 5 Dow & L 79.

[184] See *Sharp* v. *Wakefield* [1891] AC 173; *Boulter* v. *Kent Justices* [1897] AC 556 at 569. This was equally so when the London County Council was exercising its licensing powers: *Royal Aquarium and Summer and Winter Garden Society Ltd* v. *Parkinson* [1892] 1 QB 431; see too *Copartnership Farms* v. *Harvey-Smith* [1918] 2 KB 405 and *Shell Company of Australia Ltd* v. *Federal Commissioner of Taxation* [1931] AC 275.

[185] *R.* v. *Assessment Committee of St Mary Abbotts, Kensington* [1891] 1 QB 378 *per* Lord Esher MR at 382.

make use of certiorari. As the nature of the tax tribunals as courts was finely balanced, a judicial denial of certiorari was as credible as its allowance. But the interest of the judges in this respect coincided with that of the taxpayer, and it was primarily the judiciary who in the later years of the nineteenth century pressed for and created an extended supervisory jurisdiction into the tax field. Indeed, of all the protective provisions of the law, it was the only one which not only resisted its undermining, but was actually strengthened. Viewing the immense growth in adjudicating bodies in a variety of fields with professional concern, the judges desired to control the conduct of all inferior statutory jurisdictions. In 1882 Brett LJ justified this objective on the grounds of public policy. '[W]herever the legislature', he said,

> entrusts to any body of persons other than to the superior Courts the power of imposing an obligation upon individuals, the Courts ought to exercise as widely as they can the power of controlling those bodies of persons if those persons admittedly attempt to exercise powers beyond the powers given to them by Act of Parliament.[186]

Such a body, remarked Farwell LJ some thirty years later, 'is not an autocrat free to act as it pleases, but is an inferior tribunal subject to the jurisdiction which the Court of King's Bench for centuries, and the High Court since the Judicature Acts, has exercised over such tribunals'.[187]

The judges were able to ignore the contrary authorities simply because most did not expressly address certiorari, and accordingly did not constitute a legal hindrance to finding that full status as court of law was unnecessary for certiorari to apply.[188] The judges regarded themselves as free to act creatively with respect to the meaning of 'court'. They turned instead to the term 'judicial act' as distinguished from a ministerial act. In 1891 Lord Halsbury observed that licensing justices were given extensive powers to be exercised judicially and according to their discretion, which, he said, must be exercised 'according to the rules of reason and justice, not according to private opinion … according to law, and not humour. It is to be, not arbitrary, vague, and fanciful, but legal and regular'.[189] In the following year Lopes LJ stated that the term 'judicial' could refer to the discharge of the duties of a judge in court, or alternatively to administrative duties, which had to be discharged with a 'judicial mind', namely 'a

---

[186] R. v. Local Government Board (1882) 10 QBD 309 at 321.
[187] R. v. Board of Education [1910] 2 KB 165 at 179.
[188] R. v. Assessment Committee of St Mary Abbotts, Kensington [1891] 1 QB 378.
[189] Sharp v. Wakefield [1891] AC 173 at 179.

mind to determine what is fair and just in respect of the matters under consideration'.[190] The latter meaning was much wider in scope than the order of an inferior court, and it was adopted for the purposes of certiorari.[191] Indeed in 1901, Vaughan Williams LJ remarked that it did not necessarily follow from the finding that the licensing justices were not a court of summary jurisdiction,[192] that certiorari should not lie, and shortly afterwards the decisions of licensing justices were held to be of a sufficiently judicial nature to allow its application.[193]

It was clearly easier for the courts to come to that conclusion in relation to justices than other tribunals, for justices were legal officers with predominantly judicial duties, but with a natural predisposition to discharge their many administrative duties in a judicial manner. This cloaking of administrative functions in judicial form served the tax commissioners well. It enabled the courts to follow their inclination and allow the more general application of certiorari. They took the view that if a tribunal had the duty to hear and determine issues which affected the rights of subjects,[194] and had to act judicially in the sense of conducting its proceedings with fairness, impartiality and in good faith, then there was sufficient analogy with a court to allow the application of the writs.[195] This was so even if the matter was one which to modern eyes would be regarded as administrative. 'In short', commented Fletcher Moulton LJ in 1906, 'there must be the exercise of some right or duty to decide in order to provide scope for a writ of certiorari at common law'.[196] The General Commissioners satisfied this requirement, for their governing Act laid down that their duty was to hear and determine all appeals made in pursuance of the Tax Act,[197] and also provided that each commissioner should take an oath whereby he swore that he would 'judge and determine upon all Matters and Things which shall be brought before [him] under the said Act, without Favour,

---

[190] *Royal Aquarium and Summer and Winter Garden Society Ltd* v. *Parkinson* [1892] 1 QB 431 at 452.

[191] For similar developments in nineteenth-century America, see Frank J. Goodnow, 'The Writ of Certiorari', *Political Science Quarterly* 6 (1891), 493 at 505–13.

[192] It had been so held in the case of *Boulter* v. *Kent Justices* [1897] AC 556.

[193] *R.* v. *Woodhouse* [1906] 2 KB 501; see too *R.* v. *Sunderland Justices* [1901] 2 KB 357 and *R.* v. *Johnson* [1905] 2 KB 59.

[194] See *R.* v. *Electricity Commissioners* [1924] 1 KB 171.

[195] *R.* v. *North Worcestershire Assessment Committee* [1929] 2 KB 397; see *R.* v. *London County Council* [1892] 1 QB 190; *R.* v. *Legislative Committee of the Church Assembly* [1928] 1 KB 411.

[196] *R.* v. *Woodhouse* [1906] 2 KB 501 at 535.

[197] 43 Geo. III c. 122 s. 144 (1803).

Affection, or Malice'.[198] Implicit in these requirements was a duty to act fairly, impartially, and in good faith, in other words, to act judicially. The tax tribunals, therefore, with a judicial function inherent in the duty to hear and determine disputes and the duty on all commissioners to bind themselves by oath to act judicially, satisfied these judicially revised conditions for the application of certiorari.

Though the principle of control of statutory tribunals by the superior courts was firmly established by the end of the nineteenth century, and was applied to each new tribunal as it was created,[199] the first recorded instance of the application of certiorari to the General Commissioners was in 1904.[200] It was a striking example of a creative response of the judges to changing conditions and new circumstances, even though their motive in so doing was to ensure the superior courts retained their traditional control over all inferior courts, in this case even peripheral aspects of judicial activity. The judges proved to be remarkably flexible and pragmatic in their approach, and unusually generous in their interpretation, so as to allow a remedy which strictly should not have been applicable, to be widely available to statutory tribunals, including the tax tribunals. As such it constituted a significant and enduring strengthening of the supervisory safeguard.

Conclusion

The independence, power and political standing of the judiciary in the nineteenth century resulted in the overall strengthening of the judicial safeguard the law provided for the taxpayer. The judges were able to resist an encroaching executive, in a way that neither Parliament nor the local tax administration system had been able to. The judges were conservative in their approach to their interpretative safeguard, which they accordingly maintained unchanged, though it inherently protected the taxpayer by limiting any charge to tax to the clear words of an Act of Parliament. An overall policy of restrictive appeals was upheld, the outcome of competing interests of the taxpayer, the judges, the executive and the legislature,

---

[198] *Ibid.*, Schedule F.
[199] *R. v. Poor Law Commissioners* (1837) 6 Ad & E 1; *Re Dent Commutation* (1845) 8 QB 43; *Re Crosby Tithes* (1849) 13 QB 761; *Chabot* v. *Lord Morpeth* (1844) 15 QB 446 at 457 (Commissioners of Woods and Forests); *Board of Education* v. *Rice* [1911] AC 179; *R. v. Light Railway Commissioners* [1915] 3 KB 536; *R. v. Electricity Commissioners* [1924] 1 KB 171. See too *Church* v. *Inclosure Commissioners* (1862) 31 LJ CP 201 (prohibition).
[200] *R. v. Commissioners of Income Tax for the City of London* (1904) 91 LT 94.

but reforms in the wider legal system demanded some extension in the field of income tax and the new death duties. The strengthening of the legal protection of the taxpayer occurred principally through the pro-active attitude of the judges towards their supervisory jurisdiction. In this the tax tribunals benefited primarily because of the growth of a new class of statutory tribunals, of which they could claim to be members, and the control of which the judges, in the interests of their own position within the legal system, were impelled to ensure. The judges succeeded, through the albeit cautious extension of appeal provision, and the unambiguous development of their supervisory jurisdiction, in claiming a formal place for the tax tribunals in the established legal hierarchy and, accordingly, bringing them under their formal control. Although this confirmed the tax tribunals as subordinate adjudicatory bodies, whose decisions and processes were subject to an overriding power of amendment and there-fore restraint, in achieving it the judges, by the end of the Victorian period, constituted a formidable bulwark against the encroaching executive.

5

The taxpayer's access to the safeguards

Introduction

The taxpayer's three principal legal safeguards of Parliament, the local administrative process and the judiciary were as much dependent for their efficacy on the taxpayer's ability to access them in 1837 as they had been in the previous two hundred years. In direct taxation, where the fundamental voluntaryism of customs and excise was absent, access to the safeguards was of prime importance. Access comprised a knowledge and understanding of the duties which tax law and practice imposed on the taxpayer, and of the appellate bodies permitted by the law, as well as the affordability of recourse to the latter. It also encompassed the availability of expert advice to make the best possible use of the legal safeguards. Only then could the taxpayers' constitutional right to pay only the tax they had consented to through Parliament effectively be safeguarded.

Educated taxpayers in the nineteenth century could learn a great deal about the taxes applicable to them and the passage of any new tax laws through Parliament, through readily available sources. The debates of the House of Commons were published, and the numerous Select Committee reports, and those of Royal Commissions, were printed and could be purchased by the public at a relatively low price from the beginning of Victoria's reign, as well as often being available in local public libraries. Taxpayers could read informed comment about taxation in publications such as *The Times*, for as a general publication it provided information about all taxes if they happened to be topical. A regular and detailed coverage of parliamentary proceedings provided its readers with details of the passage of any new and relevant legislation. Similarly the printing of extracts from official inquiries informed taxpayers as to issues of contemporary debate, and the numerous letters to the editor and comments in leading articles provided current and practical information for taxpayers. It also regularly published the annual reports of the central revenue boards, which contained up-to-date information as to the administration of taxes, and occasionally explanations of the individual taxes for popular use. Local newspapers also carried detailed reports of parliamentary proceedings, as well as articles on aspects of tax law. In the first year of the revived income tax, most newspapers featured comment on the substance of the Act and its machinery. In January 1843, for example, the *Exeter Flying Post* featured an article accepting the necessity and fairness of the new tax but condemning its inquisitorial machinery, and in subsequent months it published extracts from the legislation.[1] Specialist commercial journals for businessmen and those in financial circles regularly discussed commercial tax issues and drew matters of urgent importance to the attention of their readers.

The accessibility of tax law

The legal charge to tax imposed on taxpayers was derived entirely from statute. The accepted ideal was that the primary legislation be sufficiently intelligible to enable them to familiarise themselves with the safeguards the law provided for them and to allow them to invoke them if necessary. They should be able to find out the nature of the charge to tax and whether it applied to their own personal situation or not. If aggrieved by an assessment or other decision of the tax authorities, they should be able to ascertain whether they had a right of appeal and, if so, how to set about putting it in motion. 'Precision of expression', it was said in 1854, 'is universally felt to be necessary, when every man is to be compelled to make definite sacrifices, and submits to the law with reluctance'.[2] As one member observed in relation to the Provisional Collection of Taxes Bill in 1913, '[t]his is a Taxing Act, which affects the subject, and which everyone who runs ought to be able to read'.[3] Similarly a leading member of the tax bar maintained in 1919 that tax legislation should be 'clear and simple, or at least expressed in clear and simple language'. 'I do not say', he continued, 'that you can have a simple tax, but you can have a tax expressed in simple language. Make it as simple as you can'. 'I want to have the whole thing plain', he said, 'so that any man of ordinary intelligence can look at the Act himself or can look at a pamphlet concerning it and understand it. That

---

[1] *Trewman's Exeter Flying Post*, 19 January 1843.
[2] First Report of Mr H. Bellenden Ker on the Proceedings of the Board for the Revision of the Statute Law, *HCPP* (1854) (301) xxiv 153 at p. 224, Appendix 1 *per* George Coode.
[3] *Parl. Deb.*, vol. 51, ser. 5, col. 1219, 9 April 1913 (HC) *per* William Joynson-Hicks.

would be a splendid thing'.[4] This view naturally had popular support, and was widely promoted.[5]

It has been seen, however, that the overall standard of the drafting of tax legislation in the nineteenth century was low, and that even the judges found its inherent absence of principle and its immense complexity a considerable challenge.[6] If it was a test for the judiciary, experienced in the construction of the most complex deeds and legislation in property law and other fields, it was clear that it would overwhelm the ordinary taxpayer. And indeed, the primary tax legislation was acknowledged by most taxpayers and tax experts as utterly inaccessible to the public. This had been a feature of the legislation in the eighteenth and early nineteenth centuries, and it continued and indeed worsened in the Victorian period.

Physical access to the legislation was difficult though not impossible, for a few taxpayers enjoyed the membership of the private libraries and reading rooms which existed in most towns and cities, though printed series of authoritative statutes with explanatory commentary and helpful indexes were a feature of the latter part of the nineteenth century. Traders subject to the excise laws regularly complained that they had considerable difficulty in finding out the regulations under which they were to operate. In the early 1830s, for example, a paper manufacturer from Aberdeen wanted to see the recent statutes affecting his trade, and though he wrote asking for them, neither he nor his agent could acquire them. He ultimately had to go to the Record Office and copy them out.[7] Of more moment, however, was that the legislation was more intellectually inaccessible than ever. Even if a taxpayer had access to the volumes of statutes, only a trained legal or tax mind could understand them. Whereas the early tax Acts had been problematic in their generality and the marked absence of the definition of key terms, the principal and growing problem of Victorian tax legislation was its expression and its complexity.

---

[4] Minutes of Evidence before the Royal Commission on the Income Tax, *HCPP* (1919) (288) xxiii, qq. 15,947, 16,032 *per* A. M. Bremner, barrister, on behalf of the General Council of the Bar of England. In 1894 Arthur Balfour maintained that every tax ought to be simple, easily calculated by the taxpayer, and have low compliance costs, and that the new estate duty had fallen short of each: *Parl. Deb.*, vol. 27, ser. 4, cols. 260–8, 17 July 1894 (HC).

[5] See, for example, H. Lloyd Reid, *The British Tax-Payers' Rights* (London: T. Fisher Unwin, 1898), pp. 263–5.

[6] See above, pp. 125–8.

[7] Fourteenth Report of the Commissioners of Inquiry into the Excise Establishment (Paper), *HCPP* (1835) (16) xxxi 159 at p. 312, Appendix 59 *per* Alexander Pirie, paper manufacture.

The taxpayer found the length, form and language of the tax Acts an impenetrable barrier to his understanding. The old convention of drafting sections in long unbroken unpunctuated sentences and the absence of any coherent plan continued,[8] as did the use of obscure language. This was the result of using terms ambiguously, or of using terms which had a certain meaning in the past and giving them new meanings, or simply of poor drafting. Technical terms, while clear to lawyers, were not generally understood. The antiquity of many of the taxing Acts could not be penetrated by the taxpayer, both in their language and in their context of enactment. Much of current tax law was nearly forty years old when Victoria came to the throne. The law relating to the appointment of collectors, for example, could only be ascertained by reference to a statute of 1803, an Act originally passed in relation to the assessed taxes and predating the introduction of the modern income tax entirely. Furthermore, the legislation rarely displayed any coherent plan. Even if taxpayers could locate the Act in question, they could rarely take it at its face value. To ascertain the current state of the law they would have to be alert to the likelihood of subsequent repeal or amendment which might extend or restrict the application of the provision they were consulting, and read those into the text in order to arrive at the law in force. For example, the 1842 Income Tax Act remained the principal Act for the nineteenth century, but was amended by the 1853 Act and numerous Acts thereafter. As late as 1870 there were 42 Acts for the land tax, 32 for income tax,[9] 23 for duties on spirits and 24 for duties on silver. Indeed, the bulk of legislation was particularly problematic in the excise. In 1836 the *Derby Mercury*, reporting on the publication of a report of the Commissioners of Excise Inquiry, observed in astonishment that there existed over 400 Acts relating to the excise. The law which it said should be 'brief, clear, and level to the apprehension of everyone, is dispersed over a multitude of statutes, and is in the last degree confused, contradictory, and unintelligible'.[10] The lengthy schedules which tax Acts almost invariably included suffered from the same difficulties, and with the added confusion resulting from the inclusion therein of unconnected topics.[11] The drafting of the first major tax Act of the new reign, the Income and Property Taxes Act

---

[8] The estate duty, however, though like all the death duties a complex tax, was at least expressed in 'short and crisp' sentences: *Parl. Deb.*, vol. 25, ser. 4, col. 385, 4 June 1894 (HC) *per* Robert Reid.
[9] CIR Thirteenth Report, *HCPP* (1870) (82, 82–1) xx 193, 377 at pp. 314, 326.
[10] *The Derby Mercury*, 7 September 1836.
[11] See G. S. A. Wheatcroft, 'The Present State of the Tax Statute Law', *BTR* (1968), 377 at 386.

1842,[12] did not show any improvements in this respect. It contained 194 sections and seven schedules. Of those schedules, five were integral to the income tax itself in that they laid down the property which was to be subject to the tax according to its source. The sixth contained the various oaths to be taken by the personnel involved in the administration of the tax, while the seventh contained detailed rules relating to the first five schedules. The Succession Duty Act passed eleven years later was better in this respect, being a new tax and as such not encumbered by earlier statutory expression. It contained only fifty-five sections, though it included a copious schedule of three tables setting out the value of certain annuities.

Furthermore, the practice of legislation by reference which so irritated the judges effectively closed the tax legislation to ordinary taxpayers. It made it impossible for them to ascertain the law from one Act alone. Members of Parliament condemned the practice in relation to the Income and Property Taxes Act 1853, one saying that not more than one in ten, or even one in fifty, of all income-tax payers in the country would be able to ascertain and understand the law under which they paid their taxes.[13] Another said that no evil could be worse than this practice for taxpayers who wanted to know what their rights were. 'If this Act', he continued,

> had been prepared by a Hindoo, he believed it would have been urged as a proof of the incapacity of the Hindoo mind. If it was important that any Act should be intelligible, it was so in the case of one affecting the interests of five or six millions of British subjects.[14]

And finally, the large body of material incorporating the interpretation of tax legislation by the central board was problematic. When Bellenden Ker examined the revision of the statute law in 1854, he said that the power of 'superseding statutory regulation by board orders adds to the difficulty of ascertaining the precise state of this branch of the statute law'.[15] Furthermore, this material was unavailable to the taxpayer. The thousands of general orders in the excise, for example, were published in one volume of over 600 pages in 1829[16] but the excise board consistently refused either to provide the traders with detailed instructions or to permit the official guidance to be shown to the traders, on the grounds that it might bind the

---

[12] 5 & 6 Vict. c. 35.
[13] *Parl. Deb.*, vol. 127, ser. 3, cols. 716–7, 27 May 1853 (HC) *per* John Bright.
[14] *Ibid.*, col. 725 *per* John Phillimore; see too *ibid.* col. 731 *per* Isaac Butt.
[15] Second Report of Mr H. Bellenden Ker on the Proceedings of the Board for the Revision of the Statute Law, *HCPP* (1854) (302) xxiv 363 at p. 383.
[16] John Owens, *Plain Papers relating to the Excise Branch of the Inland Revenue Department* (Linlithgow, 1879), p. 261.

board and be pleaded in any litigation.[17] The board even refused to supply the traders with copies of the regulations applicable to them, tending
to assume that they had a sufficient knowledge of the laws through the
daily conduct of their business,[18] and even though at the end of the eighteenth century a complete analysis of all the excise laws was printed, the
board refused to allow anyone other than its own officers to obtain a copy.
Despite a strong request from the Committee of Finance in 1787 to make
the volume more widely available, and a stern rebuke in 1835,[19] the practice of the board did not change and continued into the Victorian period.
Very occasionally instructions from the board to its surveyors found their
way into the local press, as when an official explanation of the proper basis
of assessment under Schedules A and B was published in the *Exeter Flying
Post*,[20] but in general the Treasury minutes, instructions and circulars
which revealed the nature and exercise of the powers of the central board
were regarded as confidential and so were utterly inaccessible to anyone
outside the closed circles of the central revenue boards.

The complexity of the tax Acts was necessarily reflected in the tax
forms of the central boards, the return for commercial income, known
as Form 11, being notorious in this respect.[21] If the forms did not accurately reflect the legislation, it would amount to the interpretation of the
legislation by the board[22] and could work an injustice to taxpayers and
undermine their right to be taxed only according to statute. And so in
relation to the income tax, all limits, exemptions, allowances and reliefs,
each source of income had to be clearly stated on the form. These forms
could have constituted the ideal and obvious occasion on which to supply
the taxpayer with explanations of the technical aspects of the taxes, but in
practice they were often unintelligible to those who had to pay.

The expression of complex and technical law in an obsolescent form
and the need to integrate the provisions of the different Acts rendered the
law wholly obscure to the ordinary taxpayers who found it almost impossible to even begin to grasp the laws which affected them in that capacity,

---

[17] Twentieth Report of the Commissioners of Inquiry (Excise Establishment), *HCPP* (1836)
(22) xxvi 179 at p. 525 *per* John Freeling, Secretary to the Board of Excise.

[18] *Ibid.*, at p. 567 *per* William Hetherington, Surveying-General-Examiner.

[19] Fourteenth Report of the Commissioners of Inquiry into the Excise Establishment
(Paper), *HCPP* 1835 (16) xxxi 159 at pp. 181–2.

[20] *Trewman's Exeter Flying Post*, 5 January 1843.

[21] For a copy of Form 11, see appendix to CIR First Report, *HCPP* (1857) (2199) iv 65.

[22] Minutes of Evidence before the Royal Commission on the Income Tax, *HCPP* (1919) (288)
xxiii, q. 15,952 *per* A. M. Bremner, where he pointed out the use of the term 'casual profits'
in the form, an expression not found in the legislation.

let alone find any clarity or precision in them.[23] While they could discern the charge to tax and some description of the property it applied to, they would be most unlikely to be able to ascertain with certainty whether the tax applied to their own situation or not and could not know in advance what the fiscal consequences of certain transactions were; while they could learn that if they were aggrieved by a decision of the assessing body they could appeal and probably discover how to set about doing so, they could not ascertain exactly how their appeal would be conducted. They would also be quite unable to understand the requirements of the central boards. The traders in particular expressed their 'feelings of disgust and dissatisfaction' at being subject to punitive excise laws which were impossible to conform to because of their 'multiplicity and complexity'.[24] Bellenden Ker found that the excise law was 'most difficult to ascertain' among the 'multifarious provisions' of the various Acts.[25] And in income tax too, the taxpayers realised the laws were 'spread over a vast variety of statutes, extending to several reigns, and [requiring] a great knowledge of the statute book … to know what the law is'.[26] A contemporary commentator observed that '[a]n Englishman is generally satisfied if he is quite clear what is the law, whether he likes the law or not, but now no Englishman is satisfied that he gets quite the right law in income tax matters'.[27]

By the dawn of the twentieth century the complexity of tax legislation and the intricacy of its language had got out of hand, and a judge could observe in relation to a taxing Act that '[m]ost of the operative clauses are unintelligible to those who have to pay the taxes'.[28] Lord Decies complained to *The Times* in 1927 that it was now 'beyond the comprehension

---

[23] See, for example, Minutes of Evidence before the Select Committee on Inland Revenue and Customs Establishments, *HCPP* (1863) (424) vi 303, qq. 427–40 *per* Christopher Bushell, wine and spirit merchant.

[24] Digest of the Reports of the Commissioners of Inquiry into the Excise Establishment, *HCPP* (1837) (84) xxx 139 at p. 156.

[25] Second Report of Mr H. Bellenden Ker on the Proceedings of the Board for the Revision of the Statute Law, *HCPP* (1854) (302) xxiv 363 at p. 383.

[26] Minutes of Evidence before the Select Committee on Inland Revenue and Customs Establishments, *HCPP* (1862) (370) xii 131, q. 500.

[27] Minutes of Evidence before the Departmental Committee on Income Tax, *HCPP* (1905) (2576) xliv 245, q. 1967 *per* Arthur Chamberlain JP, representing the Birmingham Chamber of Commerce.

[28] *Brown* v. *National Provident Institution* [1921] 2 AC 222 at 257 *per* Lord Sumner. In 1948 Singleton J famously advised a taxpayer thus: 'I hope you will not trouble your head further with tax matters, because you seem to have spent a lot of time in going through these various Acts, and if you go on spending your time on Finance Acts and the like, it will drive you silly': *Briggenshaw* v. *Crabb* (1948) 30 TC 331 at 333.

of any layman to make head or tail of the majority of the clauses', and in 1929 Lord Hewart condemned 'the complicated and unintelligible form' of tax statutes and pointed out that if the judges were bewildered by them, what hope for ordinary taxpayers.[29] For it was they who suffered, since ultimately they were the ones who, faced with a new and unexpected demand, found that they were committed to some provision of which they disapproved and could only elucidate the law by going to the courts of law and bearing the cost.[30] As late as 1937 a taxpayer objected violently to the confused state of the law. He protested against 'being governed in an alien language, in the language of a small body of men, aloof from the industrial and commercial life of the nation'.[31]

The taxpayer was as subject to the jurisprudence of tax as to the statutes, and the number of decided cases inevitably grew as the provision for appeals increased. Though the tax Acts were complex and obscure, it was the task of the judges to interpret and clarify their meaning. Even if this had resulted in a real coherence of tax law, it availed the taxpayer little, for the reports of tax cases were even more inaccessible than the legislation itself. For example, the discrete jurisprudence of the assessed taxes, constituting the outcome of the right of appeal by case stated which had existed from 1748, was regarded as specialised and did not form part of all law libraries, themselves anyway not easily accessible to non-lawyers. The reports of other tax cases, when they existed at all, were buried among many hundreds of case reports covering the whole span of English law and were difficult to locate, even if a taxpayer had access to the physical volumes. In the case of income tax, of course, there was no jurisprudence of the regular courts since appeals beyond the local commissioners were forbidden until 1874.

Desirable as it was to have tax laws intelligible to the lay taxpayer, most governments believed it was an almost impossible task.[32] By its very nature taxation was complicated, and was becoming increasingly so as daily commercial affairs grew in sophistication.[33] It possessed an intrinsic importance which meant it could not be rendered either simple or informal, for it interfered with property rights which in Britain were notoriously complicated in themselves, and had profound political and economic implications for the country. It also had a wide social

---

[29] Lord Hewart, *The New Despotism* (London: Ernest Benn Ltd, 1929), p. 77.
[30] *The Times*, 25 May 1927, p.12 col. d.
[31] Income Tax Codification Committee Bill Memoranda (1937–47), TNA: PRO IR 40/5274.
[32] See Wheatcroft, 'Tax Statute Law' at 390–3.
[33] Report of the Royal Commission on the Income Tax, *HCPP* (1920) (615) xviii 97 at para. 374.

dimension. The fundamental demands placed for example on income tax, notably that it should be equitable and reflect each subject's ability to pay, inevitably introduced a considerable complexity. If tax were explained in simple and comprehensible terms to the lay reader, there was always the danger that it could be misleading and could work unfairness to the taxpayer in that it would necessarily ignore the sometimes fine differences between individuals' situations. Such pragmatic considerations led to the official belief that it was impossible with respect to any law to 'bring [it] home to every man's bosom and business', to have it, in a popular contemporary expression, 'understanded of the people'.[34] If this was the view in relation to general legislation, how much more so for tax Acts. In that respect Gladstone admitted it was 'very far from being easy',[35] and in relation to the income tax, Lord John Russell thought that any such attempt would lead to 'great public inconvenience'.[36]

One partial but practical and constructive step was the consolidation of the extensive statutory law, a practice supported by many lawyers and commentators. James Fitzjames Stephens, for example, believed strongly in it as the key to simplification, praising the consolidation of civil and criminal procedure, and of certain revenue laws, in India.[37] In 1854 Bellenden Ker reported that at the end of 1853 there were 16,579 public general Acts.[38] He recommended the gradual consolidation or re-writing of the statute law in a uniform and careful way and as quickly as possible. His proposals were modest, suggesting improvement where possible, the removal of obsolete and unnecessary provisions, and better draftsmanship.[39] And though it was a feature principally of the later nineteenth century, consolidation occurred sporadically in English law, notably in the various clauses consolidation Acts, in commercial law and, at the end of the century, in trusts administration.[40] In tax, the need was clear. In his first report Bellenden Ker drew particular attention to the 'loose way' in which successive statutes had been drafted. He said it was unclear which

[34] Minutes of Evidence before the Select Committee on Means of Improving Manner and Language of Current Legislation, *HCPP* (1875) (280) viii 213, qq. 509, 526 *per* Francis Reilly, barrister.

[35] *Parl. Deb.*, vol. 127, ser. 3, col. 722, 27 May 1853 (HC).   [36] *Ibid.*, col. 732.

[37] Minutes of Evidence before the Select Committee on Means of improving Manner and Language of Current Legislation, *HCPP* (1875) (280) viii 213, q. 266.

[38] Second Report of Mr H. Bellenden Ker on the Proceedings of the Board for the Revision of the Statute Law, *HCPP* (1854) (302) xxiv 363 at p. 379.

[39] Third Report of Mr H. Bellenden Ker on the Proceedings of the Board for the Revision of the Statute Law, *HCPP* (1854) (302–1) xxiv 407 at p. 409.

[40] See generally Manchester, *Modern Legal History*, pp. 38–49.

ones had been repealed and which were still in force and that as a result revision would be very difficult, but that consolidation into one statute for each class of tax would be straightforward and an essential preliminary exercise.[41] The demand for consolidation in tax was frequent from the eighteenth century, especially in relation to the customs and excise laws. Merchants believed it would simplify these and enable them to be more easily understood, and it was certainly urgently needed, for so complicated were customs computations that merchants did not know what they had to pay, and it was said that it even acted as a deterrent to foreign merchants.[42] The demand bore fruit early, for in 1825 the 1,500 laws relating to the customs were reduced to six Acts of Parliament, were consolidated again in 1835 and 1836, and in 1853 were reduced to one Act[43] using 'plain, simple language, that no man reading English can misunderstand'.[44] Indeed, the Commissioners of Customs maintained the law was 'equally clear and notorious to those who have to administer it as to those who have to obey it'.[45] Less progress was made in relation to the excise, however, despite the equally forceful complaints of the traders. There were an average of some 500 excise Acts in force at any one time in the nineteenth century, and while the early consolidations of 1803[46] and 1827[47] effected some improvements, they were imperfect and limited exercises falling far short of the customs. Accordingly the Commissioners of Excise Inquiry in the 1830s said that a programme of thorough and expert revision, simplification and consolidation was urgently required to address the obsolete, ineffective and 'unnecessarily vexatious and oppressive'[48] excise laws. The repeal of certain duties, the defeat of the bill in Parliament, or the resistance of the trade itself meant progress was slow, and by 1837 only the laws in three trades, and the rules of general management, had been consolidated. In the case of the stamp duties, they were consolidated in three Acts in 1870, though with considerable difficulty, and two more were necessary by 1891.[49]

---

[41] First Report of Mr H. Bellenden Ker on the Proceedings of the Board for the Revision of the Statute Law, *HCPP* 1854 (301) xxiv 153 at p. 160.

[42] First Report of the Commissioners of Customs, *HCPP* (1857) (2186) iii 301 at p. 374.

[43] 16 & 17 Vict. c. 107.

[44] *Parl. Deb.*, vol. 126, ser. 3, col. 199, 21 April 1853 (HC) *per* James Wilson.

[45] First Report of the Commissioners of Customs, *HCPP* (1857) (2186) iii 301 at p. 326. In the following two years, however, two supplements had to be published.

[46] 43 Geo. III c. 69.   [47] 7 & 8 Geo. IV c. 53.

[48] Digest of the Reports of the Commissioners of Inquiry into the Excise Establishment, *HCPP* (1837) (84) xxx 139 at p. 156.

[49] 33 & 34 Vict. c. 97, c. 98, c. 99; 54 & 55 Vict. c. 38, c. 39.

In the field of direct taxation the century saw even less progress. In 1877 the Statute Law Committee recommended that the legislation administered by the Board of Inland Revenue be consolidated, and Albert Dicey, then junior counsel to the board, began the work which resulted in the Taxes Management Act 1880,[50] consolidating the law on the appointment and duties of officers relating to all taxes other than the land tax. It left the complexity and obscurity of the language, however, unaltered. In 1906 a Select Committee called for the simplification of the substance of income tax,[51] but the first consolidation did not take place till 1918, and even then was described as 'a mass of confused patchwork'.[52] Though later consolidations would follow, taxpayers would have to wait nearly one hundred years for a central initiative such as the Tax Rewrite Project for the recasting of the direct tax legislation in clearer and simpler language and its restructuring in a more logical form so as to render it easier to use. In the nineteenth century the whole of tax law remained isolated by its complexity, and consequently inaccessible to all except those who were involved with it on a daily and professional basis.

The persistent intricacy of tax legislation, its inaccessible language and the complexity of modern commercial life made the reform of the tax forms correspondingly difficult and consequently neglected. Again the customs had led the way, for they were notorious for the number and complexity of forms employed, and their board addressed the removal of all unnecessary forms and the simplification of those remaining. The only improvement in this respect in income tax was when in 1873 an Act provided that only notices prescribed or approved by the board were to be used,[53] for it put an end to the common practice of the regional production of forms and notices and introduced a welcome measure of uniformity. Although the forms were carefully and regularly revised by the board, who received and considered suggestions from taxpayers and representative groups, it believed that to simplify the language at the expense of accuracy would leave it open 'to the charge that they were giving the taxpayer garbled information, and seeing to pass off an official gloss or interpretation of the law as the law itself'.[54] Few improvements followed and the matter became

---

[50] 43 & 44 Vict. c. 19.
[51] Minutes of Evidence before the Select Committee on Income Tax, *HCPP* (1906) (365) ix 659, qq. 2781–2.
[52] Minutes of Evidence before the Royal Commission on the Income Tax, *HCPP* (1919) (288) xxiii, q. 15,952, and also q. 15,990 *per* A. M. Bremner. On the drafting of the 1918 Act, see *ibid.*, qq. 16,026–30.
[53] 36 & 37 Vict. c. 18 s. 9. See too 43 & 44 Vict. c. 19 s. 15 (2) (1880).
[54] *The Times*, 15 September 1922, p. 7 col. c.

one of the most important campaigns of the Income Taxpayers' Society in the 1920s. The director of the society, Lord Decies, wrote repeatedly to *The Times* pressing for the urgent simplification of official forms. Thousands of taxpayers in all walks of life, he wrote,

> are almost despairing in their efforts to steer a clear course through intricacies which are as unnecessary as they are confusing, and which would almost seem to have been designed for the express purpose of befogging the unhappy taxpayer and accentuating the trouble he has in paying by making it as difficult as possible for him to arrive at the basis on which he has to pay.[55]

It was largely due to the pressure of that society that the Chancellor of the Exchequer agreed to appoint a committee to consider the matter. The Departmental Committee on the Simplification of Income Tax and Super Tax Forms in 1924, however, felt unable to recommend any far-reaching or fundamental re-casting of forms.[56] It was even regarded as impractical, in view of the constant modification of tax law, to simplify the forms and place the explanatory material in an accompanying booklet.[57] Only when the legislation itself was simplified could the forms follow suit.

The accessibility of the appellate bodies

Denial of access to the overtly protective appellate processes in all taxes amounted to the denial of the major legal safeguard which enabled the taxpayer to question the decisions of the taxing authorities. Whether to appeal or not was, of course, the taxpayers' choice, but inaccessible processes effectively denied them that choice. Lack of access, either practical or intellectual, rendered these appellate bodies of no realistic use. The greater the ease with which taxpayers aggrieved by any decision of the administrative process could make any objection, dissent or appeal to a tribunal to have it heard and determined, the more they were able to benefit from the legislative provision for their protection, and the more the government could enjoy the full political benefit of making provision for appeal.

The right of appeal

In theory all taxpayers were to be made aware of their rights of appeal to the tax tribunals by the issue and publication of formal notices. The

---

[55] *Ibid.*, 14 September 1922, p. 6 col. b.   [56] *HCPP* (1924) (2019) xi 41 at para. 6.
[57] *Ibid.*, at para. 16.

tradition of publicity by affixing notices to the church door continued throughout the nineteenth century, and as the availability of newspapers continued to increase, so the publication of relevant notices became common. The church door notices were unchanged in their clear and straightforward statement of the date, time and place where a meeting of the commissioners would be held to hear the complaints of any aggrieved taxpayers.[58] Although these could be understood by the general community of taxpayers, they were perceived as antiquated and were not particularly reliable. Church door notices were required for many purposes other than tax,[59] were often ignored, and did not by law need to be placed on the doors of Catholic churches or dissenting chapels.[60] Nevertheless as late as 1932 they were still regarded as having some value, as, though not all taxpayers went to church, it was still a well-known landmark and such notices would catch the eye of some taxpayers.[61] The right of taxpayers to appeal against their tax assessment was also publicised in the official forms and notices of the income tax process sent to individual taxpayers, though they were not all particularly clear.[62] In relation to appealing to the Special Commissioners of Income Tax, the taxpayer was entirely reliant on these forms, since the church door notices did not mention the right at all. However, the form relating to commercial income did not include any explanation of the nature of the tribunal, nor did it mention the right of appeal. So while the right to assessment by the Special Commissioners was publicised to some extent,[63] the right of appealing to them was kept remarkably obscure. The official notice of first assessment included an instruction to appeal by notice in writing to the surveyor, but the fact that the appeal was to the Special Commissioners was implicit and not explicit.[64] And there was a further problem caused by the common practice before 1873 for districts to produce their own personalised

---

[58] See, for example, TNA: PRO IR 9/6A, Form 7 (1854).

[59] For example, railway and inclosure bills.

[60] Third Report of Select Committee to inquire into the Private Business of the House of Commons, HCPP (1847) (705) xii 357, qq. 831–35 per George Ellicombe, parliamentary agent; ibid., qq. 1395–1401 per Joseph Parkes.

[61] TNA: PRO IR 75/1 at p.186 (1932).

[62] TNA: PRO IR 9/2, Form 64 (1868); TNA: PRO IR 9/4 Pt 2, Form 65 (1850s).

[63] TNA: PRO IR 9/4 Pt 2, Form 11 (1857); TNA: PRO IR 88/1, Form 11 (1887).

[64] TNA: PRO IR 9/4 Pt 2, Form 65 (1850s). See too Minutes of Evidence before the Select Committee on Inland Revenue and Customs Establishments, HCPP (1862) (370) xii 131, qq. 122, 406 per Charles Pressly, chairman of the Inland Revenue Department. The Act itself made it clear that the appeal in such circumstances was to the Special Commissioners: 5 & 6 Vict. c. 35 s. 131.

income tax forms and notices, in which this minimal official information was often not included at all.[65] It was here that the system failed the taxpayer, for the right to appeal to the Special Commissioners was probably the least known of all appellate rights. It was not helped by the universal appellation of the various tribunals 'commissioners'. The 'cloud of commissioners'[66] left many taxpayers bemused and unable to distinguish with any precision between the General, Additional, Special, Assessed Tax and Land Tax Commissioners, or indeed the Commissioners of Inland Revenue. So complete was the absence of general knowledge of the Special Commissioners that most nineteenth-century taxpayers were quite unaware of the tribunal's existence, let alone its functions.[67] So when a number of surcharges caused a tax rebellion in Exeter in 1871,[68] the very tribunal which would have addressed the grievances of the taxpayers was entirely unknown to them. Accessibility to the Special Commissioners only improved after 1873 when the notices of first assessment had to be explicit in this respect.[69] It was an ignorance which persisted, even among well-informed commercial men, well into the twentieth century,[70] and which resulted in the slight use of the tribunal throughout the nineteenth century. Even in 1863, by which time the Special Commissioners as an appellate body had been established for twenty years, they were hearing only some 150 appeals a year in England.[71]

The inadequacies of the provision for formal notice of a taxpayer's right to appeal to the local income tax tribunals and the Special Commissioners were not mitigated, as they could have been, by any profound cultural knowledge of their existence, let alone their operation. The jurisdiction and

---

[65] The confidence of the board in its forms and notices was considerably undermined. See CIR Fifteenth Report, *HCPP* (1872) (646) xviii 259 at p. 312; CIR Sixteenth Report, *HCPP* (1873) (844) xxi 651 at p. 686.

[66] *Parl. Deb.*, vol. 62, ser. 3, col. 999, 22 April 1842 (HC) *per* Charles Buller.

[67] See generally, C. Stebbings, 'Access to Justice before the Special Commissioners of Income Tax in the Nineteenth Century', *BTR* (2005), 114.

[68] C. Stebbings, 'Popular Perceptions of Income Tax Law in the Nineteenth Century: A Local Tax Rebellion', *Journal of Legal History* 22 (2001), 45.

[69] TNA: PRO IR 9/2, Form 64 (1873).

[70] See the confusion of Arthur Chamberlain, representing the Birmingham Chamber of Commerce: Minutes of Evidence before the Departmental Committee on Income Tax, *HCPP* (1905) (2576) xliv 245, qq. 1950–3; see too Minutes of Evidence before the Royal Commission on the Income Tax, *HCPP* (1919) (288) xxiii, qq. 15,923, 16,032 *per* A. M. Bremner; *ibid.*, qq. 19,854–5 *per* C. Hewetson Nelson, accountant; H. H. Monroe, *Intolerable Inquisition? Reflections on the Law of Tax* (London: Stevens & Sons, 1981), p. 78.

[71] Return of Number of Special Commissioners appointed to make Assessments and hear Appeals against the Property and Income Tax, *HCPP* (1863) (528) xxxi 607.

procedures of the Excise Court of Summary Jurisdiction and the Justices of the Peace in excise matters, and those of the Land Tax Commissioners, and of the Assessed Taxes Commissioners, were relatively well known because their hearings were all public. Taxpayers became familiar with their existence and processes through normal social and commercial intercourse. It was quite different in relation to the income tax, for there all local income tax commissioners and their subordinate officials, and all officers of central government, had to swear not to disclose any information received in the course of their duties. This meant that all reports of income tax cases before the commissioners were unavailable. Even though they consisted, at least in relation to the General Commissioners, of nothing more than a note whether the assessment was confirmed, reduced or increased,[72] they could not be published, and only became public if they went on appeal to the regular courts. Similarly, the Special Commissioners did not keep reports of their decisions until the closing years of the following century. Only very occasionally did the proceedings before income tax commissioners become public. They were sometimes reported in general terms, and revealing no personal details, in order to inform the tax-paying public. For example, a meeting of the General Commissioners in Devon was reported in the local press under a headline 'Important Decision, Property and Income Tax', where many appellants had claimed certain deductions to income tax, and the commissioners unanimously held that this was not permitted by the Act.[73] While the secrecy provisions effectively stifled press reporting of individual appeals, no scruples were felt when a taxpayer was found guilty of any kind of tax fraud. Such cases took on the nature of criminal proceedings and local newspapers published them in full detail, in much the same way as they published bankruptcy court and magistrates' court hearings.[74] Though not addressing directly the appellate safeguards the law provided, and intended primarily to deter tax evaders, such reports served to increase local awareness of the administration of income tax. Again, tax proceedings could be reported when an aggrieved taxpayer, the only participant in the proceedings not bound by an oath of secrecy, wished for publicity for his or her own purposes, though such reporting was rare. In 1856, for example, *The Times* reported an appeal hearing of income tax commissioners in Ireland, where the appellant, a Roman Catholic priest, took the

---

[72] See, for example, TNA: PRO IR 86/3; Income Tax Minute Book of the Kingsbridge Division, 1853–1866: TNA 3625Z/OA1–2.
[73] *Trewman's Exeter Flying Post*, 9 February 1843.
[74] See for example *ibid.*, 2 February 1843 and 16 March 1843.

opportunity of stating his objection to the taxation of his income when it consisted of the voluntary offerings of his flock, and generally to the treatment of the Roman Catholic clergy by the British government.[75] Not only did lack of publicity result in a widespread ignorance of the rights of appeal against assessment, it meant that taxpayers entered their appeal hearing with minimal information as to the procedures the case would follow and, on some occasions, its very substance. Apart from giving rise to suspicion of bias and arbitrary adjudication, fuelled by gossip and hearsay, it meant it was impossible for ordinary taxpayers to anticipate with any confidence the view the commissioners would take were an appeal to be made. Appellants felt this keenly, and one taxpayer remarked in 1905:

> Now, half the beauty of the law, is that when one is arguing before judges one can quote previous cases, and we know where we are. We say, 'This has been decided there, and that has been decided there', and so you can go from one to the other. But with the Commissioners we do not know what they have decided in the cases of the last thirty men they have had before them. We do not know how much they have allowed off Brown and refused off Smith, because Brown had a more pleasing manner or a more ready wit. That is where the income tax appealer is at a disadvantage, that he has no knowledge of their proceedings.[76]

The initiation of the appeal

Once aware of the existence of their right to challenge the decision of the assessing commissioners, the effectiveness of the taxpayers' right of appeal depended on their being able to initiate it with relative ease. In this the tax tribunals were highly accessible. The tax legislation continued to give clear guidance, and the simple and relatively informal process of direct written communication with the commissioners or a central tax officer was maintained in all taxes. So in relation to an assessment under Schedule D income tax, the notice of the sum with which a taxpayer had been charged included a brief instruction to give notice in writing to the surveyor if the taxpayer wished to appeal.[77] Only if the surveyor omitted to publicise his address, as happened in the Kensington scandal,[78] was initiating an appeal problematic. This was in striking contrast to litigation

---

[75] *The Times*, 10 October 1856, p. 7 col. e and 13 October 1856, p. 7 col. d.
[76] Minutes of Evidence before the Departmental Committee on Income Tax, *HCPP* (1905) (2576) xliv 245, q. 1940 *per* Arthur Chamberlain JP. See too *ibid* q. 1953; *The Times*, 11 March 1854, p. 8 col. a.
[77] TNA: PRO IR 9/2, Form 64 (1868).   [78] See above, p. 99.

before the regular courts of law. That was a complex and formal process which a litigant could not undertake without the assistance of a professional lawyer. The process in both the common law and equity courts was stultified by a dependence on form and a rigorous adherence to complex and detailed rules, exacerbated by fictions, verbosity and repetition.[79] Charles Dickens reinforced popular perceptions of the legal process in many of his works, but notably in *Bleak House* published in 1853. After preliminary procedural reforms in the middle of the nineteenth century,[80] and the introduction of the county court system in 1846,[81] the demand for an accessible system of regular courts ultimately resulted in the complete recasting of the system of superior courts and a uniform code of procedure in the Judicature Acts 1873–1875.[82] This went far towards achieving the 'cheap justice, and near justice, and speedy justice' Henry Brougham had called for forty years before.[83] Nevertheless, litigation in the regular courts remained slow, because the process of writ of summons, indorsements, pleadings, statements of claim, defences, demurrers and interrogatories was technical and complex, with demanding standards of proof and evidence, and a pervasive inflexibility. And this was self-perpetuating, as a complex process required the involvement of lawyers, and that in turn rendered the process complex. So when in 1874 the surveyor and the appellant were permitted to appeal to the High Court by way of case stated on a point of law in income tax cases,[84] though generally welcomed, it was understood that it would expose the taxpayer to considerable potential difficulty. Invoking the developing supervisory jurisdiction of the superior courts was equally difficult.

[79] See First Report of the Common Law Commissioners, *HCPP* (1829) (46) ix 1; First Report of the Commissioners for Inquiring into the Process, Practice and System of Pleading in the Superior Courts of the Common Law', *HCPP* (1851) (1389) xxii 567. See generally The Law Society, *A Compendium of the Practice of the Common Law* (London: R. Hastings, 1847).

[80] 2 Will. IV c. 39 (1832); 3 & 4 Will. IV c. 27 (1833); 15 & 16 Vict. c. 76 (1852); 17 & 18 Vict. c. 125 (1854). See W. S. Holdsworth, 'The New Rules of Pleading of the Hilary Term, 1834', *Cambridge Law Journal* 1 (1923), 26; Baron Bowen, 'Progress in the Administration of Justice during the Victorian Period' in *Select Essays in Anglo-American Legal History*, 3 vols. (Boston: Little, Brown & Co., 1907), vol. i, pp. 516–57.

[81] 9 & 10 Vict. c. 95.

[82] 36 & 37 Vict. c. 66; 38 & 39 Vict. c. 77. See generally W. R. Cornish and G. de N. Clark, *Law and Society in England 1750–1950* (London: Sweet & Maxwell, 1989), pp. 38–45.

[83] *Parl. Deb.*, vol. 18, ser. 3, col. 891, 17 June 1833 (HL). Similar arguments were made in the debates on the Supreme Court of Judicature Bill in 1873, for example by the Attorney General in *Parl. Deb.*, vol. 216, ser. 3, col. 643, 9 June 1873 (HC). See too *ibid.*, vol. 214, ser. 3, col. 337, 13 February 1873 (HL).

[84] See above, pp. 137–9.

Expense

The essential and determining element in the accessibility of the appellate process was that of expense. It is clear that by definition the tax tribunals administering the direct taxes were not for the abject poor: if an individual were paying income tax at all, it meant that his or her income came above the exemption allowed by the taxing Acts. Taxpayers assessed on their luxury goods clearly initially at least had the means to afford them. Accordingly the local lay tribunals were used by the middle and lower middle classes, principally the commercial and professional classes. Nevertheless, if the expense of bringing an appeal were excessive, the great majority of taxpayers would be unable or unwilling to challenge the taxing authorities. The expense of litigation, whether in the fiscal tribunals or in the regular courts, lay partly in any demand for court fees, but primarily in the need to employ lawyers and, to a lesser extent, in the location of the proceedings.

All the fiscal tribunals, including the excise courts, were highly accessible in all these respects. The expenses involved in appealing to them were described as 'trifling'.[85] None charged court fees, and though the fees of solicitors and counsel could be considerable, it was not a widespread problem. The formal prohibition on solicitors or barristers appearing before the income tax commissioners was continued by the Act of 1842,[86] and expressly included in the Taxes Management Act 1880.[87] Parties therefore either represented themselves, or, as in the case of commercial taxpayers appearing before the Special Commissioners, were represented by a partner, director or company officer. In the case of other tax tribunals, legal representation was permitted but never compulsory, and was anyway rendered unnecessary by the informality and simplicity of the procedures. In assessed taxes appeals and cases before the excise court, for example, taxpayers could be represented by an agent if they so chose but in practice rarely were. This mandatory or practical avoidance of legal representation was not with an eye to the accessibility of the tribunal or the benefit of the taxpayer but stemmed from public policy considerations. In the case of a general tax such as the income tax, potential litigants numbered in their thousands, and its unpopularity could only exacerbate any tendency

---

[85] Ninth Report of the Commissioners of Inquiry into the Collection and Management of the Revenue arising in Ireland and Scotland, *HCPP* (1824) (340) xi 305 at Appendix 4 *per* Thomas Carr, solicitor of Excise.

[86] As 43 Geo. III c. 99 s. 26 (1803) was incorporated by reference.

[87] 43 & 44 Vict. c. 19 s. 57 (9).

to appeal. The participation of lawyers in the legal process introduced a 'nicety of discussion, and subtlety of argument'[88] that invariably added to the length and complexity of any proceedings. From the point of view of the government this delay in the expeditious determination of appeals would affect the efficient collection of tax and the consistency of the tax yield.

Though the prohibition of legal representation in the income tax tribunals ensured they were financially accessible to most taxpayers wishing to bring an appeal, it could in another way undermine the very protection the tribunals purported to provide for them. In the regular courts of law, the legal representation of litigants was regarded as essential to fair adjudication and was accepted as one of their most important safeguards. It ensured that evidence was thoroughly tested and the material facts correctly found through rigorous expert oral examination and cross-examination. This was arguably all the more necessary in the lay tax tribunals, where the commissioners' only expert legal knowledge lay in their clerk. There was the added factor of the imbalance of power between the taxpayer and the executive. It was clear that when faced with the power, authority and undoubted experience of the board, ordinary individual taxpayers needed all the help they could get in putting their case properly and effectively to the commissioners. Any potential undermining of the taxpayer's safeguard weighed little, however, when balanced against the government's needs.

The Victorian taxpayer was not quiescent in this respect, and there was a public demand for legal representation. The prohibition had been shown to cause hardship, particularly among female appellants,[89] taxpayers in Wales with limited knowledge of English, and those businessmen who were 'utterly unable to cope with a smart Surveyor of Taxes who had every line of the Statute Law at his finger ends'.[90] It is clear that a practice had grown up of allowing solicitors and barristers to appear before the General Commissioners, at the request of the appellants and with the commissioners' consent, and experience had shown that proceedings had been unchanged in terms of delay and cost. As a result reform followed swiftly, and the right to legal representation was granted in 1898.[91]

---

[88] *Collier* v. *Hicks* (1831) 2 B & Ad 663 at 670 *per* Lord Tenterden CJ.
[89] See the introduction of the new clause by Lord Edmond Fitzmaurice in *Parl. Deb.*, vol. 59, ser. 4, cols. 128–9, 13 June 1898 (HC); Minutes of Evidence before the Departmental Committee on Income Tax, *HCPP* (1905) (2576) xliv 245, q. 55 *per* W. Gayler.
[90] *Parl. Deb.*, vol. 26, ser. 4, col. 749, 2 July 1894 (HC) *per* John Roberts.
[91] 61 & 62 Vict. c. 10 s. 16; 8 & 9 Geo. V c. 40 s. 137 (3) (a) (1918); 13 & 14 Geo. V c. 14 s. 25 (1923).

It was of neutral effect in relation to the localist safeguard, for its benefits of testing evidence were balanced by its disadvantage of expense. Since it was not mandatory it did not increase the inaccessibility of the tribunals. The evidence suggests, furthermore, that despite this demand for, and ultimate granting of, the right to legal representation, it was used only slightly. In cases before the income tax and assessed taxes commissioners, most taxpayers represented themselves, but where in income tax matters they desired professional representation they would appoint an accountant. Not surprisingly, perhaps, they employed tax barristers only for cases where the sums at stake were large, and where a party had the means and the will to fight the board to the highest court, or where the case was taken to the Special Commissioners because of technical complexity.

Whereas legal representation before the tax tribunals was either forbidden or a matter of choice, it was quite another matter if taxpayers took their appeal to the regular courts of law. The formality of the procedures made legal representation necessary, and the complexity and relative novelty of tax as a matter of litigation made tax barristers such as A. M. Bremner both few and highly paid. When the necessary court fees were included, along with the time and attention of the taxpayers, the expense of residence in London and the danger of having costs awarded against them were they to lose the appeal, the scale of the expense was such that the right of appeal to the regular courts was rendered inaccessible to all but the wealthiest litigant. Indeed it was not unreasonable to argue that the more the permitted stages in a tax appeal, the more the safeguard itself was rendered nugatory. Though the appeal by case stated in the assessed taxes was said to be obtained 'with so little trouble or expense as to be scarcely worth mentioning',[92] and that for the income tax 'comparatively inexpensive',[93] it was all relative, and the costs of litigation made most taxpayers reluctant to challenge the central revenue boards in the courts of law. The inequality in the respective standing of the parties was undeniable and meant that the board would have resources few individual taxpayers could match. With the funds of the exchequer behind it, the board not only could and would afford the best counsel it could find, it would not hesitate to fight an adverse decision through every court open to it. Expensive litigation invariably favoured the wealthier party, and this would undermine a fundamental objective of the local tax tribunals, namely to hold the balance between the taxpayer and the

[92] CIR Sixth Report, *HCPP* (1862) (3047) xxvii 327 at pp. 346–7.
[93] CIR Seventeenth Report, *HCPP* (1874) (1098) xv 673 at p. 712.

state. Legislators were aware of this, and whenever appeals to the regular courts were suggested in relation to the new taxes of the nineteenth century, the expense involved was always a matter of concern. The Court of Exchequer was objected to as the appeal court for the succession duty on the basis of the enormous expenses involved. And when it was initially proposed that a taxpayer should pay the whole liability to the new estate duty in 1894 before being permitted to appeal against the valuation of the estate, there was strong criticism in Parliament on the grounds that it compounded the expense involved and rendered the appellate safeguard unusable.

Location

Another significant factor contributing to the expense, and therefore the accessibility, of tax appeals, was that of the distance taxpayers had to travel to put their case to a tribunal or a court. Though travel was easier in the 1830s than it had ever been, with the public benefiting from the improvements in road building of the previous century, it was by no means easy. Carriages were the preserve of the wealthy, and for most people travel was on horseback or on foot. This was restricted by the weather, and entailed personal practical difficulty. The greater the distance to travel, the more time taxpayers would have to spend away from their trade or employment, and the greater the expense of securing board and lodging away from home. The location of tax appeal hearings was, accordingly, an issue of real practical importance. In 1833 the House of Commons was told how nine farmers had to appear before the tax commissioners fourteen miles from their home, on a market day, to find that no evidence was adduced against them for sporting without a licence.[94] Indeed, the distance litigants had to travel to recover small debts, in some instances some fifty miles to recover a debt of less than forty shillings, was one of the problems which gave rise to the creation of the county courts in 1846, and when new tribunals were established in relation to the restructuring of land rights in the 1830s and 1840s, the importance of an easily accessible location in the locality and its effect of keeping the cost of summoning witnesses to a minimum was clearly recognised. Location was a real problem with appeals to the superior courts in London. The inconvenience and expense to a litigant of court proceedings in the capital had been a major complaint against the regular courts for years. The cost to the parties of taking themselves

---

[94] *Parl. Deb.*, vol. 17, ser. 3, col. 799, 30 April 1833 (HC) *per* William Cobbett.

and their witnesses to London, and remaining there for the possibly long duration of the trial, rendered much litigation prohibitively expensive. In this respect the lay tax tribunals, like the Justices of the Peace, were highly accessible, for they sat in small divisions over the whole country, and in general taxpayers were never far from a panel to hear their case. This high degree of geographical accessibility meant that complaints were few.

Even the Special Commissioners of Income Tax, who constituted a notable exception to the localism of income tax administration, were equally accessible in a physical sense. Although they were based in London their duties extended over the whole country, and 'for the convenience of taxpayers' they went on circuit all over the country, once or twice a year for some three or four weeks, solely to hear appeals. In practice they sat in the main towns and cities, in 1849 visiting twenty-seven towns and cities in England, from Truro to Newcastle.[95] Any geographical inaccessibility in the small towns where the Special Commissioners did not sit was mitigated to some extent by the expansion of the railways, but significantly so by the new facility of the uniform penny post, whereby all letters were charged by weight and at the flat rate of one penny per ounce, irrespective of the distance. This had been introduced by Rowland Hill in the third year of Victoria's reign, and it was soon enthusiastically adopted by the tax tribunals. The availability of fast, reliable and cheap postage enabled some appeals to be settled without requiring personal attendance at a hearing, and cut down considerably on the potential expense to individual taxpayers.[96]

Within the local centres too the specific venues for appeal hearings were generally convenient. There was little concern in the nineteenth century with the appropriateness of the buildings in which hearings were held, no awareness of any desirability to strike a balance between the formality appropriate to judicial or quasi-judicial proceedings and the informality necessary to prevent the intimidation of an appellant. Local tax commissioners usually sat in a local hotel, inn or coffee house, or used the same courtrooms as those used by the Justices of the Peace. The Special Commissioners heard most appeals at their own offices in London, and

[95] Minutes of Evidence before the Select Committee on the Income and Property Tax, *HCPP* (1852) (354) ix 1, qq. 1068–71, 1106 *per* James Dickens, Special Commissioner; Minutes of Evidence before the Select Committee on Inland Revenue and Customs Establishments, *HCPP* (1863) (424) vi 303, q. 2511; Minutes of Evidence before the Royal Commission on the Income Tax, *HCPP* (1919) (288) xxiii, q. 13,730 *per* G. F. Howe, Presiding Special Commissioner.

[96] TNA: PRO IR 86/2, Board Minute, 8 October 1850.

when out on circuit they sat at an hotel or at the offices of the surveyor, all of which were convenient for the taxpayer.

Where communications were difficult, the organisation of appeal hearings was all the more important. Taxpayers appealing to or summoned to appear at a distant court should not, having made the journey, find their case was not being heard. This was an important issue in the debates as to the provision for the trial of excise prosecutions in Ireland, communication in that country remaining difficult for most of the nineteenth century. There were frequent complaints throughout the century at appellants before the General Commissioners being summoned all at the same time, and obliged to wait, often for many hours in uncomfortable conditions, to be heard.

Expert advice

Such was the complexity and technicality of tax law and practice that the need for expert advice and assistance was self-evident. There were a number of sources of such advice, namely the clerk or other subordinate officials of the local commissioners, the surveyor, the central board itself, the members of the legal profession and the emerging accountancy profession. The evidence suggests that the provision of advice from all these increased throughout the nineteenth century, as tax became more complicated and taxpayers found themselves unable to manage their tax affairs entirely on their own. Certainly taxpayers became more demanding in the Victorian period, being largely members of the emerging middle class, a class with unprecedented power and influence in national life. It comprised businessmen, bankers, lawyers, medical doctors, clergymen, civil servants and shopkeepers. As a class they were self-reliant, educated and commercially astute, as well as possessing considerable confidence in themselves and indeed in their country's political and economic standing.

Although the names of the various local tax commissioners in each district were publicised in city directories,[97] taxpayers could not approach them directly for advice any more than they could a judge of the regular courts. Their subordinate officials, however, being well known to the taxpaying public, were an obvious source of information and guidance.

---

[97] In Exeter, as in most cities, the *Directories* named the lay commissioners for all taxes: *Besley's Exeter Directory for 1835* (Exeter: Henry Besley, 1835), p. 9; *Household Almanack* (Exeter: William Pollard & Co., 1891), p. 19. Furthermore, from 1869 the names of persons qualified to act as Land Tax Commissioners were to be published in the *London Gazette*: 32 & 33 Vict. c. 64.

The clerk was not as expert in tax practice as the surveyor, and lacked the ear of the board, but he did possess the considerable advantage of being perceived as being on the taxpayer's side and not tainted by any government connection. Taxpayers constantly went to his office seeking advice on completing returns, to question a particular assessment, for a view on the meaning of a statutory provision or for advice as to how to appeal or claim a repayment. And since the public was not admitted to the hearings of the income tax commissioners, the clerk, as one of the few persons familiar with the substance and machinery of the process, was very frequently asked as to the conduct of appeal hearings. The local assessors too were often approached for advice. Though lacking any profound tax knowledge, they were in the front line of tax administration, delivering and collecting the returns, and it was inevitable that they would be asked for advice on the doorstep if taxpayers had experienced any difficulties in this first stage of the assessment process. It was argued before the Royal Commission on the Income Tax in 1920 that assessors were essential to the large body of poorer taxpayers.[98]

As the surveyor came to dominate the administration of tax in the nineteenth century, so he became the principal source of advice for taxpayers[99] and the ultimate one for the assessors, clerks, and often the local commissioners too. So though clerks and surveyors vied with each other for recognition as the provider of expert advice to the taxpayer, it was the surveyor who came to be acknowledged as the source of accurate and authoritative advice and information. He was recognised from the first days of the reintroduction of the income tax as the expert in the field, who not only understood local conditions and the tax laws, but equally knew the policies and usages of his board. These practices, central to tax administration, were available to the public only through the medium of the surveyor. Not being remunerated by poundage he had no personal interest and had no reason to give anything other than honest advice and fully to inform the taxpayers of the options open to them. Although the surveyor was the representative of the taxing authority, with an overriding duty to protect the interests of the crown, there was a traditional ethos and expectation within the service that officers should act impartially and with integrity and skill. The chairman of the Board of Inland Revenue said in 1862 that the surveyor 'always acts as adviser' and was constantly

---

[98] Minutes of Evidence before the Royal Commission on the Income Tax, *HCPP* (1919) (288) xxiii, q. 23,890; see too q. 23,983 *per* Randle Holme, on behalf of the Law Society.
[99] David Williams, 'Surveying Taxes, 1900–14', *BTR* (2005), 222 at 229.

available to the taxpaying public to respond to queries[100] and by 1878 the board itself was recommending the surveyor as a ready source of explanation or information.[101] When approached, therefore, the surveyor was generally prepared to discuss the taxpayers' tax affairs with them and advise them as to the law. Despite a considerable burden of work on the surveyor, taxpayers were sufficiently few in number for this to be a practical possibility. Whether a taxpayer approached the surveyor personally depended on the character of the surveyor and his standing in the community. All surveyors worked in a degree of social isolation caused by both the nature of the work and the constant moving between districts insisted on by the board, but if a surveyor were known as an independent and just man, taxpayers tended to approach him. If he was perceived as a 'government man', they tended to rely on other sources of advice. The officers of the central boards gave advice in relation to whichever tax came within their personal remit. In relation to the stamp duties, for example, taxpayers with simple queries would normally go to their local stamp offices for advice, though stamp distributors were under no duty to give it, and often did not possess sufficient knowledge to do so, in which case it became largely a matter of chance. Taxpayers in the metropolis had access to more skilled advice, so where they had complex queries in relation to the stamp duties they could call at Somerset House. Charles Trevor, the comptroller of the legacy and succession duties, while the subject of considerable popular hostility,[102] repeatedly stated, although somewhat unfortunately, that his office was 'as open as a police office' for advice to any taxpayer who cared to come in.[103] The board's officers were, furthermore, geographically accessible, for though the central boards came to dislike localism in tax administration, they were not opposed to decentralisation. To assist the public and promote its own internal efficiency, the Board of Inland Revenue not only ensured that offices of its various branches were situated across the country, with an officer in all the principal towns, but also

---

[100] Minutes of Evidence before the Select Committee on Inland Revenue and Customs Establishments, *HCPP* (1862) (370) xii 131, q. 504 *per* Charles Pressly.

[101] CIR Twentieth Report, *HCPP* (1878) (1896) xxvi 593 at p. 646. Occasionally the surveyor gave general advice through the medium of the local newspaper, as when in 1843 the Exeter surveyor published a letter in which he carefully explained the nature of income tax appeal proceedings: see *Trewman's Exeter Flying Post*, 12 January and 19 January 1843.

[102] See *The Times*, 4 August 1864, p. 6 col. b; 5 August 1864, p. 4 col. d; 13 August 1864, p. 7 col. e; 13 August 1864, p. 8 col. d; 16 August 1864, p. 5 col. f; CIR Tenth Report, *HCPP* (1866) (3724) xxvi 131 at pp. 148–62.

[103] Minutes of Evidence before the Select Committee on Inland Revenue and Customs Establishments, *HCPP* (1862) (370) xii 131, qq. 2155, 2244, 2283–5.

as far as possible located together.[104] Only in Ireland, where the districts were large and surveyors usually lived in Dublin, were there recorded difficulties of access, with taxpayers having to make long rail journeys to discuss their assessments.[105]

In advising taxpayers, however, it was the board which could potentially play an active role in protecting them against any incursion of their fundamental right resulting from external factors such as the complexity and ambiguity of tax legislation, or again the inexperience or ignorance of local tax officials. During the nineteenth century there developed a practice of taxpayers directly consulting the central boards. Early in the century this practice was particularly prevalent in relation to the excise, as a result of the prominence of that tax, the complexity of its laws and the central importance of the Board of Excise in their administration. The board, however, was found wanting, for the official inquiries of the 1830s revealed an almost total lack of communication between it and the traders and a pervasive and ingrained culture of inaccessibility. The board ignored routine technical queries or delayed in replying to them. 'We have never heard from them; we never get a direct answer; they take no notice',[106] complained a papermaker in 1835. In many instances communications were often not even acknowledged, and so traders did not know if their letters had reached the board.[107] Furthermore, even if the board did respond, it refused to provide a full written response with reasons, and relied instead on the oral communication of the mere decision through an officer. This was to save time and to ensure that no written statement could be used against the board in future communication or litigation but it often left the trader uncertain as to the correctness or scope of the decision.[108] As a result, taxpayers were reluctant to petition the board, even if they had been injured in some way, and felt this 'most severely'.[109] The stern

---

[104] CIR First Report, *HCPP* (1857) (2199 sess. 1) iv 65 at p. 116.

[105] Minutes of Evidence before the Royal Commission on the Income Tax, *HCPP* (1919) (288) xxiii, q. 13,740 *per* G. F. Howe.

[106] Fourteenth Report of the Commissioners of Inquiry into the Excise Establishment (Paper), *HCPP* (1835) (16) xxxi 159 at p. 285 *per* John Gater.

[107] Seventeenth Report of the Commissioners of Inquiry (Soap), *HCPP* (1836) (20) xxvi 1 at p. 94 Appendix 51 *per* William Hawes; Fourteenth Report of the Commissioners of Inquiry into the Excise Establishment (Paper), *HCPP* (1835) (16) xxxi 159 at p. 182.

[108] See, for example, the views of the principal distillers in Cork in Seventh Report of the Commissioners of Inquiry into the Excise Establishment (British Spirits Part 1), *HCPP* (1834) (7) xxv 1 at p.179.

[109] Fourteenth Report of the Commissioners of Inquiry into the Excise Establishment (Paper), *HCPP* (1835) (16) xxxi 159 at p. 182.

criticism of the Commissioners of Excise Inquiry in 1835[110] had a salutary effect on the board, for by 1862 it was said that the traders' queries were not only directly answered, but were incessant and increasing enormously in number.[111] The attitude of the board at the beginning of Victoria's reign had been particularly objectionable in the context of the complex and punitive excise laws, but all the more so because it was in striking contrast with the practice in the other revenue boards of customs, stamps and taxes. The Board of Inland Revenue was remarkably accessible to the taxpayer, with much of its daily business consisting of applications from individuals about their own personal assessment. The minute books of the board abound with examples of minor queries from taxpayers of all kinds, in relation to all the taxes within the board's charge, answered individually with patience and courtesy. The board would clearly go even further and meet taxpayers in person on request.[112] In the twenty years following the reintroduction of the income tax the number of such inquiries rose considerably.

Taxpayers could turn for advice outside the specialist tax world to their own solicitor. Although the work of such lawyers was often dominated by conveyancing,[113] it inevitably included taxation matters. For most of the nineteenth century taxation was a pervasive if not major element of solicitors' work, demanding a familiarity with stamp duties, the land tax[114] and all death duties, and when income tax entered the era of case law in 1874 great opportunities were given to solicitors as well as barristers as a new field of operation opened up for them.[115] The formal and legalistic approach to the interpretation of taxing Acts certainly ensured, whether

---

[110] *Ibid.*

[111] Minutes of Evidence before the Select Committee on Inland Revenue and Customs Establishments, *HCPP* (1862) (370) xii 131, qq. 1341, 1658 *per* Thomas Dobson, Principal Secretary, Board of Inland Revenue.

[112] Minutes of Board of Inland Revenue, 22 January 1849: TNA: PRO: IR 31/141.

[113] Avner Offer, *Property and Politics, 1870–1914: Landownership, Law Ideology and Urban Development in England* (Cambridge University Press, 1981), pp. 11–20, 31–2.

[114] When in 1843 an equalisation of the assessment for the land tax took place in Exeter, the parishes benefiting from the measure raised money to cover the expenses of the solicitors who had so expertly advised them, and presented them with a purse of fifty guineas: *Trewman's Exeter Flying Post*, 13 April 1843.

[115] R. Cocks, 'Victorian Barristers, Judges and Taxation: A Study in the Expansion of Legal Work' in G. R. Rubin and David Sugarman (eds.), *Law, Economy and Society, 1750–1914: Essays in the History of English Law* (Abingdon: Professional Books Ltd, 1984), pp. 445–69, at pp. 445–6. See too David Sugarman, 'Simple Images and Complex Realities: English Lawyers and their Relationship to Business and Politics, 1750–1950', *Law and History Review* 11 (1993), 257 at 277.

deliberately or not, that lawyers were essential figures in the process,[116] though solicitors, like members of Parliament, judges and taxpayers, were often baffled by matters of tax law and the often incomprehensible legislation.[117] Moreover, solicitors did not have access to the official practices of the central boards, nor their interpretation of tax legislation, which were of vital importance in advising clients. Solicitors often had to consult the assessors, valuing their detailed local knowledge and their easy accessibility. They also perceived the assessor to be relatively independent of the case at issue, for he did not represent the taxpayer to the extent the surveyor represented the board. By the end of Victoria's reign the tax work of solicitors had greatly increased, stimulated in part by high exemption limits which gave many taxpayers the right to rebates. As a body too the legal profession began assisting the taxpayer, with the new Incorporated Law Society bringing particular problems in the tax law to the notice of Parliament. The Victorian taxpayer could also have recourse to the emerging accountancy profession. For the whole of the Victorian period the accountant was unable to oust the solicitor from his position as tax adviser, but after the First World War, when rates rose and the number of taxpayers continued to grow, so he undertook more tax work, particularly on behalf of commercial clients.[118] He would come to match the surveyor in his technical knowledge and understanding of tax matters[119] and to surpass the solicitor.[120] So while the poorer taxpayer relied on the assessor, clerk or surveyor for advice, the wealthier traders and companies made use of accountants both for advice and to negotiate with the surveyor directly and attempt to arrive at some kind of settlement. Accountants and their clients, observed a solicitor in 1919, 'are quite able to take care of themselves'.[121] In the twentieth century the accountant would establish himself firmly in the tax world, both at the administrative

---

[116] Cocks, 'Victorian Barristers', pp. 449–51. Professor Cocks concludes that the bench and bar of the late nineteenth century did not have a sufficiently coherent identity to make this a deliberate policy.

[117] Minutes of Evidence before the Select Committee on Inland Revenue and Customs Establishments, *HCPP* (1863) (424) vi 303, q. 427 *per* Christopher Bushell, wine and spirit merchant. See generally John Prebble, 'Why is Tax Law incomprehensible?', *BTR* (1994), 380.

[118] Wyn Griffith, *A Hundred Years, The Board of Inland Revenue 1849–1949* (London: Inland Revenue, 1949), pp. 40–1.

[119] See Martin Daunton, *Trusting Leviathan: the Politics of Taxation in Britain, 1799–1914* (Cambridge University Press, 2001), pp. 200–4.

[120] Minutes of Evidence before the Royal Commission on the Income Tax, *HCPP* (1919) (288) xxiii, qq. 15,992–4 *per* A. M. Bremner.

[121] *Ibid.*, q. 23,890 *per* Randle Holme.

stage of taxation and as the preferred expert representative before the local tax commissioners.[122]

Finally, a taxpayer could attempt to seek advice from a self-help organisation. In the earlier years of the nineteenth century these tended to take the form of pressure groups campaigning for the reform of certain aspects of the tax laws to lessen the burden on specific groups of taxpayers. One example of many is the Liverpool Financial Reform Association which in 1849 led a campaign against the burden of customs and excise duties on trade and industry.[123] Membership of the association was open to all on payment of 5 shillings per annum, but for 10 shillings the member was entitled to the association's publications, some of which directly addressed taxation issues. But it was the Income Taxpayers' Society which was the most important of the self-help groups, though one which came into existence after the close of the Victorian period. It campaigned actively in the 1920s and 1930s to improve the lot of the ordinary taxpayer. It had an expert staff which assisted all taxpayers, rich and poor, who were in need of advice on income tax matters and lobbied members in the house on income tax issues.[124]

Conclusion

The nineteenth century saw an increased awareness of accessibility as an issue, an appreciation that law should be understandable and that expensive justice was no justice, but it saw relatively slight improvement. The inherent nature of tax law and a governmental inertia towards addressing a topic of difficulty and potential loss to the revenue meant that there was little material alleviation of the difficulties of access to the primary sources of tax law[125] and a total failure to simplify tax forms. As a matter of knowledge and understanding, public accessibility showed some minor improvement during the nineteenth century only through a stronger culture of giving advice from the organs of the central revenue boards. Access to the regular courts was improved through the general reform of court procedures in the 1850s and the major restructuring of the

---

[122] David Stopforth, 'Settlements and the Avoidance of Tax on Income – the Period to 1920', *BTR* (1990), 225 at 242–4.

[123] Liverpool Financial Reform Association, *Address of the Council of the Liverpool Financial Reform Association to the Tax-Payers of the United Kingdom* (London: printed at office of The Standard of Freedom, 1849).

[124] *The Times*, 23 July 1926, p. 11 col. c.

[125] Though see Manchester, *Modern Legal History*, p. 32.

courts themselves in the 1870s, and as the movement made no distinction between tax and other matters, the taxpayer benefited from these easier and cheaper appeals. The question of the expense of legal representation was untouched, however, and while the introduction of the appeal by case stated strengthened the appellate safeguard, it was itself undermined by its technicality and attendant expense. The remaining faults of the regular court system were, however, of marginal significance to taxpayers, since they benefited from a highly accessible system of first-tier appeals to the various fiscal tribunals, which, whatever their shortcomings, were undoubtedly cheap, expeditious and entirely informal and which, in practical terms, obviated the need for further appeal in the vast majority of cases. The improvements to accessibility were thus piecemeal, and in many instances balanced by consequent disadvantages.

A consideration of the accessibility of the safeguards which characterised the relationship of the taxpayer with the law reveals the perception which the organs of the executive had of their own functions and the place of the taxpayer. It is seen that access to the safeguards was as much controlled by the executive as were the safeguards themselves. The central boards' caution in pressing for the reform, consolidation and simplification of tax law was the result of a fear of disruption to the fiscal process. It was also the result of the insular and close-knit culture of the nineteenth-century civil service,[126] for that bred a certain detachment from the wider context of its activity, and a lack of sensitivity to the needs and aspirations of the taxpaying public. This was exacerbated by the revenue boards' total familiarity with the law, practice and institutions of tax, for it became harder for them to appreciate the problems the taxpayer experienced in this respect. Indeed, the familiarity of tax officers with the legislation often made them underestimate its difficulty,[127] as when in 1862 the chairman of the Board of Inland Revenue said of income tax that 'it is so simple that there can be no difficulty in understanding it'.[128] Many observers also wondered whether tax was kept deliberately obscure to prevent its mastery by taxpayers and indeed by members of Parliament.[129] Either way,

---

[126] See generally Daunton, *Trusting Leviathan*, pp. 180–223. See too *The Times*, 17 October 1866, p. 10 col. c.

[127] Minutes of Evidence before the Royal Commission on the Income Tax, *HCPP* (1919) (288) xxiii, q. 15,992 *per* A. M. Bremner.

[128] Minutes of Evidence before the Select Committee on Inland Revenue and Customs Establishments, *HCPP* (1862) (370) xii 131, q. 500 *per* Charles Pressly.

[129] See, for example, TNA: PRO IR 40/5274, Income Tax Codification Committee Bill Memoranda (1937–47).

it left the central boards pre-eminent in this respect. Their reluctance to publish their own regulations and practice whereby they administered the laws stemmed from a fear that they would be committed by them. It was above all in relation to the Special Commissioners of Income Tax that more disturbing official attitudes to the accessibility of legal safeguards for the taxpayer are revealed. The board's inertia in publicising them stemmed from an appreciation that it was the very existence of the right to appeal to this inexpensive and efficient tribunal, and a few cases to confirm it in the public mind, which were of real value to the public revenue, for it encouraged compliance. From that perspective its actual use was not necessary. Indeed, any extensive use following wide publicity might have led to a substantial increase in litigation which would delay the fiscal process. Too many appeals, like too much knowledge, could hinder the collection of the public revenue. And so the tribunal's inaccessibility through its limited promotion was nothing less than an expression of the board's control. Lacking a real incentive to publicise any appellate tribunal, the evidence suggests that the board paid lip service to publicity, rarely being proactive in that respect, and was somewhat disingenuous in its repeatedly expressed concern as to its minimal use.[130] Even in their provision of advice, which the boards did increasingly in the nineteenth century, they did so on their own terms. Accessibility was desirable only insofar as it promoted compliance with tax process, and accordingly the central boards, as far as they could, astutely kept the legislation, practice and legal process of tax firmly within their own control. Only well-informed, robust and articulate taxpayers could penetrate the system; for the great majority, they had little choice but to accept the views and the decisions of the central boards without question.

---

[130]   CIR First Report, *HCPP* (1857) (2199 sess. 1) iv 65 at p. 96. In 1868–9 there were nearly 2,400 special assessments out of a total of 380,000 people assessed under Schedule D: CIR Thirteenth Report *HCPP* (1870) (82, 82–1) xx 193, 377 at p. 328.

6

The taxpayer, the constitution and consent

The Victorian taxpayer's protection under the law

A number of factors combined to force a re-evaluation of the traditional relationship between the taxpayer and the law in the nineteenth century. These included changes in fiscal policy and culture, shifting ideologies, rapidly increasing national wealth, the sophistication of commerce and industry and the pragmatic and political demands arising from these. English law had always recognised the inequality inherent in the relationship between the state and the taxpayer, and had made provision to place them, as far as possible, on an equal footing before it to ensure the taxpayer was not subjected to any illegal exaction. This it did by giving extra, and special, protection to the taxpayer as such, and that protection lay primarily in founding the legal right to impose taxes in the taxpayer's own consent and the legal authority to administer them in the hands of his or her own representatives. It has been seen that by the start of the Great War in 1914, when the world took on a greater fight to defend its fundamental freedoms, the three safeguards constructed by the law and for the maintenance of which the civil war of the seventeenth century had in part been fought, had been significantly undermined. They had been revealed as outdated and restrictive,[1] pragmatically if not ideologically, unacceptably impeding the efficient collection of the public revenue and the implementation of its wider policies, which central government demanded. Taxes were no longer imposed only by the taxpayers' representatives in Parliament after full debate and investigation prior to being administered by their local and independent lay representatives. By the Parliament Act 1911 the imposition of tax had become a matter entirely for the lower house, with any authority in the House of Lords having been formally eclipsed by the will of the House of Commons and indeed ejected

---

[1] See, for example, Robert Colley, 'Mid-Victorian Employees and the Taxman: A Study in Information Gathering by the State in 1860', *Oxford Journal of Legal Studies* 21 (2001), 593.

entirely from the process. Furthermore, by the Provisional Collection of Taxes Act 1913 the Commons legally could impose a tax by mere parliamentary resolution, albeit temporarily. The administration of the direct taxes now resembled that of the indirect taxes, for the local commissioners and their staff no longer undertook the task in its entirety, it having been transferred elsewhere in large measure. The notable exception to the undermining of the law's protection for the taxpayer lay in the judicial sphere. The judicial safeguard was not only maintained, but expanded, achieved principally through a combination of judicial self-interest and robust political independence. Overall, however, the legal protection afforded to the taxpayer by the law had been materially diminished by the end of the Victorian period.

It was not merely that the safeguards had as such been eroded, it was the instrument and the victor of that erosion which was of particular significance to the taxpayer. The potency of the law's protection had lain in the requirement enshrined in the law that the imposition and administration of taxation be undertaken by institutions independent of the executive. By the end of the Victorian period it was this very independence that had been formally or covertly diminished. It was the executive, precisely the organ from which independence had been sought, that had pervaded the traditional safeguards of the law and encroached so as to render them if not nugatory, then considerably less robust in 1914 than they had been at the beginning of the reign. The exercise of arbitrary powers by the executive was the result of the nature of the tax legislation, the demands of a bureaucracy of growing sophistication and momentum, and the inevitable tension between centralism and localism in tax administration. Although such powers might well be necessary in practice, their very existence undermined the legal protection of the taxpayer.

Though the fundamental right of the taxpayer to be taxed only by Parliament was in legal theory unaffected by the right and duty in the central revenue boards to ensure the care and management of the revenue, the taxpayer was, by the end of the Victorian period, overwhelmed by their power and authority. This was despite a determination to ensure the control of taxation and finance was in the democratically elected House of Commons and not in either the House of Lords or the executive. Other elements in the legal sphere facilitated the undermining of the legal safeguards by the executive, elements which were less evident, obscured by certain rigid divisions within the law and traditional classification and not necessarily grounded in substantive rules of tax law or procedure. Of particular significance were the physical and intellectual inaccessibility of the substantive and procedural rules of tax law and the inevitable dominance of the internal quasi-legal rules and practices of the executive in its administration of tax. The selective inertia of the executive in relation to the accessibility of the safeguards themselves compounded its dominance. Only on their own terms would the boards permit easier access to a law which only they understood, to an administrative practice which they controlled, and to institutions which they dominated. The central boards came to control the administration of all taxes from the middle of the nineteenth century and, like any department of the executive, they had resources and expertise which placed them in a considerably stronger position than the ordinary taxpayer. Furthermore, their statutory duty to manage the public revenue, the extensive powers they were given to do so, the natural development of a bureaucracy with its internal rules and practices, a strong united culture and the lack of any robust control, served to strengthen their position and power inexorably. The taxpayers' vulnerability to the dominance of the executive was increased through the lack of any established complaints procedure they could follow if they had a grievance as to the administration of tax by the central boards, for the Ombudsman, the Revenue Adjudicator and human rights legislation were safeguards of a later age. They could appeal against an assessment to the various bodies of commissioners, and sometimes to the courts of law, but they had no formal remedy for poor administration, for any mistakes made, or delays in the handling of their tax affairs, or any incompetence in the central boards. They could only hope for redress out of their bounty. If taxpayers had overpaid as the result of a mistake of law they could do nothing. Taxpayers could only petition the boards, the Treasury and Parliament to air their grievances.[2] Finally, while the exercise of the judicial power of the state was legally and constitutionally in the hands of the judges of the regular courts of law, even here the executive exerted its influence. As tax adjudication could legitimately be argued to be part of the administrative process of assessment to tax, it came under the control of the executive and was left, until the very end of the Victorian period, largely outside the control of the regular courts.

The taxpayer's traditional legal safeguards had lost their essential independence and had become in many instances little more than the tools of the bureaucracy, with the taxpayer reduced to dependence on civil servants, albeit expert and responsible officers of integrity who were not

[2] See Sir Norman Chester, *The English Administrative System 1780–1870* (Oxford: Clarendon Press, 1981), p. 112.

insensitive to the nature of the constitutional rules underlying taxation in England.[3] Though the revenue authorities saw themselves as the 'guardians of the Revenue',[4] it increasingly seemed to the taxpayers that the delicate balance which the law had achieved between them and the infinitely more powerful interests of the state had been upset, and that it had swung towards the government, thereby compromising their essential protection in the constitutional requirement for their consent. The past struggles which had been fought to restrain the executive's power to tax now seemed in vain. Tax had become professional and bureaucratic. The executive had undermined the law's protection of the taxpayer, and had emerged dominant, with the law seeming both powerless and indifferent.

It has been seen that the undermining of the legal safeguards by the increasing dominance of the executive was principally effected through informal practices, and as such was generally not reflected in the legislation. There was, in this respect, a striking dislocation between the theoretical legal position and its actual application. At the close of the nineteenth century the provision in the Bill of Rights that taxes could only be imposed by Parliament remained in full theoretical force. Every charge imposed upon the taxpayer had to be embodied in a statute properly passed by Parliament. However, the provision had been undermined in practice by the growing influence of the Commons over the Lords and the domination of the former by the executive. Legally, the Parliament referred to in the Bill of Rights, and whose consent to taxation was necessary, constituted the Commons, Lords and crown. In practice, however, the House of Commons jealously maintained its traditional usage of dominance in tax matters to the exclusion of the Lords. Ultimately of course, it was given statutory expression in the Parliament Act 1911 and was then no longer a matter of debate. What was equally clear, and not reflected in the legislation, was that there was a traditional domination of the House of Commons by the executive, and it was in this that the fundamental safeguard of parliamentary consent was most forcibly undermined in real terms in the nineteenth century. The development was a gradual one, culminating in the legal imposition, albeit temporarily, of tax by parliamentary resolution in 1913, a development which undoubtedly increased the power of government.

But there had been earlier, more insidious, undermining, notably the growth of the party system and the corresponding weakening of the influence of the private member, as well as the limitation on time for

---

[3] See H. H. Monroe, 'The Constitution in Danger', *BTR* (1969), 24.
[4] CIR Second Report, *HCPP* (1857–8) (2387) xxv 477 at p. 497.

debate due to the introduction of procedural restrictions. Furthermore, the undoubted ability of the Commons to reject or amend the tax proposals of the government was rendered almost worthless by the inability of many individual members fully to understand the subject-matter of tax legislation. Growing pressures on parliamentary time combined with increasingly voluminous and technical legislation to put tax statutes beyond the full comprehension of ordinary members of the house. The executive thus dominated in this respect, for it conceived and drafted the legislation in line with its own policies, and was accordingly considerably better informed and understanding of the detail than the rank and file of parliamentary members. Though debate was limited in both time and quality, some debate necessarily took place, and the government could, to some extent, be held to account for its tax proposals. Furthermore, the executive was unable to tax by regulation, nor could it attempt to impose a tax under another guise. Nevertheless, the outcome was an unambiguous legal provision that tax could only be levied with the consent of Parliament, and a practical application and development which meant that consent was a mere formal consent to the will of the executive. The legal requirement for parliamentary consent was thus, as a safeguard, robust in law but materially diminished in practice.

The same dislocation between law and practice arising from the undermining of the safeguard through practice without reflecting it in the formal law is seen even more strikingly in relation to the legal safeguard which dominated the law of taxpayer protection during the formative years of the modern fiscal and legal systems in the nineteenth century. This was the taxpayers' right to have their direct taxes, notably the income tax, administered by their fellow taxpayers in the locality. Statute continued expressly to provide that the taxes in question were to be implemented by local lay commissioners, with the executive officers having merely the supervision of them, but it had become in practice a shadow of its theoretical self and had collapsed in all but name by the end of Victoria's reign. The duties of the lay commissioners had come to be fulfilled almost in their entirety by the executive officer and their role reduced to a formality. As with formal parliamentary consent, the undermining had received some statutory recognition, but for the most part the diminishing of the local commissioners' role and the ascendancy of that of the surveyor to the extent that he was described as the 'pivotal figure' in the income tax administration[5] was the outcome of informal usage.

[5] Report of the Royal Commission on the Income Tax, *HCPP* (1920) (615) xviii 97 at para. 375.

The loss of any effective independent scrutiny of tax assessments to act as a buffer between the taxpayer and the state meant that to Victorian taxpayers this legal safeguard was ineffectual. They recognised that this was a clear extension of bureaucratic control at the expense of local control.[6] They were at the mercy of the executive, and though for the most part the government official was both expert and honourable, he was not independent. It could still operate as a safeguard where the commissioners were conscientious and well informed, but that was increasingly unlikely and difficult. The Royal Commission on the Income Tax in 1920 acknowledged this dislocation between theory and practice, but admitted that had it not happened, the machinery of income tax administration would have been 'hopelessly inadequate'.[7]

Popular support for change

In harmony with the age, the Victorian taxpayer was generally inquiring, open-minded and receptive to change. The intense curiosity many Victorians showed about art, literature, history, science, medicine and the natural world was continued into the more prosaic sphere of government and social and legal institutions, including taxation. The Victorian age saw legal concepts and devices addressed, examined, reformed, refined and developed, and, thus adapted, playing their full part in the vibrant society of Victorian England. And so in an age which was dominated by a culture of social and political inquiry, debate and reform, and was pervaded by new ideas and perspectives, taxpayers understood that their traditional protective relationship with the law might legitimately require a re-evaluation and possible reform to suit it to a new dynamic commercial society. Many taxpayers were aware of the shortcomings of the safeguards, revealed to them through personal experience, that of their friends and colleagues, correspondence in the newspapers, the growing number of journals addressing issues of contemporary life and, significantly, through the many detailed investigations into every aspect of the tax system which took place regularly throughout the nineteenth century. Chambers of Commerce and professional organisations also played their part in publicising tax issues. With a popular appreciation of the weaknesses of the legal safeguards, some adjustments to them were likely

---

[6] *Parl. Deb.*, vol. 76, ser. 5, col. 1118, 6 December 1915 (HC) *per* George Barnes. See too *The Times*, 25 October 1915, p. 9 col. e and 26 October 1915, p. 10 col. b.
[7] Report of the Royal Commission on the Income Tax, *HCPP* (1920) (615) xviii 97 at para. 331.

to be acceptable to the taxpaying public, and indeed some support was articulated.

Accordingly, Victorian taxpayers recognised the weaknesses of the parliamentary process for enacting the legislation imposing taxes. They understood that strictly the safeguard comprised the consent of both the House of Commons and the House of Lords, but saw the dangers in allowing the Lords too great a role in the taxation process. It was, indeed, a fear addressed by the constitutional usage of limiting the upper house's powers in this respect and making the Commons, the only representative chamber, supreme in matters of taxation. To remove the Lords from any role in the tax process would support this usage and would reinforce taxation by a representative body. And so when the Lords purported to reject the paper duty bill in 1860, most taxpayers objected because the popular consensus was that the upper house had exceeded its authority and that the Commons should stand firm to ensure that the safeguard of representative consent to taxation was maintained. One member of Parliament, having met with his constituents on the matter, warned the house of the 'dangerous elements' who could be aroused and agitated by such an action.[8] Protest meetings were held all over the country, many yielding large petitions. One meeting in London was attended by representatives from fifty of the principal towns in England,[9] and another in Birmingham was attended by some two hundred protestors.[10] These events were publicised by placards bearing slogans such as 'Is the House of Lords to govern the finances of the people and the country?'[11] The radical Liberal John Bright observed that however inadequately the House of Commons represented the people on matters of taxation, yet its members could protest in the name of their constituents against any injustice the government might try to inflict upon them. The House of Lords, being unelected, included no representatives of the people. 'What would become of the liberty of England', he asked, 'if any irresponsible, unelected, hereditary House of Parliament was to be committed, without check, to rifle the pockets and tills of the industrious populations of this country?'[12] There was an appreciation that this was an issue going well beyond the tax sphere, and there was a serious questioning of the role of representative government and the very basis of the House of Lords.

---

[8] *Parl. Deb.*, vol. 159, ser. 3, col. 1416, 5 July 1860 (HC) *per* William Coningham.
[9] *Ibid.*, col. 2079, 17 July 1860 *per* Lord Fermoy.
[10] *The Times*, 18 May 1860, p. 8 col. b.
[11] *Ibid.*, 16 May 1860, p. 12 col. b.
[12] *Ibid.*

One member predicted that if the upper house were to have any control over the finances of the country, 'it might become an important question whether we should not do well to substitute an elective for an hereditary peerage'.[13] The chairman of one of the London public meetings called the Lords 'an obvious anomaly', and observed that if it were to usurp any of the privileges of the Commons, 'the days of hereditary legislation were numbered'.[14] Support for the undermining of the role of the Lords in the parliamentary safeguard was, for wider political reasons, strong. In relation to the other undermining of the parliamentary safeguard, namely the permitting of taxation by parliamentary resolution, support was minimal. Indeed, it was limited to those taxpayers inconvenienced by the fact that bankers, brokers and agents could not legally deduct income tax when they paid dividends to the taxpayers during the period of hiatus, to those bankers who accordingly had to keep detailed records of each transaction, and to the government of the day.

Similarly the more sophisticated and critical taxpayers of the late Victorian period saw that the legal framework of local tax administration had become anachronistic and appreciated many of its shortcomings. First, they had considerable reservations as to the method of appointment of the local commissioners.[15] It was indeed neither open nor understood,[16] and it was condemned in 1853 as nothing short of 'hocuspocus'.[17] There was support expressed for the adoption of the American system of electing assessors in order to prevent the appointment of commissioners who might be prone to bias.[18] Secondly, many taxpayers were increasingly concerned as to the competence of the local commissioners, their lack of responsibility and uniformity and, in particular, their lack of technical knowledge and of legal procedures. Commercial taxpayers especially were acutely aware that in many cases the commissioners' local knowledge, which in theory was central to arriving at an assessment to tax, was all too often little more than a general impression of the income

[13] *Parl. Deb.*, vol. 159, ser. 3, col. 1808, 12 July 1860 (HC) *per* Sir John Trelawny.
[14] *The Times*, 16 May 1860, p. 12 col. b.
[15] For an acute criticism of local tax administration by a surveyor, see *The Times*, 4 February 1873, p. 7 col. f.
[16] CIR Sixth Report, *HCPP* (1862) (3047) xxvii 327 at pp. 342–3.
[17] *Parl. Deb.*, vol. 127, ser. 3, col. 717, 27 May 1853 (HC) *per* John Bright. See too *The Times*, 5 January 1893, p. 2 col. f. For the appointment process see CIR Thirteenth Report, *HCPP* (1870) (82, 82–1) xx 193 at p. 308.
[18] *Parl. Deb.*, vol. 127, ser. 3, col. 536, 23 May 1853 (HC) *per* John Blackett; *ibid.*, cols. 717–18, 27 May 1853 (HC) *per* John Bright; *ibid.*, vol. 126, ser. 3, cols. 689–90, 28 April 1853 (HC) *per* Richard Cobden.

of taxpayers, gleaned from gossip and outward appearances of their style of living. That the growing complexity of the income tax was outstripping the intellectual and physical abilities of local commissioners was plain for the taxpayer to see. They were regarded as providing 'rough justice'.[19] One businessman in 1905 condemned them as 'no good at all'. 'They do little', he said, 'they know little. Hardly one of them could open a set of books in double entry'.[20] It was widely understood that an ignorant local commissioner, with his monopoly on establishing questions of fact, and a right to decide on questions of law which remained unchallengeable in the case of income tax until 1874, could seriously undermine a taxpayer's right to be correctly assessed to tax. This was the sacrifice demanded in return for the safeguard of local tax administration and an informal process, but as the safeguard itself was undermined, the cost appeared to some taxpayers to be too high. And thirdly, taxpayers continued to resent the disclosure of their private financial affairs to their neighbours and colleagues on the grounds of the invasion of privacy and the danger of commercial or social bias. It was a problem inherent in the administration of an inquisitorial tax by local lay commissioners who inevitably were geographically and socially in constant and necessary contact with the taxpayers. Suspicions of bias and of arbitrary adjudication, even if they were not justified, undermined taxpayers' confidence in an administrative system constructed to protect them from unjust taxation. A lack of confidence led to a reluctance to engage with the process, with all the political and fiscal consequences that entailed. In this the access to the lay tier of the appellate process was undermined, and the protection it offered weakened. Such disclosure was, however, again a price taxpayers had to pay for lay involvement in the assessment process which in turn – in theory at least – kept the government at a distance. This was small comfort when the taxpayers saw that the government officer was not being kept at arm's length at all. As taxpayers realised they were enjoying none of the advantages of the localist system, so their resentment of disclosure continued.

Accordingly there was some support by taxpayers for the greater involvement of central government in tax administration, as they began to see that the criticisms which the board had long expressed about the

---

[19] Minutes of Evidence before the Royal Commission on the Income Tax, *HCPP* (1919) (288) xxiii, qq. 4903, 4905, 4912.
[20] Minutes of Evidence before the Departmental Committee on Income Tax, *HCPP* (1905) (2576) xliv 245, qq. 1978 *per* Arthur Chamberlain JP, putting forward the views of the Birmingham Chamber of Commerce on income tax.

localist system were often justified and that the surveyor was the real expert in the tax process who understood their tax affairs and was more likely to arrive at a correct assessment than the local commissioners. This positive perception was encouraged in other ways. First, by the Victorian public's increased familiarity with state intervention and a lessening of resentment of centralised tax administration. The intense unpopularity of the centrally administered excise, for example, had diminished to a large extent. Secondly, it was strengthened by the practical limitation of local tax administration. Localism related only to the direct taxes, and was primarily an English phenomenon. It did not exist in Ireland, and was rapidly diminishing in Scotland. Scottish taxpayers had always been far more receptive to the undermining of localism, for they had voluntarily abandoned most local administration of tax to official administration preferring central administration, with any resentment which might have been felt towards the surveyors undertaking assessment both small and fast disappearing by 1862. The Board of Inland Revenue noted this change in public opinion in 1869.[21] Thirdly, although the Special Commissioners were not extensively used, taxpayers who did use them found they were an excellent tribunal.[22] Though not constituting an undermining of the localist system, they were certainly an extension of the authority of the executive in tax matters. The Special Commissioners' lack of independence as permanent employees of the very government department whose function was the direction and control of the machinery and systems necessary to raise the revenue, was not perceived as a problem in the nineteenth century,[23] and indeed they were the object of almost universal praise.[24] And finally, attitudes to disclosure of personal financial information were changing. There was a growing understanding by taxpayers that the surveyor was as discreet as he was expert, and that disclosure to him was preferable to disclosure to their peers.

---

[21] CIR Twelfth Report, *HCPP* (1869) (4094) xviii 607 at p. 635.

[22] Minutes of Evidence before the Royal Commission on the Income Tax, *HCPP* (1919) (288) xxiii, q. 8185 *per* H. Lakin-Smith, on behalf of the Association of British Chambers of Commerce.

[23] Only in later years were their conflicting duties a matter of concern: *ibid.*, qq. 23,891, 23,898; 24,017 *per* Randle Holme, solicitor, on behalf of the Law Society.

[24] *Ibid.*, q. 8185 *per* H. Lakin-Smith; *ibid.*, q. 1853 *per* G. O. Parsons, secretary to the Income Tax Reform League; *ibid.*, q. 13,770 *per* D. M. Kerly KC, member of the Commission; Report of the Royal Commission on the Income Tax, *HCPP* (1920) (615) xviii 97 at para. 359; Report of the Committee on Ministers' Powers, *HCPP* (1931–2) (4060) xii 341 at pp. 86–7.

Opposition to the safeguards' undermining

Such expressions of sympathy for the shortcomings of the law in its protective provisions did not, however, extend to support for the undermining of the safeguards themselves. On the contrary, while Victorian taxpayers were sensitive to the need for the re-evaluation of the safeguards in a changing society, when they saw that in some instances it amounted to their abrogation, it was unacceptable to them. They were prepared to recast the safeguards to suit the changing conditions of the age, but not to sacrifice them entirely.

Popular objection to the undermining of the rights of individuals in relation to the state was not limited to the tax sphere. Debates as to individual rights in the face of increasing powers of central government permeated British society and politics in the nineteenth century, notably in fields associated with the origins of the welfare state. Those reforms, resulting from the agrarian and industrial revolutions of the eighteenth and early nineteenth centuries and addressing factories, public health, mines, education and the relief of poverty, all undermined to some degree the private rights of individuals. Much of the legislation undermined property rights, as where owners were obliged by statute to fence dangerous machinery and take other measures to ensure the health and safety of factory workers, to build sewerage systems or ensure clean water supplies. The undermining of individual property rights was particularly evident in the reconstruction of land rights where property interests were permanently recast.[25] As with all property rights, compulsion was a last resort, and wherever possible the commutation of tithes,[26] the enfranchisement of copyholds[27] and the inclosure of land[28] were, initially at least, voluntary. All, nevertheless, raised popular resentment,[29] though most of the reforms succeeded on their merits because of the undeniable need to remedy obvious evils. Personal rights were similarly undermined in many areas but notably through new mental health and public health legislation, though such legislation was more consistently compulsory

---

[25] C. Stebbings, 'State Intervention and Private Property Rights in Victorian England', in Alastair Hudson (ed.), *New Perspectives on Family Law, Human Rights and the Home* (London: Cavendish Publishing, 2004), pp. 217–37.

[26] 6 & 7 Will. IV c. 71 (1836).   [27] 4 & 5 Vict. c. 35 (1841).

[28] 8 & 9 Vict. c. 118 (1845).

[29] The central board created to implement the public health legislation aroused particularly strong opposition. See David Roberts, *Victorian Origins of the British Welfare State* (New Haven, Connecticut: Yale University Press 1960; reprinted Archon Books 1969), pp. 70–85.

in character. For example, legislation ultimately made the vaccination of babies against contagious diseases, notably smallpox, compulsory,[30] a reform which was widely condemned as undermining individual rights. Similarly government powers providing that prostitutes undergo compulsory medical examination for venereal diseases were powers of central government interfering directly with individual liberties,[31] as was the lunacy legislation which gave central government extensive powers over the person and property of individuals.[32]

It was, therefore, within a wider political and legislative context of the undermining of individual rights, and a culture of sensitivity and protest, that taxpayers experienced the erosion of their own legal safeguards. While most taxpayers opposed the excessive interference of the Lords in taxing legislation, perceiving it as an undermining of representative parliamentary consent[33] and therefore wanting them to have a limited role, they did not necessarily want the Lords to be ousted altogether, for that amounted to the abrogation of the safeguard. Accordingly the Parliament Act 1911, though a logical outcome, was for many a step too far. The formal legal safeguard of parliamentary consent was effected by strict rules of parliamentary procedure ensuring successive stages of full debate and scrutiny in both chambers. To some taxpayers the formal removal of the Lords from taxing legislation amounted to an abrogation of a forum for the critical analysis and debate of taxing legislation, and as such an undermining of the safeguard of parliamentary process. Again others saw the Lords' right to reject money bills as an important restraint on the power of the Commons. It, and only it, could 'stem the progress of popular fury',[34] a check some saw as of unprecedented importance as the lower house became increasingly dominated by the executive. *The Times* supported the upper house's assertion of its right to reject the paper duty bill in 1860, though did so in measured terms. It said the government had brought the Lords' action on themselves, because the 'largest, most comprehensive, and most perilous Budget ever known' had been too ambitious and the repeal of the paper duty had been a step too far.[35] It felt that the Lords had

---

[30]   16 & 17 Vict. c. 100 (1853).
[31]   27 & 28 Vict. c. 85 (1864); 29 & 30 Vict. c. 35 (1866); 32 & 33 Vict. c. 96 (1869).
[32]   16 & 17 Vict. c. 70 (1853); 16 & 17 Vict. c. 96 (1853); 16 & 17 Vict. c. 97 (1853).
[33]   The representation of the House of Lords was, at most, indirect: *Parl. Deb.*, vol. 163, ser. 3, col. 103, 27 May 1861 (HC) *per* Richard Milnes.
[34]   William Paley, *The Works of William Paley*, Edmund Paley (ed.), 7 vols. (London, C. & J. Rivington, 1825), vol. iv, pp. 388–9.
[35]   *The Times*, 23 May 1860, p. 8 col. f.

'vindicated a privilege and established a right', though it expressed a hope that it would not be used other than on 'some equally proper occasion'.[36] The assessment and payment of tax under a mere parliamentary resolution rather than enacted legislation excited no such ambivalent responses in the taxpaying public, and it was almost invariably regarded as threatening the essence of the safeguard and was vigorously resisted. It was unequivocally perceived as undermining parliamentary consent with no mitigating factor beyond the convenience of a dilatory government and a grasping executive. It was a 'revolutionary',[37] momentous, remarkable change. 'It is a new thing', said one member. 'I am sure that it is a dangerous thing. I think that it is an unnecessary thing'.[38]

While taxpayers' attitudes to localism were equivocal, recognising the evident shortcomings in the system, its underlying premise remained highly valued. It was clear that there was a limit beyond which taxpayers were not prepared to go, and which would entail a vigorous political battle to breach. Indeed, of the four guiding principles of taxation extant at the beginning of the nineteenth century, namely that the direct taxes should be voluntary, exceptional, non-inquisitorial and locally administered, the first three were effectively eliminated from the fiscal system with intense but relatively brief opposition. It was recognised that to retain them was economically unsustainable. The undermining of local tax administration, however, was faced with unremitting resistance throughout the nineteenth century, and the challenge to localism proved remarkably intractable. So while the French were not much interested in it and their political and social systems allowed only a limited and integrated localism, and the Americans effectively side-stepped the issue but then used it or rejected it as it suited them, the English were tenacious in their support of it. It was said that there existed 'ample testimony' showing the public were very unwilling to be 'under the uncontrolled power or influence, direct or indirect, of the Inland Revenue Department'.[39] As late as 1919 a solicitor observed that one of the reasons why income tax was collected with so little friction was the system whereby it was administered by individuals who were not servants of the revenue.[40] 'As a taxpayer', he said, 'and a representative of taxpayers, I have always comforted myself by imagining that that work was done, not by the Inland Revenue … but by

---

[36] *Ibid.*   [37] *Parl. Deb.*, vol. 51, ser. 5, col. 857, 7 April 1913 (HC) *per* William Fisher.
[38] *Ibid.*, col. 1047, 8 April 1913 (HC) *per* George Cave.   [39] TNA: PRO IR 74/20 (1906).
[40] Minutes of Evidence before the Royal Commission on the Income Tax, *HCPP* (1919) (288) xxiii, q. 23,890 *per* Randle Holme.

a neutral body',[41] the local commissioners 'representing not the taxpayer, strictly, and certainly not representing the Inland Revenue'.[42] Local commissioners were to administer the legislation fairly between the crown and the taxpayer, and 'to secure to the public every privilege which the spirit or letter of the law provides'.[43] Even the author of the highly critical *The Income Tax in Utopia* in 1917 wanted to retain local assessors.[44] The maintenance of local tax commissioners as a buffer between the taxpayer and the powerful interests of the state, a 'natural safeguard',[45] emerged as largely non-negotiable by the tax-paying public. An entirely central administration was still unacceptable, and when the principle of localism was breached either in law or in practice in such a way as to threaten its very existence, taxpayers understood it was of real significance and resented it strongly. Its undermining provoked the most vehement outcry in Parliament, in the press and among taxpayers in public meetings, the most sustained popular resistance and the most equivocal response by the government. The measure of taxpayers' disquiet revealed the extent to which they valued it.

Formal erosions of the system by specific legislation were invariably opposed, though the source of that opposition was often the clerks,[46] who naturally feared losing an important element in their earnings, and the local commissioners themselves, who understandably feared being reduced to mere figureheads. Local officials alarmed the public by suggesting that all elasticity and personal attention to individual taxpayers would be lost if the central board took over their functions.[47] Taxpayers were urged not to surrender the protection afforded to them by the system.[48] Even when the undermining was suggested by a body of taxpayers, as when the Associated Chambers of Commerce proposed in 1883 that the government fill all future vacancies for collectors of commercial and employment income, it was strongly resisted and the right jealously guarded. One member of Parliament believed it undermined 'one of the ancient safeguards which were thought to be necessary in raising the tax

---

[41] *Ibid.*, q. 23,969.   [42] *Ibid.*, q. 23,986.   [43] TNA: PRO IR 74/20 (1906).
[44] Arthur Herald, *The Income Tax in Utopia* (Letchworth: Garden City Press Ltd, 1917), p. 14.
[45] Report of the Royal Commission on the Income Tax, *HCPP* (1920) (615) xviii 97 at para. 344.
[46] Minutes of Evidence before the Select Committee on Inland Revenue and Customs Establishments, *HCPP* (1862) (370) xii 131, q. 2476 *per* Edward Welsh, surveyor of taxes for the City of London.
[47] *The Times*, 'Hunting the Taxpayer', 20 April 1921, p. 11 col. f.
[48] For later opposition, see *ibid.*, 19 May 1931, p. 12, col. b; *ibid*, 25 April 1931, p. 13 col. f.

originally'.[49] A further unsuccessful attempt in 1887 was opposed in the press[50] and a large meeting of commercial taxpayers in London formally protested against it as depriving the tax-paying public of some measure of legislative protection.[51] An appreciation of the profound implications of any changes in local administration, and their resentment, was unremitting.[52] *The Times* called assessment by independent local commissioners representing the taxpayer 'the cardinal principle of income-tax assessment'.[53] It was well established, trusted and economic,[54] and essential to protect all taxpayers, especially those who were vulnerable and generally unable to obtain or afford expert technical advice.

Popular opposition to the informal undermining of localism was just as intense. While taxpayers knew the local commissioners' knowledge was imprecise and insufficient and that of the surveyor was accurate and expert and to that extent preferable, they nevertheless resented the latter's inevitable dominance over their representatives. Their resentment was widespread and passionate, primarily with respect to his role in the exercise of the local commissioners' appellate jurisdiction. There were of course problems of inadequate time and knowledge at the assessment stage, but there the dominance of the surveyor was acceptable as it resulted in an accurate charge to tax. At the appellate stage, however, the character of the issue changed completely, and the undermining of the localist safeguard through the practice of the executive was met with considerable hostility. The adjudication of a dispute was no ministerial task. Parties presented themselves before independent adjudicators with every expectation of equal and impartial treatment, and for one of the parties to influence the adjudicators was utterly unacceptable to the English taxpayer's sense of justice. If the views of the surveyor, the officer of a government which had a clear material interest in raising taxation, were given greater weight than those of the taxpayer, if he could address the commissioners in the absence of the taxpayer, or if his view was accepted without

---

[49] *Parl. Deb.*, vol. 279, ser. 3, col. 500, 10 May 1883 (HC) *per* William Smith.
[50] *The Times*, 15 August 1887, p. 14 col. a.
[51] *The Times*, 'The Inland Revenue Bill', 19 August 1887, p. 10 col. c.
[52] *Parl. Deb.*, vol. 155, ser. 4, cols. 1476–7, 25 April 1906 (HC); *ibid.*, vol. 158, ser. 4, cols. 1146–8, 14 June 1906 (HC); *ibid.*, vol. 163, ser. 4, cols. 861–2, 30 October 1906 (HC); *The Times*, 25 October 1915, p. 9 col. e and 26 October 1915, p. 10 col. b.
[53] *The Times*, 'More Bureaucratic Finance', 29 October 1915 p. 9 col. b, complaining about the increased power of the Inland Revenue in relation to the excess profits tax. See too *ibid.*, 29 June 1927, p. 17 col. b.
[54] *Parl. Deb.*, vol. 76, ser. 5, cols. 1098–1129, 6 December 1915 (HC). See too *The Times*, 30 October 1915, p. 9 col. f.

question or examination, then the futility of the taxpayer's appeal was clear. Suspicion grew of the commissioners' subordination to the will of the executive and a popular and understandable view was formed that in so doing the members of the tribunal could not be impartial and independent in their adjudication. The state became, in effect, judge in its own cause. This perception was in many instances correct. Opposition was sustained well into the twentieth century, for when it was proposed to formalise the practice in 1921 and transfer all assessing powers to central officers, though leaving the local commissioners with their appellate powers, it was condemned as vicious[55] and as unequivocally promoting an increased control by the Inland Revenue. Headlines such as 'Hunting the Taxpayer: Safeguards to be Withdrawn',[56] and 'A Principle at Stake',[57] were typical of the popular rhetoric of the time. So fiercely were the proposals opposed that not only did the bill have to be abandoned,[58] it led to the founding of the Income Taxpayers' Society.[59] This strength of feeling does not mask the ambivalence and complexity of taxpayers' attitudes to localism in tax administration. They wanted the commissioners retained as the embodiment of independence from the executive, of local government, of decentralisation. What they wanted was the localist system to work properly, with well-informed commissioners who would demand that the surveyor defend and explain his assessments and who would apply common sense to the process. The principle of independence was crucial, and the esteem in which it was held was revealed by the degree of resentment when the commissioners appeared to lack it.

The strength of the taxpayer's response to the undermining of his traditional legal safeguards is striking. The language was almost invariably extreme, public meetings of opposition well-attended, pamphlets and letters to the newspapers abundant, and, on occasion, the opposition took violent expression. The reasons for this depth of feeling were twofold: first, an intense dislike of state intervention in Victorian England, and secondly a belief that the undermining of the safeguards amounted to nothing less than an undermining of the constitution itself.

Attitudes to state intervention

The undermining of individual property and personal rights in all spheres was almost invariably effected by central government, and was the result

---

[55] *The Times*, 18 March 1920, p. 17 col. c.   [56] *Ibid.*, 20 April 1921, p. 11 col. f.
[57] *Ibid.*, 18 March 1920, p. 17 col. c.
[58] *The Times*, 'Protection for the Taxpayer', 28 July 1921, p. 11 col. e.   [59] See above p. 174.

of the intervention of the state in fields of human activity it had hitherto largely ignored. This movement began in the 1830s when legislation was enacted to address, among other things, the growing problem of pauperism, to promote public health in increasingly squalid and overcrowded towns, and the improvement of the dangerous and unhealthy conditions in mines and factories. The restructuring of property rights to allow the improvement of land to feed a growing population and the regulation of railways were among other activities which were subject to parliamentary scrutiny and then central government control as the century progressed. The growth of a centralised administration was the only solution to the magnitude of these problems for only central government could provide the necessary authority, uniform standards and national control.[60]

This new legislation, which covered an astonishingly wide field of activity in the nineteenth century, was interventionist, centralist and increasingly collective. As a result of such intensive government activity, the nature and extent of state interference was a topic of considerable debate throughout the nineteenth century.[61] Attitudes depended on individual philosophies, but in general ideologies were complex, fluid and inconsistent in this respect. Whigs, Liberals and Tories were broadly united in a humanitarian concern to address the most pressing and undeniable social evils, and accepted this would best be done through central agencies. Similarly the Utilitarians, though individualists, believed that governments could ensure the greatest happiness of the greatest number through efficient centralised state intervention.[62] Radicals favoured it only in extreme instances. Popular attitudes were, in general, ones of hostility or, at best, suspicion and apprehension. The degree and tone of the opposition is revealing. At one extreme sat critics such as Joshua Toulmin Smith, who founded the Anti-Centralisation Union in 1854. For him government was either local self-government or centralised control and they

---

[60] See generally Roberts, *Victorian Origins*; J. B. Brebner, 'Laissez Faire and State Intervention in Nineteenth Century Britain', *Journal of Economic History* 8 (1948), Supplement 59; M. W. Thomas, 'The Origins of Administrative Centralisation', *Current Legal Problems* 3 (1950), 214; W. C. Lubenow, *The Politics of Government Growth* (Newton Abbot: David and Charles, 1971); Derek Fraser, *The Evolution of the British Welfare State* (London: Macmillan, 1973); Martin Daunton, *Trusting Leviathan: the Politics of Taxation in Britain, 1799–1914* (Cambridge University Press, 2001), p. 194.

[61] J. S. Mill, *Principles of Political Economy,* 6th edition, People's Edition (London: Longmans, Green & Co, 1896), Book V, Chapter 1, sections 1–3 pp. 479–83.

[62] For the complexities and contradictions of ideologies, see Brebner, 'Laissez Faire and State Intervention'. See too Oliver MacDonagh, 'The Nineteenth Century Revolution in Government: A Reappraisal', *Historical Journal* 1 (1958), 52; J. D. Chambers, *The Workshop of the World*, 2nd edition (Oxford University Press, 1968), pp. 130–9; Roberts, *Victorian Origins*, pp. 22–34.

sat at opposite extremes; the first was good, the second comprehensively evil.[63] He called centralisation 'mere charlatan legislative experiments', and 'a miserable but mischievous abortion'.[64] Other than where the evils exposed could not be denied, it was generally disliked, particularly in those areas regarded as essentially private in nature. It was popularly, and derogatively, known as 'officialism'.[65]

Reasons for opposing state intervention were many. It undermined the dominant doctrine of laissez-faire which imported a principle of non- or minimal interference of the state and was opposed by the promulgators of that ideology in all but cases of real necessity;[66] it has been seen that it was vigorously resented by those whose vested interests of property were undermined, as nothing less than the undermining of the sanctity of private property; it was resented by those who maintained the importance of the traditional orthodox values[67] of individualism, independence and self-reliance; it was distrusted by those who venerated the common law and found the statute law arbitrary and lacking in individual sensitivity; and it was opposed by all those who valued local self-government. Individual freedoms were jealously guarded, particularly in the early years of the nineteenth century when the French revolution was still fresh in the popular and parliamentary mind. From this independence grew a powerful, emotional and practical attachment to local self-government which in turn engendered a widespread, long-standing and strong distrust of any interference by central government.

The undermining of the taxpayer's legal safeguards took its place in this ideological debate surrounding interventionist legislation. In taxation, which constituted the epitome of state intervention with its compulsory interference with property rights by central government, it was

---

[63] Lubenow, *Government Growth*, pp. 89–95. See too Joshua Toulmin Smith, *Government by Commissions, Illegal and Pernicious* (London: S. Sweet, 1849). Toulmin Smith had had his own personal problems with the excise: see Documents relative to Petition of J. Toulmin Smith, *HCPP* (1846) (167) xxxiii 395.

[64] Joshua Toulmin Smith, *Centralization or Representation? A Letter to the Metropolitan Sanatory Commissioners*, 2nd edition (London: S. Sweet, 1848), pp. v, viii.

[65] *The Times*, 'The Growth of Officialism', 5 April 1893, p. 3 col. d; 'Counterblast against Officialism', *The Times*, 1 June 1895, p. 11 col. e. See generally C. Stebbings, ' "Officialism": Law, Bureaucracy and Ideology in late Victorian England', in Andrew Lewis and Michael Lobban (eds.), *Law and History*, Current Legal Issues (Oxford University Press, 2003), vol. vi, p. 317.

[66] Arthur J. Taylor, *Laissez-faire and State Intervention in Nineteenth-century Britain*, Studies in Economic History (London: Macmillan, 1972); Fraser, *British Welfare State*, pp. 91–114.

[67] Roberts, *Victorian Origins*, pp. 315–26.

disliked but, having been so long established, was accepted. The principle of taxation was not perceived as innovative centralisation, but as a necessary evil. Its unequivocally interventionist character, however, contributed to a particular sensitivity not as to its substance but its manner of implementation, namely its machinery. Opposition to state intervention in tax was an opposition to the encroachment of the executive into the legal safeguards, and while it pervaded each of the safeguards, it was particularly prevalent in attitudes to the undermining of local tax administration, especially in relation to a tax as inquisitorial as income tax. So whereas in other spheres of national life, lay tribunals were seen as the response to the special challenges of the age and the embodiment of the centralisation of government and interference of the state, in tax they were quite the opposite. They were expressions of the old localism, of vested interests, of individualism and independence from central government. They were nothing less than an expression of resistance to centralism rather than an expression of it. The acute degree of resentment of the domination of local tax administration by the surveyor had its roots in an antipathy to state intervention. The excise had always been centrally administered and this had traditionally exacerbated the intense popular dislike with which it was regarded. Though time had accustomed taxpayers to that impost, the reintroduction of the income tax in 1842 revived the traditional resentment and fear. This intensified as the tax establishments grew in both personnel and their influence on the local tax process. The staff of the central revenue boards were numerous and placed all over the country, implementing a host of regulations, rules, policies, circulars and instructions. This bureaucracy of tax, and all state intervention, was resented. The antipathy comprised a perception not only that it was displacing local institutions through an invidious extension of power, but that all bureaucrats, including revenue officials, were more concerned with processes rather than substance,[68] that they were inflexible, prone to misconduct as a result of the sums of money they daily handled and open to corruption. An encroaching state served to intensify the perception of the local administration of taxes by an impartial and independent body as an indispensable principle of taxpayer protection. The effects of centralisation roused unabated popular opposition which was particularly evident in the tax sphere. For example, the ostensibly sensible reform proposed in 1883 to allow the board to fill all future vacancies among collectors was condemned as 'a serious step in the direction of compulsory

---

[68] *The Times*, 'The Evils of Bureaucracy', 17 October 1866, p. 10 col. c.

centralization',[69] that in 1915 'a clear extension of bureaucratic control',[70] and the clothing of the custom to tax by resolution in statutory form was a particularly dangerous form of 'officialism'.[71]

The intensity with which the English disliked the interference of central government in tax matters is revealed when it is compared to French and American attitudes in the same period. Both France and America experienced central involvement in tax administration, but reactions to it were very different. In France, centralism was dominant. The administrative state introduced by Napoleon after the revolution was highly centralised.[72] Nevertheless, opposition to it in tax terms was minor. Local tax administration, the principal expression of a decentralised tax process, was neither liked nor valued,[73] even though it reflected the ideology of the revolution and was provided for in the constitution.[74] It was strictly controlled and limited, and while there is some evidence of support of local administration, it was slight. The strongest resentment of centralised tax administration was in relation to inquisitorial powers given to central tax officers,[75] but that was a universal complaint in all commercial societies where property was of social and economic importance. The overall view of the French tax-paying public was of support for the uniformity, control and efficiency that centralised tax administration provided.[76] Indeed, localism was feared as an undermining of the administrative unity

---

[69] *Parl. Deb.*, vol. 279, ser. 3, col. 492, 10 May 1883 (HC) *per* John Slagg.

[70] *Ibid.*, vol. 76, ser. 5, col. 1118, 6 December 1915 (HC) *per* George Barnes.

[71] *Ibid.*, vol. 51, ser. 5, col. 1033, 8 April 1913 (HC) *per* Sir Alfred Cripps.

[72] See generally Louis Bergeron, *France under Napoleon*, R. R. Palmer (trans.) (New Jersey: Princeton University Press, 1981), pp. 37–51; Alan Forrest, *The French Revolution* (Oxford: Basil Blackwell, 1995), pp. 57–64; René Stourm, *The Budget*, Thaddeus Plazinski (trans.), W. F. McCaleb (ed.) (New York and London: D. Appleton & Co., 1917), pp. 393–421; Geoffrey Ellis, *The Napoleonic Empire* (Basingstoke and London: Macmillan Education Ltd, 1991), pp. 26–35.

[73] René Stourm, *Les Finances de l'Ancien Régime et de la Révolution*, 2 vols. First published Paris, 1885 (New York: Burt Franklin, 1968), vol. i, p.176.

[74] The constitution of 1793 provided that 'Tous les citoyens ont le droit de concourir à l'établissement des contributions, d'en surveiller l'emploi, et de s'en faire rendre compte': Jacques Godechot (ed.), *Les Constitutions de la France depuis 1789* (Paris: Garnier-Flammarion, 1970), p. 82.

[75] See Félix Ponteil, 'Le Ministre des Finances Georges Humann et les Emeutes Antifiscales en 1841', *Revue Historique* 179 (1937), 311 ; Robert L. Koepke, 'The Loi des Patentes of 1844', *French Historical Studies* 11 (1980), 398 at 412.

[76] Local administration was introduced for the new land tax from 1790 but proved a failure, and it was thereafter strictly limited and controlled: Stourm, *Finances*, vol. i, pp. 178–80; Stourm, *Budget*, pp. 395–6. As to preference for centralism, see Koepke, 'Loi des Patentes', 414.

achieved by the constitution which could lead to anarchy.[77] American attitudes to central government involvement in tax administration were more complex, primarily because of their own constitutional arrangements. American taxpayers felt a profound attachment to their own state rather than the federal government, which led them to prefer state institutions to federal ones. Indeed, they regarded their state assemblies much as the English regarded their Parliament.[78] And since the constitution provided that state property taxation dominated over federal taxation,[79] American taxpayers enjoyed an institutionalised decentralisation which recognised local allegiances and limited the power of central government. As federal officers were not involved in state taxation, there was no cause for conflict between localism and centralism as there was in England. In relation to federal taxes, however, administered by federal officers, it was a different matter, and resentment was clear.[80]

Constitutionality

Strong though the Victorian dislike of central government was, their veneration for the constitution was even stronger. It was the essence of their national identity, the embodiment of their liberties as Englishmen and women, reflecting hundreds of years of evolution and embodying their hard-won victory in the civil war. When their legal safeguards as taxpayers were undermined, they felt it far more intensely than a mere dislike of an encroaching executive, because they saw it as nothing less than a breach of the constitution. Their resentment to the breaches of their legal safeguards was accordingly almost invariably couched in terms of constitutionality, particularly in the nineteenth century when political turmoil in France and America made them particularly sensitive to any infringement of their own constitution. Again, this was not confined to tax, for

---

[77] Ponteil, 'Emeutes Antifiscales', 351–2. Throughout most of the nineteenth century, France was in a state of political upheaval with eleven constitutions between 1789 and 1875: see generally Maurice Duverger, *Le Système Politique Français*, 21st edition (Paris: Presses Universitaires de France, 1996), pp. 21–105.

[78] David Ramsay, *The History of the American Revolution*, Lester H. Cohen (ed.) (Indianapolis: Liberty Classics, 1990), pp. 18–19.

[79] See W. Elliot Brownlee, *Federal Taxation in America*, 2nd edition (Cambridge University Press; Washington DC: Woodrow Wilson Center Press, 2004), pp. 13–21.

[80] See, for example, *Congressional Globe*, 37 Cong., 1 sess., 24 July 1861 at 247; 25 July 1861, at 272, 285–6; Charles F. Dunbar, 'The Direct Tax of 1861', *Quarterly Journal of Economics* 3 (1889), 436; Joseph A. Hill, 'The Civil War Income Tax', *Quarterly Journal of Economics* 8 (1894), 416.

popular objections to many centralising measures in other spheres, or those which resulted in a decline in lay participation in government, commonly took constitutional expression. A notable example, which has a number of parallels with contemporary developments in tax administration, was the coroner's inquest. This 'institutional bulwark of English liberties',[81] which was perceived as providing a check on the abuse of central authority, became increasingly dominated by the medical profession at the expense of the local lay jury, a development which was repeatedly condemned as unconstitutional.[82] The debates as to the nature of the role of the House of Lords in the taxing process, which culminated in its removal from that process and the undermining thereby of the parliamentary safeguard, were entirely constitutional in nature. In the context of the Lords' rejection of the paper duty bill in 1860, which was a debate as to the balance of the powers between the two chambers, it was perceived as arguably legal, but unconstitutional.[83] It breached the tacit understanding between the two houses that the Commons were supreme in relation to money bills, and the nationwide meetings objecting to the undermining of the Commons' privileges expressed their feelings in constitutional terms. The fundamental principle of the English constitution that the people were not to be taxed except through their elected representatives in Parliament was asserted; some felt the Lords' excessive interference brought them into 'dangerous collision' with the Commons and was 'subversive of the sound constitutional principle' that only the representatives of the people should have the legal power to impose national taxes.[84] The Commons, understandably vociferous in maintaining their chamber's constitutional privilege, vigorously condemned the Lords' action as 'so incredible an usurpation',[85] 'a stretch of the prerogative',[86] a 'gigantic innovation',[87] and 'a rash and unjustifiable proceeding'.[88] The government argued that the Lords' action was not 'with the spirit of the constitution … nor … consistent with the dictates either of justice or

[81] Ian A. Burney, *Bodies of Evidence* (Baltimore and London: John Hopkins University Press, 2000), p. 16; Daunton, *Trusting Leviathan*, p. 182. See too, in relation to bankruptcy and insolvency in Victorian England, V. Markham Lester, *Victorian Insolvency* (Oxford: Clarendon Press, 1995).

[82] See Burney, *Bodies of Evidence*, pp. 7, 19, 20, 27, 29; Daunton, *Trusting Leviathan*, p. 182.

[83] *Parl. Deb.*, vol. 158, ser. 3, col. 1458, 21 May 1860 (HL) *per* Earl Granville; *ibid.*, col. 1521 *per* Duke of Argyll.

[84] *The Times*, 18 May 1860, p. 8 col. b.

[85] *Parl. Deb.*, vol. 159, ser. 3, col. 1424, 5 July 1860 (HC) *per* Edward Leatham.

[86] *Ibid.*, col. 1430 *per* Edwin James.   [87] *Ibid.*, col. 1457 *per* Lord Fermoy.

[88] *Ibid.*, col. 1501 *per* Lord John Russell.

wisdom'.[89] When half a century later the unwritten constitutional relationship between the two houses in relation to money bills was given an extreme and statutory form in the Parliament Act 1911, constitutional objections were raised as to the overall desirability of a bicameral legislature. Taxpayers were aware that the Parliament Act, even if arguably it reflected the proper constitutional position, nevertheless resulted in their representatives in Parliament having little power to contain the executive in any taxing measure, and furthermore reduced the degree of debate and consideration of money bills, even by a non-representative element of Parliament. By expunging one major element of Parliament, the Act changed the meaning of parliamentary consent for the purposes of taxation and thereby undermined the spirit of the Bill of Rights. Money bills were now the work of a single chamber and the consent of Parliament had become the consent of the House of Commons. The degree of security had been reduced.

Constitutional objections lay at the heart of objections to the practice of taxation by parliamentary resolution. Gibson Bowles' legal challenge in 1913 was on the basis that the practice undermined the substantive constitutional principle of parliamentary consent to taxation, 'a constitutional reality' constituting the safeguard of the subject and an essential and unalterable part of the law.[90] The practice removed the independence of the Commons in imposing taxes and that was perceived as being unconstitutional. Indeed the judge accepted that it raised an issue of considerable constitutional and legal importance.[91] When the decision forced the passing of the Provisional Collection of Taxes Act 1913 to cast the custom in statutory form, it was perceived as evidence of the unwritten constitution of the country breaking down.[92] The Act was called 'constitutionally an outrage',[93] 'monstrous'[94] and 'unconstitutional, unnecessary, and harmful'.[95] Sir Alfred Cripps, an eminent lawyer and strong proponent of the constitutional argument, reminded the house of its duty. 'We, who represent the taxpayers of this country, are bound … not to give up

---

[89] *Ibid.*, vol. 158, col. 1457, 21 May 1860 (HL) *per* Earl Granville.

[90] T. Gibson Bowles, *Bowles v. The Bank of England: the Proceedings in Court and Official Court Documents* (London: Butterworth & Co. 1914), p. 79.

[91] *Bowles v. Bank of England* [1913] 1 Ch 57 at 66.

[92] See, for example, *Parl. Deb.*, vol. 51, ser. 5, col. 882, 7 April 1913 (HC) *per* James Hope; *ibid.*, col. 924 *per* Arthur Steel-Maitland. Austen Chamberlain saw it as parting with an element of the constitution: *ibid.*, col. 851.

[93] *Ibid.*, col. 1219, 9 April 1913 (HC) *per* William Joynson-Hicks.

[94] *Ibid.*, col. 1033, 8 April 1913 (HC) *per* Sir Alfred Cripps.

[95] *Ibid.*, col. 1670, 14 April 1913 (HC) *per* Felix Cassel.

the great constitutional safeguards we now enjoy at the dictation of any government, or at the mere suggestion of Treasury convenience'.[96] The Act diminished the role of the Commons as the 'guardian and custodian' of the people in matters of finance.[97] Whereas the Parliament Act had undermined the spirit of the Bill of Rights, the Provisional Collection of Taxes Act undermined its letter.[98]

Although the local administration of the direct taxes was not as clearly a constitutional safeguard as formal parliamentary consent to taxation, its undermining was nevertheless invariably perceived as a weakening of the constitutional principle of taxation. Taxpayers saw their institutions of local government as enshrining their very liberties, and their importance remained immensely strong. Indeed they saw the constitution as lying in these local institutions rather than in Parliament.[99] They saw the right to assess and collect their own taxes in their own communities as a constitutional right.[100] As 'self-taxation'[101] or 'self-assessment' were the expressions of self-government in the tax sphere, so opposition to its undermining consistently took constitutional expression.[102] As early as 1842, when Robert Peel introduced the Special Commissioners to assess commercial income in some cases, it was remarked that the tax was even more unconstitutional now that it included commissioners appointed by the crown.[103] The proposal in 1883 to allow the board to appoint collectors narrowly failed because it was a 'striking change, which really aimed at the alteration of … the Constitutional collection of the Income Tax'.[104] One member recalled Peel's words in 1842, and observed that the constitutional principle of localism in tax administration was 'a sound principle of human nature'.[105] A repeated attempt in 1887 failed, the bill being withdrawn when the constitutional right of taxpayers to assess themselves was strongly and widely asserted.[106] And again, the proposal in 1915 that

---

[96] *Ibid.*, col. 873, 7 April 1913 (HC) *per* Sir Alfred Cripps.

[97] *Ibid.*, vol. 52, ser. 5, col. 74, 21 April 1913 (HC) *per* William Fisher.

[98] *Ibid.*, vol. 51, ser. 5, cols. 889–90, 7 April 1913 (HC) *per* Felix Cassel.

[99] M. Sheldon Amos, *Fifty Years of the English Constitution* (London: Longmans, Green and Co., 1880), pp. 137–8.

[100] See A. Farnsworth, 'The Income Tax Commissioners', *Law Quarterly Review* 64 (1948), 372 at 388 where he calls it 'a sacrosanct constitutional principle'.

[101] CIR Twelfth Report, *HCPP* (1869) (4049) xviii 607 at p. 635.

[102] Daunton, *Trusting Leviathan*, pp. 193–4.

[103] *Parl. Deb.*, vol. 62, ser. 3, col. 1001, 22 April 1842 (HC) *per* Charles Buller.

[104] *Ibid.*, vol. 279, ser. 3, col. 492, 10 May 1883 (HC) *per* John Slagg.

[105] *Ibid.*, col. 501 *per* William Smith.

[106] See *The Times*, 15 August 1887, p. 14 col. a; *ibid.*, 19 August 1887, p. 10 col. c.

weekly wage earners should be assessed by the surveyor, and their tax collected by an Inland Revenue collector, was opposed as undermining 'constitutional usage'.[107] The Income Taxpayers' Society's object was 'the protection of the liberties and rights of the taxpaying public'[108] and to defend 'what is regarded as the constitutional issue – assessment independent of the bureaucracy – against further attacks'.[109] Even the central boards themselves acknowledged the 'great constitutional principle' of local tax administration[110] and called it 'undoubtedly a well-recognized and cherished principle of our constitution'.[111]

It was not just the erosion of parliamentary consent and local administration which the taxpayer resented and condemned as unconstitutional. It has been seen that the clarity of the parliamentary authority to tax embodied in the legislation was theoretical rather than real, since while lawyers might be able to understand and discern its meaning, it was highly unlikely that an individual taxpayer could. The complexity of the law of tax which challenged the judges and prevented the members of Parliament from being able to debate, question, and hold the government to account on tax matters equally prevented taxpayers from ascertaining the legal authority and capabilities of their representatives in tax administration. Indeed it went further, and prevented them from fully exploiting those remnants of the safeguards which were still effective. There was a growing feeling that the almost total inaccessibility of tax legislation which left taxpayers ignorant or uncertain as to the charge to tax placed upon them constituted a pervasive and insidious undermining of their legal safeguards and prevented them from exploiting them and was itself unconstitutional. Again it was John Bright who identified the constitutional infraction, and he did so in relation to the practice of incorporating legislation by reference into taxing Acts. 'It was unquestionably unconstitutional', he said in 1853, 'to tax men by Acts which they could not comprehend'.[112]

---

[107] *Parl. Deb.*, vol. 76, ser. 5, col. 1101, 6 December 1915 (HC) *per* John Butcher. See too *The Times*, 25 October 1915, p. 9 col. e.

[108] *The Times*, 'Protection for the Taxpayer', 28 July 1921, p. 11 col. e.

[109] *Ibid.*, 'Income-Tax Administration', 10 April 1931, p. 13 col. c.

[110] Minutes of Evidence before the Select Committee on Inland Revenue and Customs Establishments, *HCPP* (1862) (370) xii 131, q. 1630 *per* Thomas Dobson, Principal Secretary, Board of Inland Revenue.

[111] CIR Sixth Report, *HCPP* (1862) (3047) xxvii 327 at p. 351.

[112] *Parl Deb.*, vol. 127, ser. 3, col. 723, 27 May 1853 (HC) *per* John Bright. See too *ibid.*, cols. 724–5 *per* John Phillimore; H. Lloyd Reid, *The British Tax-Payers' Rights* (London: T. Fisher Unwin, 1898), pp. 263–5.

The legitimacy of the constitutional arguments

Despite the constitution, like the law, being essentially inaccessible to them, the Victorian taxpayers' sense of constitutionality, so lacking in medieval England,[113] was both acute and abundant. Most did not understand the complex and opaque relationships which comprised the constitution, but the expression 'liberty of the subject' embodied what they understood by it,[114] and taxpayers felt they had a very clear idea of what was constitutional or unconstitutional about a tax. Indeed, though they might struggle to articulate it in a coherent and systematic way, they had just as highly developed a sense of the constitution as did their American and French counterparts. They were emotionally and intellectually convinced that the undermining of their legal safeguards in taxation amounted to the undermining of their fundamental liberties and therefore of the constitution itself, another skirmish in 'the battle-field of the liberties and privileges of the House of Commons'.[115]

That the undermining of the legal safeguards amounted to the undermining of the constitution as the taxpayer maintained, however, was not self-evident. Indeed it was problematic, if only because the real undermining of the safeguards had been achieved by informal practices by the executive and was not reflected in the law itself. While in real terms the safeguards had indeed lost much of their effect, the legislation retained for the most part the full statutory expression of the safeguards in their original form of the seventeenth century and so remained essentially static. That made it difficult to argue that any principle, let alone a constitutional one, had been undermined at all. Certainly when taxpayers complained that their legal safeguards had been undermined, the official view was that no such deterioration had occurred as the legislative expression of the safeguards was largely intact and theoretically robust.[116] The popular view that their undermining was unconstitutional was dismissed as mere rhetoric. Nevertheless, it is arguable that the taxpayer's view had a legitimate basis. In undermining the various legal safeguards through informal practices of the central revenue boards and piecemeal legislation, it was not just a matter of the natural process of the evolution of the law,

---

[113] A. L. Brown, *The Governance of Late Medieval England 1272–1461* (London: Edward Arnold, 1989), p. 207.

[114] Amos, *English Constitution*, pp. 422–3.

[115] *Parl. Deb.*, vol. 159, ser. 3, col. 1430, 5 July 1860 (HC) *per* Edwin James.

[116] For discussion as to the distinction between legal and constitutional, see Jeffrey Goldsworthy, *The Sovereignty of Parliament* (Oxford: Clarendon Press, 1999), pp. 190–1 and the authorities there cited.

but a challenge to the cardinal principle of consent to taxation. Consent to taxation was a fundamental, undisputed right in constitutional law and so any undermining of it would amount to an undermining of the constitution. It was not merely a tension between law and practice. It was nothing less than a constitutional conflict.

It has been seen that in France and America, countries with very different fiscal structures, there existed some degree, albeit varying, of distrust and resentment of central government involvement in taxation, notably in its administration. None, however, expressed such consistently hostile objection to the encroachment of the executive into taxation, and none justified it in such unambiguously constitutional terms. Indeed, only the English sought constitutional justification for their complaints. In both France and America authority for taxation was founded, as it was in England, on notions of popular consent and the sanctity of private property, but in those countries these principles were not always expressed in their constitutions, and their constitutions were more detailed and precise as to taxation, sometimes including further provisions. Their constitutionality of taxation was narrowly conceived, both popularly and legally, and any unconstitutionality of tax was directed into recognised and specific channels.[117] With such explicit and accessible constitutions, it was clearer to American and French taxpayers what was unconstitutional about a tax and what was not. In England, however, there existed no such single-text written constitution. It has been seen that English law made Parliament the ultimate safeguard for the taxpayer, the pre-eminent principle of English law being that a tax could only be levied with the consent of Parliament.[118] This one broad express constitutional provision for the

---

[117] In America constitutional debate addressed issues such as apportionment among the states and the nature of direct taxation: Bruce Ackerman, 'Taxation and the Constitution', *Columbia Law Review* 99 (1999), 1; Roy Blough, *The Federal Taxing Process* (New York: Prentice-Hall, 1952), pp. 195–7; M. A. S., 'The Bearing of the Sixteenth Amendment on the Power of Congress to Tax Any Income Regardless of its Source', *Virginia Law Review* 7 (1920), 136; J. H. Riddle, 'The Supreme Court's Theory of a Direct Tax', *Michigan Law Review* 15 (1917), 566. In France concerns tended to address issues of equality, as article 13 of the Declaration of the Rights of Man and of the Citizen made provision for equality in taxation: Godechot, *Constitutions*, p. 35. See too *ibid.*, pp. 36, 102, 134, 219, 247, 264, 266.

[118] It was unchallenged after the fourteenth century: Brown, *Governance of Late Medieval England*, pp. 224–5. See generally Sydney Knox Mitchell, *Taxation in Medieval England*, Sidney Painter (ed.) (New Haven: Yale University Press, 1951), pp. 156–235. For tithes as a form of tax to which the taxpayer had not consented, see Laura Brace, *The Idea of Property in Seventeenth-Century England: Tithes and the Individual* (Manchester University Press, 1998), p. 96.

consensual basis of the right to tax was prominent, clear, accessible, of immense popular significance and formed part of the national consciousness and identity. It was widely believed, in England and elsewhere, that one of the great advantages of the constitution was the protection afforded to taxpayers by the need for parliamentary consent to taxation.[119] And it was jealously guarded by them.

The legitimacy of the taxpayer's argument was based on a twofold perception of legal consent to taxation. First, there was formal legal consent through the assent of his representatives in Parliament ensured by a sophisticated parliamentary procedure for the enacting of money bills. Secondly, and of central importance, there was real consent.[120] Political leaders were aware that in the popular mind the issue of consent to taxation went far beyond the formal requirement of parliamentary consent, and that active consent to taxation by the public was essential if unpopular taxes were successfully to be levied.[121] If there was significant opposition then avoidance, evasion and simple non-compliance would rise and the yield would suffer, for '[c]onsent, trust and legitimacy are crucial to the history of taxation'.[122] As Lord Holland observed in the debate in the House of Lords on Pitt's income tax in 1799, '[i]t was the business of a wise legislature to consult the prejudices as well as the interests of a nation, and to be as careful that the former should not be violated, as that the latter should not be injured'.[123]

Formal consent was expressed in the letter of the Bill of Rights; real consent in its spirit. Though formal consent had not been undermined because that had long been narrowed and limited to its express terms, namely parliamentary consent, what alarmed English taxpayers, and caused them to express their feelings in such emotive terms, was the perception that any notion of real consent to a tax was being effectively crushed. And if indeed the legal safeguards were expressions of real consent and could claim a legitimate provenance in the fundamental constitutional principle of taxation in English law, their undermining was unconstitutional as a breach of the spirit of the Bill of Rights.

---

[119] Jean-Louis De Lolme, *Constitution de L'Angleterre ou Etat du Gouvernement Anglois*, 2 vols. (London: G. Robinson and J. Murray, 1785), vol. i, p. 236.

[120] Blackstone referred to the 'real and voluntary' consent to a tax: Sir William Blackstone, *Commentaries on the Laws of England*, 1783 edition printed for W. Strahan and T. Cadell, London and D. Prince, Oxford, 4 vols. (New York: Garland Publishing Inc., 1978), vol. i, p. 140.

[121] Daunton, *Trusting Leviathan*, pp. 180–204.   [122] *Ibid.*, p. 7, and see pp. 1–31.

[123] *Parliamentary History*, vol. 34, col. 187, 8 January 1799.

Real consent was a concept embodying notions of voluntaryism, informed acquiescence and control. Though involuntary taxes were well established by the nineteenth century,[124] voluntaryism in taxation was still valued. The taxpayer persisted in regarding taxes as a gift to the government, and as such unequivocally founded in consent.[125] An involuntary tax was regarded as undesirable and unconstitutional as a national fiscal policy. Taxpayers believed that they should be able to choose whether or not they paid taxes, to modify their fiscal liability by their own personal behaviour. In denying the taxpayer choice, involuntary taxes were regarded as an invasion of private rights, showing contempt for the liberty of the person as much as for the right of private property found in all free constitutions.[126] Accordingly this issue lay at the heart of the major contemporary debate on whether direct or indirect taxes were to be preferred. Though ultimately England's policy was relatively balanced in this respect, it inexorably predisposed the English to favour taxation on luxury goods of consumption. Only there could an individual choose whether or not to pay the tax, by purchasing the item or taking the decision not to purchase it. So with the assessed taxes, excise and customs duties, though they were unpopular, they were acceptable as they were submitted to through choice. Taxes that could not be avoided in this way were always fiercely resisted. Pitt's triple assessment of 1798 had broken the principle of voluntaryism, since it was based entirely on past expenditure. Its breach of the principle of voluntaryism was a breach of consent, and was vehemently denounced. To tax on the basis of past expenditure was 'the most iniquitous rule that can possibly be adopted'[127] and the tax was compared unfavourably with that of Robespierre.[128] A forced contribution was 'a thing utterly irreconcilable to the spirit of a free and commercial country'[129] contrary 'to every rational idea of liberty'.[130] Charles

[124] See the speech of Sir William Pulteney in the debate on the income tax in 1798, *Parliamentary History*, vol. 34, cols. 134–5, 22 December 1798; William Phillips, 'The Origin of Income Tax', *BTR* (1967), 113 at 118–19.

[125] See John Dunn, 'Consent in the Political Theory of John Locke', *Historical Journal* 10 (1967), 153 at 169–71.

[126] *Parliamentary History* vol. 33, cols. 1111–12, 14 December 1797 *per* Charles James Fox; *ibid.*, cols. 1187–8, 4 January 1798 *per* Benjamin Hobhouse; *ibid.*, vol. 34, cols. 134–5, 27 December 1798 *per* Sir William Pulteney.

[127] *Parliamentary History*, vol. 33, col. 1117, 14 December 1797 *per* Charles James Fox.

[128] *Ibid.*, cols. 1280–1, 9 January 1798 *per* Lord Holland.

[129] *Ibid.*, col. 1203, 4 January 1798 *per* Richard Sheridan. See too *ibid.*, cols. 1080–3, 4 December 1797 *per* John Nicholls, William Plumer, Benjamin Hobhouse.

[130] *Ibid.*, col. 1190, 4 January 1798 *per* Benjamin Hobhouse.

James Fox was incensed by the breach of voluntaryism. '[Y]ou are called upon to regulate your future exactions', he said,

> not by the future prudence of men, which would be a fair rule of impost in certain cases; but by the most iniquitous rule that can be possibly adopted – that of the past expenditure of men.[131]

The income tax of the following year constituted an even more radical blow to voluntaryism. The compulsory taxation of income and its enforcement by strict regulations was a new principle which alarmed contemporaries.[132] To allow the taxpayer no option constituted 'a new system of taxation, which would give away much of the controlling power of taxes'.[133] It has been argued that this breach of the principle of voluntaryism constituted the principal objection to the new income tax.[134] As voluntaryism was an aspect of the fundamental right to consent to taxes, when a tax was involuntary, the cry of unconstitutionality was not entirely misplaced.

The orthodox view was that acquiescence to taxation was achieved through the debate and voting by representative members of Parliament. Through representation in the Commons, taxpayers were directly involved in the imposition of taxes upon themselves. Though only formal, this had traditionally been thought, in tax terms, to constitute an approximation of real agreement. The bloody conflicts of the seventeenth century between the state and the people established a firm and clear relationship between taxation and representation with the executive only levying taxes granted by the representatives of the people in Parliament. Indeed this principle was central to the argument that the House of Lords should be ejected from the taxing process entirely and that thereby real consent to taxation would not be affected. The members of Parliament of the seventeenth century, being landowners and professional men, were in some real sense representative of the classes who were subject to the direct taxes, sharing common values, though not admittedly of the majority of those who paid indirect taxes on the goods they consumed. There thus originally existed, to some extent, a genuine nexus between the taxpayers and their representatives in Parliament which resulted in the fusion of formal and real consent since true representation in Parliament gave the ordinary taxpayer a measure of agreement to the imposition of

---

[131] *Ibid.*, col. 1117, 14 December 1797 *per* Charles James Fox.
[132] *Ibid.*, vol. 34, col. 86, 14 December 1798 *per* Sir John Sinclair.
[133] *Ibid.*, col. 135, 27 December 1798 *per* Sir William Pulteney.
[134] See William Phillips, 'The Real Objection to the Income Tax of 1799', *BTR* (1967), 177.

tax. This acquiescence embodied in formal parliamentary consent was diminished in the nineteenth century as members of Parliament became less representative of the tax-paying classes. This inevitably happened as the scope of direct taxation widened to bring into charge taxpayers who were not landowners and who had relatively modest incomes. There was, furthermore, no corresponding widening of the franchise which might have given taxpayers a greater say in the choice of their representatives.[135] Though the Reform Act 1832[136] moved power from the titled nobility to the new middle class, it extended the suffrage only to propertied individuals and so did not improve that 'irregularity of the popular representation' noted by William Paley.[137] Not until after the Second Reform Act 1867[138] did consent to taxation by representatives in Parliament begin to approach a real representation.

Real consent was particularly threatened when the members of Parliament, who were at least representative of the taxpayer to some degree, became unable to assimilate or understand the tax measures to which they were being asked to consent.[139] It has been seen that as society and its commercial context grew in sophistication and complexity, so the fiscal system followed suit. Tax measures were expressed in complex and technical legislation which, in the nineteenth century, was as obscure to the ordinary member of Parliament as it was to the lay commissioners attempting to implement it, or the ordinary taxpayers attempting to find out the scope of the charge imposed upon them. Most members were ignorant about technical tax matters, and debate was consequently ill-informed, and this lessened any notion of real consent to tax legislation. Contemporaries were aware of this. Toulmin Smith said that to call a measure law which had been hurried through the house or with only a few members present was 'a mockery of the Constitution and a fraud upon the public'.[140] Specifically, the requirement that Parliament must consent to any charge laid on the people was 'a reality, and not an empty form',[141] and to do so without real assent and careful consideration[142] was 'a clear and open violation of the fundamental laws of the land'.[143] As late as 1927 Lord Decies made the point that the language of tax legislation 'should

---

[135] See generally W. R. Cornish and G. de N. Clark, *Law and Society in England 1750–1950* (London: Sweet & Maxwell, 1989), pp. 9–16; Norman McCord, *British History 1815–1906* (Oxford University Press, 1991), pp. 135–6.
[136] 2 & 3 Will. IV c. 45.   [137] Paley, *Works*, p. 390.   [138] 30 & 31 Vict. c. 102.
[139] See H. H. Monroe, 'The Constitution in Danger', *BTR* (1969), 24 at 27.
[140] Toulmin Smith, *Government by Commissions*, p. 98.
[141] *Ibid.*, p. 95.   [142] *Ibid.*, pp. 98–9, 100.   [143] *Ibid.*, p. 92.

be understandable by the member of Parliament, if not by the man in the street'. At present, he argued, it was not even so understood, and there was the very real danger that legislation could be passed without members of Parliament grasping its full significance. In the same way the restrictions on independent members and the growth of the party system reduced the degree of independent scrutiny of tax legislation in Parliament and thereby lessened real consent to taxing measures. The reduction of parliamentary consent to consent by a House of Commons dominated by the executive, with less debate by less informed members, and thus considerably more limited than its original form in practice, was a clear diminution of real consent. All elements of independent, voluntary and informed consent to taxation were no longer present. In this way the fundamental constitutional principle of taxation was itself undermined.

Finally, real consent imported control by the taxpayer over the taxing process, a reinforcement of the notion of a voluntary gift which was of especial importance in direct taxation where voluntaryism was not inherent in the taxes themselves. Such control was regarded as part of the tradition of consensual taxation and took the form of the administration of tax by the taxpayers themselves. The land tax, for example, had traditionally been raised entirely through the real consent of the taxpayer, administered by responsible local men with a keen sense of civic duty. The strict legal provenance was not as robust, but nevertheless the localist system of tax administration undoubtedly emphasised the consensual nature of taxation,[144] promoting tax as a contribution, assessed by the taxpayers themselves and handed to the crown voluntarily, as a gift through their Parliament. The local administrative system has been shown to have gone far to ensure the consent of the taxpaying public,[145] but it went even further: it was itself a formal expression of the constitutional and legal requirement for consent. Local administration ensured that taxpayers had some control over the tax process, that they were to some extent taxing themselves, and that therefore their consent to being taxed was implicit, and this was reflected in the popular terms 'self-taxation' and 'self-assessment'.[146] As such the principle of localism was an expression of the very freedom which the English people had won in the constitutional conflict between them and their king in the seventeenth century. It lay at the heart of their constitutional liberties. It is in this context that taxpayers regarded local administration as

---

[144] See generally Colin Brooks, 'Public Finance and Political Stability', *Historical Journal* 17 (1974), 281.

[145] Daunton, *Trusting Leviathan*, pp. 182–94.

[146] CIR Twelfth Report, *HCPP* (1869) (4049) xviii 607 at p. 635.

more than merely a benchmark of conduct to remind legislators of the optimum standard of tax administration. It was of course an indicator of the system of tax administration the public would find acceptable, but it was fundamentally a legitimate aspect of the right to consent to taxation and its breach was accordingly unconstitutional. On this reasoning the administration of tax by the central government clearly undermined the fundamental notion of taxation by consent, and also challenged the sanctity of personal property. The popular perception of a centrally administered tax as unconstitutional thus had some formal legitimacy and considerable popular support. Legally and culturally, therefore, the legal safeguard of local administration was founded in consent.

The nature of the constitution permitted this popular conception of real consent. It lacked visibility and precision, with only a few broad principles expressly stated and the understanding of which was based on tradition. As such, it was much less circumscribed and less rigid than that of either France or America. Furthermore, the constitution of 1688 was a compromise and was as such not solely based on the new ideas of the fundamental rights and sovereignty of the people. Instead, having to deal with a monarch who had abdicated, it claimed simply to restore the old order dating from Anglo-Saxon times under which the king ruled with the consent of a representative assembly. So the Bill of Rights was not viewed as expressing any new notion of consent but one which had been built up through custom. This notion of a constitution built on the tradition and usages of the common law strengthened the broad view of parliamentary consent as encompassing consent in a real sense.[147] The very flexibility, uncertainty and lack of formal limits which had permitted the executive to undermine the safeguards also permitted taxpayers to maintain that such undermining was unconstitutional and that they were as a result being denied full and effective constitutional protection against a rapacious executive.

As a result the term 'constitutional' was loosely used in eighteenth- and nineteenth-century England, and tended to reflect long and established usage rather than an unambiguous legal principle. Indeed, Blackstone had observed that the fundamental right of private property, of which consent to taxation was an expression, was, like all 'liberties', 'more generally talked of, than thoroughly understood'.[148] And so when the new income tax of 1799 was condemned as being unconstitutional a distinguished

---

[147] See generally Carl S. Shoup, 'Some Distinguishing Characteristics of the British, French, and United States Public Finance Systems', *American Economic Review* 47 (1957), 187.

[148] Blackstone, *Commentaries*, vol. i, p. 144.

lawyer and politician observed that '[i]t was easy to assert this of any measure'. 'It had a popular sound', he said, 'and was calculated to excite alarm'.[149] He did not, he continued, 'regret that the people of this country should be ready to take the alarm at the very idea of a measure being unconstitutional. It was right that they should be jealous of a constitution to which they owed so much happiness'.[150] The very breadth of the principle of consent to taxation and its prominence within the constitution made it liable to wide and fluid popular interpretation[151] and it was possible that taxpayers condemned a tax as unconstitutional simply because they thought it was in some way harsh or unfair, it being the strongest condemnation they could find. But as the safeguards were an expression of real consent, itself legitimately inherent in legal consent, they did not entirely misunderstand the term 'constitutional' or confound it with expediency rather than legality.[152] The undermining of the safeguards resulted unequivocally in the lessening of this real consent inherent in the overall concept of legal consent, because it diminished the control the taxpayer enjoyed over the taxing process and thereby lessened the voluntary nature of taxation. So while formal consent remained intact and reflected in the law, the undermining of the legal safeguards had resulted in a lessening of real consent. This common foundation in consent gave the taxpayers' legal safeguards, and accordingly the taxpayers' objections to their undermining, constitutional legitimacy. The undermining of the safeguards did amount to the undermining of the constitutional rule of taxation that it could only be imposed with the consent of Parliament.

The effects of constitutional provenance

The constitutional provenance of the taxpayer's legal safeguards did not, in all respects, serve the taxpayer well. Being theoretically unmovable and static in expression, the safeguards could only be undermined informally through practice. The resulting dislocation between law and practice could not be masked by any constitutional provenance, and indeed was its cause. It was probably the most damaging legacy of the undermining of the safeguards, even more than the undermining itself. Dislocation allowed legal anachronisms to persist, resulting in the English tax system being plagued by internal conflicts and tensions throughout the nineteenth century, which it was able to resolve only with difficulty and

---

[149] *Parliamentary History*, vol. 34, col. 145, 31 December 1798 *per* Charles Abbot.
[150] *Ibid.*   [151] Amos, *English Constitution*, pp. 462–8.   [152] Paley, *Works*, vol. iv, p. 372.

discord. In particular, it burdened the machinery of tax administration with features, often major ones, which caused problems in modern tax tribunal structure and process which endure to the present day. The legislative provisions which gave the local commissioners the sole responsibility for making assessments to income tax remained unaltered in law, even when the practical responsibility had been transferred to the surveyor and thus made the General Commissioners uncertain and ambivalent in their role and jurisdiction. The original conception of the General Commissioners as a local body for tax administration resulted in a jurisdiction neither clearly inquisitorial nor adversarial, a continued insistence on appointing only commissioners with local knowledge, a cultural reluctance to give reasons for their decisions, and the secrecy of their hearings, all of which became increasingly inappropriate in a modern, accountable and cost-conscious society sensitive to the upholding of human rights. But it was the informal dominance of the surveyor which led to the most damaging modern legacy, namely a perceived lack of independence of the tribunal from the Inland Revenue. Ironically it was this very quality of independence from the executive which had been the reason behind the adoption of, and popular support for, the principle of localism in tax administration. The outcome was a divergence between law and practice of insurmountable inaccessibility for the taxpayer, and a system of tax administration which was a confused hotchpotch.

This dislocation between tax law and practice did not have the beneficial effect which it had in other branches of English law. It was potentially a motive force for law reform. Where through changing social, political or economic conditions the rules of a branch of law ceased to be suited to the needs and desires of their users, those users would attempt to avoid the law, their practice became widespread and, if not checked, new rules would be generated through the instruments of law reform. Such adaptation through stimuli was illustrative of a growing, living law. The law had to develop in this way, for if it did not it risked losing the allegiance of the community it sought to govern, and therefore its raison d'être. It was an essential progression that was seen in all branches of English law. It was, in short, the very life-blood of the law. Certainly in the early nineteenth century such law reform was slow and painstaking, with governments wary of legal change and lawyers temperamentally unsuited to reform and suspicious of it,[153] and in nearly all fields legal change was achieved only

---

[153] See generally A. H. Manchester, *A Modern Legal History of England and Wales 1750–1950* (London: Butterworths, 1980), pp. 1–20; 402–10.

after long and persistent struggles. From the middle of the century, however, movement for reform began to yield results, albeit modest ones. As the social and economic challenges of the new industrial age revealed by intensive official investigation demanded action, and any action required implementation by the law and its institutions, governments necessarily became more open to law reform. So although the law, both judge-made and statutory, was traditionally slow to respond to changes in the commercial and financial climate of the country, many of those branches of English law which had been challenged by the conditions of the new industrial age adapted in practice and in due course reflected that adaptation in the law. They became as a result among the most dynamic and innovative in English law, and were fitted to sustain the economic growth and social improvement of the country. By the outbreak of war in 1914, Britain had legislative provision in a wide range of fields,[154] for example for public health, workers' safety, the education of children, the creation of incorporated companies by registration, efficient bankruptcy processes and an increasingly coherent commercial law. It also boasted an innovative and pragmatic system of extra-judicial dispute-resolution which was to remain one of the century's most enduring legacies.[155]

Tax law, however, did not follow this pattern. The dynamic context of tax and the static form of the law certainly resulted in the dislocation of the law and practice, but that did not in turn lead to the adaptation, even slowly, of the formal tax law; the adaptation remained one of practice and the dislocation persisted. The reasons were many. The constitutional provenance of the legal safeguards made their reform possible only by amendment of the 'noble pile' of the constitution[156] and risked thereby alienating public opinion. The constitutional provenance also rendered their retention in the formal statement of the law politically necessary and resulted in that formal expression remaining static. It was therefore inherent in the nature of the legal safeguards in tax law that they retain a formal inflexibility, a tendency strengthened by a traditional political reluctance to be innovative in tax matters.[157] And as far as income tax was

---

[154] See generally Council of Legal Education, *A Century of Law Reform* (London: Macmillan & Co., 1901).

[155] See generally C. Stebbings, *Legal Foundations of Tribunals in Nineteenth Century England* (Cambridge University Press, 2006).

[156] Blackstone, *Commentaries*, vol. iv, pp. 435–6. See Manchester, *Modern Legal History*, pp. 11–12.

[157] David W. Williams, 'Three Hundred Years On: Are our Tax Bills Right Yet?', *BTR* (1989), 370 at 385.

concerned, throughout the nineteenth century there was little incentive to reform its law and administration because it tenaciously retained the character of a temporary tax, enduring for two or three years at a time. In 1853 Gladstone confirmed it would run for another seven years, and at the end of that period the demands of war led to its retention. The practice, if not the theory, of a permanent income tax began in 1874.[158] As long as it was politically necessary that the tax be truly temporary, governments were reluctant to reform the law for fear of giving the impression the tax was going to be permanent.

The principal reason, however, for the failure of tax law to respond to the new conditions of Victorian England was that its special nature militated against the natural evolution seen in other branches of law. A doctrinal study of the taxpayer's legal safeguards is a revealing and important context because it shows tax law to be one of the most isolated branches of English law. It was unique from the legal perspective as a branch of law which in many ways struggled to establish itself. Tax law was a self-contained system enjoying little interaction with other areas of legal theory, the legal system or indeed legal practice. A surveyor of taxes said in 1919 that he saw 'the Income Tax in rather a different category from ordinary legal questions'.[159] The integration of tax law and its institutions into the theory, practice and popular perception of the law, legal system and legal education was, in the nineteenth century, as it is to some extent today, a challenging issue. A number of factors were responsible for this isolation.

The constitutional underpinning of tax law was a contributory factor. It gave it a special nature savouring of public affairs and fundamental rights, with an immensely strong political context and constitutional basis not shared by other branches of law. Its public character was generally unfamiliar to the majority of those involved in the practice of law who were in their daily lives more concerned with the private law of property, contract, wills and trusts, and domestic relations between individuals. The major factor, however, was that tax law was not perceived as law in the generally accepted sense of the term, and it was a perception which was more persistent in tax than in other fields. Railway regulation, for example, a subject more novel than taxation, was condemned in the 1850s

[158] See Leone Levi, 'On the Reconstruction of the Income and Property Tax', *Journal of the Statistical Society of London*, 37 (1874), 155 at 157; H. C. G. Matthew, *Gladstone* (Oxford: Clarendon Press, 1997), pp. 121–3.

[159] Minutes of Evidence before the Royal Commission on the Income Tax, *HCPP* (1919) (288) xxiii, q. 4910 *per* Arthur Ereaut, formerly surveyor of taxes.

by the judges as being mere regulation and therefore unsuitable for the regular courts of law, and yet only twenty years later it was being proposed that there should be a railway division of the High Court. Tax law was, of course, law in the strict sense of the term, being expressed in statute and in an admittedly small body of case law. The subject-matter, however, set it apart from other branches of law and made it unfamiliar to lawyers. It was not because tax law was particularly complex, for it was not as technically demanding as it would become in the future, and anyway Victorian lawyers were accustomed to highly technical law such as the land law. The unfamiliarity of tax law was due to its own special composite nature. Even simple cases would often involve figures and accounts and as such require some knowledge of accountancy, a discipline with which lawyers were notoriously uncomfortable. This made tax law to some degree intellectually inaccessible to them. A commentator at the beginning of the reign observed that 'men of acquirement in legal knowledge are, perhaps, the least qualified to conduct business transactions, or attend to the jog-trot detail of accounts',[160] and a leading member of the tax bar showed the persistence of the view when he observed in 1919 that '[p]ersonally I dislike figures very much, and I am quite unable to deal with them, and I am delighted to put the figures on to more competent shoulders'.[161] The importance of accountancy in tax law revealed a cultural reason for lawyers having a tendency to avoid being associated with tax law: the taint of money and commerce created a tension with the perception the bar had of itself as the higher branch of the legal profession. And what was neither law nor accountancy was administration, and it was this most of all which was responsible for the isolation of tax law.

The tax legislation was implemented by bodies possessing an admixture of administrative and judicial functions. The parent Acts of the tax tribunals made it clear that the function of the various bodies of commissioners was to implement a specific legislative regime and that function was a function of the executive. The various local commissioners, the Special Commissioners of Income Tax, the excise courts and the revenue boards themselves all adjudicated on tax disputes as well as undertaking ministerial functions. In the case of income tax commissioners, they were responsible for making the actual assessments. Had the function of

---

[160] Twentieth Report of the Commissioners of Inquiry (Excise Establishment), *HCPP* (1836) (22) xxvi 179 at p. 644 *per* Peter Abbott.

[161] Minutes of Evidence before the Royal Commission on the Income Tax, *HCPP* (1919) (288) xxiii, q. 15,994 *per* A. M. Bremner, barrister, on behalf of the General Council of the Bar of England.

adjudication been discrete it would have been recognised as judicial in nature, but it was not perceived as such. The adjudication by the organs of the revenue boards and the various bodies of commissioners was regarded as no more than the final stage of the administrative process of assessing individuals to tax. Their judicial powers had not been given to them as an end in themselves, as stand-alone powers, but were embedded in the process and were subsumed by the overall administrative purpose of the tribunal. This intimate relationship between the law and its administration obscured boundaries which were clear in other branches of law. Such was the difficulty of isolating tax law from tax administration that any clarity of legal rights and processes was difficult to achieve. Even the increased exposure of the courts to tax cases did not undermine the acceptance of tax as administration not law. The perception of tax law as an anomalous species of law was far more deep-seated than that. After all, the regular courts had long been familiar with tax litigation. The assessed taxes had had the right of appeal since the mid eighteenth century, and stamp duty and excise cases abound in the law reports. Furthermore, the Court of Exchequer had been hearing revenue cases since the medieval period, providing the judges of that court with long experience of adjudicating on tax matters, while the superior courts would also have adjudicated on tax cases removed to them by certiorari.

As adjudication in tax was regarded as part of an administrative and not a judicial process, it followed that it stood outside the legal system, and it was legitimate to maintain that it should be untouched by the values and standards of that system. The special nature of tax law as savouring of administration, and that of tax adjudication as being part of the administrative process of taxation, supported the executive in its undermining of the safeguards in this way. The executive could, and did, argue that the special features of tax law demanded and justified an increased role for the executive. For example the system of the internal tax appeals of the Inland Revenue through the Special Commissioners and the board itself, which constituted a major instance of the executive asserting its control over tax administration, was permitted to thrive because the settling of appeals in the tax sphere was not regarded as a judicial act. The board did not consider its various adjudicatory powers as discrete, let alone judicial. It saw them as part of its duty to care for and manage the public revenue and so merely an aspect of the administration of tax. So while an absence of legally qualified adjudicators and of independence were totally unacceptable in the regular legal system, which maintained a long and profound training in the law and an unimpeachable independence as its two salient features, in tax they were portrayed, if not as virtues, then certainly as proper and legal. With taxation as an administrative function, a lack of independence was perceived as broadly in line with the constitutional orthodoxy of the separation of powers and legal training was neither necessary nor appropriate. Accordingly there was a marked absence of any requirement for formal legal expertise in the commissioners who implemented the law, whether lay or state-employed, and indeed in their clerk, and a minimal provision for seeking expert legal advice. This confirms that neither the letter of the law nor legal skills were thought to be important in the implementation of tax law. The view was that the issues coming before tax tribunals were not legal issues, but were factual issues of finance and accounting. Indeed of all the fiscal tribunals, only the Commissioners of Appeal for the Redemption of the Land Tax were expressly permitted to seek professional legal advice. Similarly, it has been seen that legal representation was not thought necessary in many tax tribunals, and was prohibited for most of the nineteenth century. These factors reinforced the general perception of tax law as not being law in the usually accepted sense of the term.

The corollary of this denial of any need for legal skills was the insistence that a different kind of expertise altogether was required: that of specialist knowledge of tax. The executive maintained that the tax laws could only be administered by specialists in the field and, in view of the state of tax law in the nineteenth century, it was a powerful and convincing argument. Only specialist practitioners could master the complex and technical law and regulations, apply them and, ultimately, adjudicate upon them. It has been seen that this was a potent argument against lay adjudication in the direct taxes, and it was used to justify the widespread culture of bureaucratic adjudication through formal courts such as the Special Commissioners and the excise courts, and also for the wide de facto appellate jurisdiction exercised informally by all the boards. In the case of the excise it was accepted that that law was 'confessedly of an extraordinary and anomalous character',[162] and that the excise commissioners who composed the excise court, who were indeed highly experienced in their field, had a 'superior competency' to administer it and had 'a more precise knowledge' of the cases than magistrates.[163]

The administration of tax law thus formed a self-sufficient system, isolated by its persistent classification as pure administration and essen-

---

[162]   Third Report of the Commissioners of Inquiry into the Excise Establishment: Summary Jurisdiction, *HCPP* (1834) (3) xxiv 87 at p. 97.

[163]   *Ibid.*, p. 140.

tially inward-looking, a culture fostered by the developing civil service and bureaucratic state and the special nature of tax. That tax law and its tribunals were isolated in the legal world is evidenced by the minimal impact which the tax tribunals had on the development of the statutory tribunals of the nineteenth century. Despite being one of the oldest forms of statutory tribunal, and being well established and effective, no tax tribunal was drawn upon for use as a model for newer tribunals. This tendency was encouraged by the self-sufficient nature of the tax tribunals themselves. This is illustrated by the Land Tax Commissioners who formed the basis of the Assessed Taxes Commissioners, the Land Tax Redemption Commissioners and the General Commissioners of Income Tax. Furthermore the same tribunal was often given subsequent new functions, as where the existing commissioners responsible for administering the assessed taxes were given the task of administering the triple assessment of 1798.

In only one context did the institutions of tax law manage to overcome this clear and persistent isolation and secure a place, albeit sui generis, in the regular legal system. This was the achievement of the judiciary, the outcome of the developing adjudicatory and supervisory safeguard. Though the judicial safeguards were persistently undermined by problems of access, alone among the legal safeguards they were strengthened in real terms. The judges were largely able to resist any encroachment of the executive in tax matters, being forceful and robust, despite attitudes to tax law and the place of the tax tribunals in the legal system. Rights of appeal, themselves an affirmation of the taxpayers' constitutional right to enforce their legal rights in a court of law, were increased, and supervisory jurisdiction widened into the tax sphere. In this way a firmer place was created for the tax tribunals in the regular legal system. Though that place was a subordinate one, with the tax tribunals subject to the restraint of the superior courts, it ensured the tax tribunals were not permitted to operate entirely in isolation from the judicial world. They were drawn inexorably into some relationship with the judicial system. This counteracted to some degree the isolation of tax law and tax tribunals. Furthermore, it has been seen that the interpretative safeguard had been undermined by the practice of the central boards to construe the tax legislation themselves, and for that interpretation to stand until challenged. And since appeal provision was slight, this compounded the undermining. But as appeal provision grew, so this particular undermining of the judicial interpretative safeguard was reduced.

Though the dislocation of law and practice, and its effects, was a damaging and enduring consequence of the constitutional provenance of the safeguards, it was far outweighed by the fact that it was those very origins which ensured they endured at all. In the struggle between the political and fiscal demands of modern government and the traditional safeguards constructed by the law to protect the taxpayer, it has been seen that the executive emerged the winner. It was not, however, an outright victory, because the legal safeguards were not obliterated. The reason for their survival was their constitutional provenance, and its effects were profound.

First, it ensured legislators retained the formal expression of the safeguards in tax legislation. There was no question of amending the statement of formal consent in the Bill of Rights, for being fundamental to taxation and the liberty of the subject it was politically untouchable. This was in contrast to the French constitutions of the nineteenth century where the requirement of consent, though always implicit, was not invariably given express form.[164] It therefore remained an express legislative provision that taxation could only be imposed with the consent of the taxpayers' representatives in Parliament and, moreover, that the direct taxes had to be administered by their own representatives in the locality. The right to be assessed by local commissioners and to appeal to the same body proved the most enduring, and the most important, tool of taxpayer protection. Indeed, from the middle of the twentieth century the right of appeal to local commissioners was the only formal protection afforded by the law to a taxpayer within the administrative process, ensuring the executive was not the final arbiter of the taxpayer's assessment. As legal rights, the imposition of taxation only by the consent of Parliament and local administration were protected by the courts of law.

Secondly, although the fact that the letter of the law remained unaltered served to strengthen legislators' arguments that the safeguards were not being undermined at all, this legislative expression of the safeguards ensured they constituted a constant reminder to, and enduring check on, the encroaching power of the executive and slowed down the process of undermining. Their legitimacy was continually being reinforced. The

---

[164] It was affirmed as a fundamental liberty in the Declaration of the Rights of Man and the Citizen in 1789. See S. Caudal, 'Article 14', in Gérard Conac, Marc Debene, Gérard Teboul (eds.), *La déclaration des droits de l'homme et du citoyen de 1789* (Paris: Economica, 1993), pp. 299–315. It was reiterated, expressly or implicitly, in subsequent constitutions: see Godechot, *Constitutions*, pp. 64–5, 84, 86, 134–6, 194, 222, 266, 295, 316.

political imperative of maintaining the legal expression of real consent obliged governments and legislators to proceed with the utmost caution, and to justify and account for any development which was a perceived breach of the principle of the safeguards. It gave the safeguards such political influence that governments were reluctant to breach them and would do so only when it was unavoidable. Indeed even the slightest constitutional legitimacy was potent. For example taxpayers argued an inquisitorial tax was unconstitutional, and although this was only tenuously based on the fundamental right to taxation by consent, it was nevertheless of such political sensitivity that sophisticated statutory provisions against disclosure were enacted, to a degree somewhat greater than the strength of the right warranted.[165] The safeguards' constitutional legitimacy constituted a formidable force of resistance to their encroachment. It strengthened the arguments of taxpayers resisting the complete ousting of the upper chamber from the tax process, the allocation of parliamentary time to the debate of tax measures, the accessibility of tax legislation to members of Parliament and the imposition of taxation by parliamentary resolution. It was central to the retention of local administration, for Peel admitted in 1842 that 'it was more consistent with constitutional law'.[166] The force of a constitutional provenance based to some extent on usage could, however, work against the safeguards. For example, by the early years of the twentieth century, formal and informal breaches in the principle of localism had eroded it to the extent that the Chancellor of the Exchequer could respond to objectors to the proposal of 1915 by saying that '[i]t is not unconstitutional; it is not a novelty'.[167] Whether it was the surveyor at an appeal hearing or the chancellor in Parliament, the underlying legal necessity for consent to taxation required him to justify his actions to the taxpayers or their representatives.

Thirdly the underlying requirement of consent resulted in a culture of discussion, consultation and compromise in tax matters. Even though the safeguard of local administration had been considerably undermined in practice, it left a legacy of real and striking importance to the fiscal system, and one which was particularly noticeable in England. The intimate involvement of the taxpayer in the administration of tax through the local commissioners and their officials had a deeper and more profound

---

[165] See C. Stebbings, 'The Budget of 1798: Legislative Provision for Secrecy in Income Taxation', *BTR* (1998), 651.

[166] *Parl. Deb.*, vol. 61, ser. 3, col. 912, 18 March 1842 (HC).

[167] *Ibid.*, vol. 76, ser. 5, col. 1112, 6 December 1915 (HC) *per* Reginald McKenna.

significance than just independent involvement in administration. It had the effect of achieving a far more balanced tax system than in those jurisdictions lacking the involvement of local institutions in tax administration. The taxpayer was an integral part of the system of tax administration itself, and was valued as a partner, albeit not an equal partner, in tax. This helped ensure a balance between the interests of the taxpayer and those of the government, and as such limited the power of a potentially all-powerful repressive taxing state.

Finally, because the safeguards were still expressed in law in an unchanged form, it meant that necessarily the judges did not undermine them. They continued to fulfil their constitutional function of implementing and interpreting the enacted law, and it has been seen that they adopted a strict and literal approach in so doing. This was a robust expression of the judicial interpretative safeguard and acted as a reinforcement of the fundamental principle that the taxpayer should be charged to tax only by clear terms in the enacted law. This served to strengthen the legal expression of the safeguards, which remained in existence, thereby providing a measure of resistance to their undermining by the executive. The potency of the judicial interpretative safeguard was undermined to some extent by the obscurity of the tax legislation, but it was that very obscurity which encouraged the restrictive and literal approach to the interpretation of the tax legislation. The expression of the safeguards in law gave confidence to taxpayers to enforce them before the judges in the courts of law, and the judges' insistence on a clear legal authority to tax protected the taxpayer against arbitrary taxation by the state.

Epilogue

The Victorian period saw the re-evaluation of individual rights in many spheres, not least that of tax, and in that sphere it resulted in an overall undermining of the protective provisions which formed the central element of the taxpayer's relationship with the law. An examination of this re-evaluation exposes the nature and extent of this undermining, but also reveals that the taxpayer's protection by the law was not destroyed as a result, but that in fact the safeguards were deceptively robust and their undermining was more in the character of a recasting to suit a new dynamic age. This survival in a modified form occurred because the safeguards themselves were, as taxpayers instinctively believed, not mere rules of law to be changed by indifferent Parliaments at the instigation of successive governments, but of far more profound significance. Because tax constituted a relationship of such fundamental importance between the state and the subject, the evolving legal safeguards of the nineteenth century reflect the shifting tectonic plates of the executive, Parliament and the judiciary, the component powers of the state. The historical antecedents of the safeguards show they were not a collection of individual rules with no underlying connecting principle. Instead the legal safeguards were offshoots, though not always evidently so, of an underlying, pervasive and, crucially, constitutional principle of consent: the formal consent of Parliament and the real consent expressed in informed parliamentary debate and local administration. The security of Victorian taxpayers was derived almost entirely from this constitutional principle, and they thereby enjoyed the highest formal protection possible.

This constitutional imperative combined with a number of influences, including political and practical considerations as well as public demand to shape the taxpayer's relationship with the law. The safeguards which constituted its legal expression were able to adapt to suit a new phase in the country's fiscal system.[168] They could not, and did not, ensure that 'exact justice' between the crown and the taxpayer was always done. That was, arguably, impossible.[169] Instead the notion of consent inherent in the law permeated the relationship of state and taxpayer, and despite the taxpayer being the weaker party it still was instrumental in ensuring the executive did not abuse its position. The effect and consequences of the safeguards' constitutional provenance in establishing them in the law ensured that they were not an encumbrance to be bypassed by the tax establishment and ignored by the legal establishment. It was prominent in the consciousness of legislators, judges, administrators and taxpayers and found coherent expression in the three legal safeguards, which in turn enjoyed a fundamental consistency, constitutional legitimacy and legal integrity. They emerged as the formal expression of a consensus as to how taxpayers should be protected by the law and constituted a precept of conduct regulating the imposition and administration of tax. This general concept of taxpayer protection was not peculiar to any one tax: it transcended the usual distinctions drawn between types of taxes, and between individual taxes, though it sometimes adopted a different emphasis. In redefining the relationship between the taxpayer and the law, although the safeguards themselves were undoubtedly weakened, the general concept of taxpayer

---

[168] See Philip Baker and Anne-Mieke Groenhagen, *The Protection of Taxpayers' Rights, An International Codification* (London: European Policy Forum, ICOM, 2001).

[169] See *AG v. Earl of Sefton* (1863) 2 H & C 362 at 375 *per* Wilde B.

protection through consent which they reflected was a real force in the historical continuum of taxation, providing a flexible and robust protection to the taxpayer which transcended and overcame changing social and economic conditions. The relationship itself, as part of that between the subject and the state, was one of such fundamental importance that it emerged as a connection of more than mere law. Its legal expression was just the outward asseveration of a more complex relationship of cultural, political and economic imperatives which pervaded the fiscal culture of England.

INDEX